Classroom Encounters:

Problems, Case Studies, Solutions

by R. Baird Shuman

nea PROFESSIONAL LIBRARY
National Education Association
Washington, D.C.

Printing History
    First Printing: September 1989

Note

The opinions expressed in this publication should not be construed as represent-ing the policy or position of the National Education Association. Materials pub-lished by the NEA Professional Library are intended to be discussion documents for educators who are concerned with specialized interests of the profession.

Library of Congress Cataloging-in-Publication Data

Shuman, R. Baird (Robert Baird), 1929–
    Classroom encounters : problems, case studies, solutions / by R.
Baird Shuman.
        p.   cm.—(NEA aspects of learning)
    Bibliography: p.
    ISBN 0–8106–3001–X
    1. First year teachers–United States–Case studies.   2. Teacher
-student relationships–United States–Case studies.   I. Title.
II. Series.
LB2844.1.N4S55   1989
371.1'02'0973–dc20   89–12381
                                                                                         CIP

CONTENTS

The Author

R. Baird Shuman is Professor of English and Director of English Education at the University of Illinois at Urbana-Champaign. Dr. Shuman is the author of *The First R: Fundamentals of Initial Reading Instruction*, and the author or editor of these previous NEA publications: *The Beginning Teacher: A Practical Guide to Problem Solving; Education in the 80's: English;* and *Strategies in Teaching Reading: Secondary*.

Advisory Panel

Shelton A. Gunaratne, Associate Professor of Mass Communications, Moorhead State University, Minnesota

Joan D. Hobbs, Second Grade Teacher, Orrs Elementary School, Griffin-Spalding County Schools, Griffin, Georgia

Joyce Hodges, Reading Teacher, Lovington Junior High School, New Mexico

Edna Henry Rivers, Chairperson of Guidance Department, W. P. Davidson High School, Mobile, Alabama

Gary W. Streit, Dean of the Graduate School, Olivet Nazarene University, Kankakee, Illinois

Charles Lamar Thompson, Professor of Education, Memphis State University, Tennessee

Denny Wolfe, Professor of English Education and Associate Dean, Darden College of Education, Old Dominion University, Norfolk, Virginia

INTRODUCTION

Classroom Encounters replaces an earlier publication of the National Education Association, *The Beginning Teacher: A Practical Guide to Problem Solving* (1979), by Robert J. Krajewski and me, and we had hoped to collaborate on this book. The pressures of university administration, however, left Dr. Krajewski little choice but to withdraw from the study if it was to be finished on time.

I am grateful to Dr. Krajewski for his excellent work on our former collaboration and for his initial willingness to work on this one. I appreciate the grace with which he withdrew from the project when it was apparent to him that his duties at the University of Texas, San Antonio, where he is Director of Education in the College of Social and Behavioral Sciences, would prevent his completing his part of the collaboration in time for us to go to press with the book.

I am grateful to Donna Walker and Carol Anne Moore, who helped prepare the final typescript. John Marshall Carter, Geng-Sheng and Zheng-Wu Chen, Cindy Hughes, Gideon Schlessinger, and Zohreh Sullivan all helped in their own ways. Colleagues at Carey College in Kew near Melbourne, Australia—Adrian Collins, Mark Collins, and John Marks—each provided insights and were hospitable to me when I visited their school in July 1988.

The book this one replaces evoked response and suggestions from a broad range of people who used it. Veteran teachers wrote to say that although the book addressed beginning teachers, teaching interns, and other teacher trainees, they found it useful and informative to them in their teaching. It was heartening to know this, and these comments convinced me that the scope of the present book needed to be broadened. *Classroom Encounters* still addresses the problems of beginning teachers, but most of its case studies present problems all teachers might face.

In our earlier book, we felt we should not propose solutions to the problems most of the case studies present because what is appropriate in a given teaching situation or at a particular teaching level may be inappropriate in another situation or at another level. For example, novels that parents in one locale might feel their children have to read in middle school or senior high school are often banned even in a neighboring district. Such is the diversity of a country whose diversity is a major component of its strength. In the earlier book, we posed questions for discussion and a few projects, but we refrained from going beyond that in most cases.

In the present book, I still pose questions and some projects because in thinking or talking through these questions or working through the projects, you will develop insights that you might not reach otherwise. Bowing to suggestions and to popular demand, however, I have posed either possible or alternate solutions—three or four of them—for most of the case studies. In doing so, I do not always mean to suggest that one solution is correct and the others are not. A solution is correct if it works for you in your teaching situation.

What is a correct solution in Greenwich, Connecticut, might be a disastrous or silly solution in Carversville, Pennsylvania, or Milpitas, California, or Tesuque, New Mexico. Every region of the United States, every large city, every middle-size town, every tiny hamlet, has unique philosophical colorations. It is up to you as a teacher in a community to figure out the philosophical colorations of the venue in which you teach. It is necessary to realize that no teaching situation is likely to be completely homogeneous.

You need to know as well how to make allowances for students whose physical conditions or religion proscribes some activities or readings to which your other students must legitimately be exposed. Realizing that many students are embarrassed by deviating from the norm, you will also need to learn how to deal tactfully with students who for reasons of health, handicap, or philosophical persuasion must be treated differently from the majority.

I value reactions from users of my books. Readers who write to me in care of the Department of English, University of Illinois, 608 South Wright Street #208, Urbana, Illinois 61801 will receive responses, but more importantly, they will contribute to the value and utility of my future books for teachers.

Finally, I must tell you that although details have been altered here and there to meet certain needs and to preserve the anonymity of teachers and their students, every case study in this book is based upon something that actually has happened. The case studies in Chapter 6 present the most extreme situations in the book. The writer hopes that these extreme—and at times, distressing—case studies will not dissuade people from using the book because every case study in every chapter presents a situation that has happened to some teacher somewhere.

It is unpleasant to think that some ten-year-old students push drugs, that others break into teachers' homes or bring guns to class. You may never in a long teaching career encounter even one such student, and I hope you won't. If, however, you encounter just one student like this in a forty-year teaching career, perhaps having thought through a case study that reflects problems of this sort will enable you to recover from your initial shock sufficiently to deal professionally with the threatening situation.

Teachers unprepared to deal with the extremes of human behavior sometimes leave the profession when such extremes surface in one or more of their classes or in their dealings with students outside the classroom. Teachers who have dealt theoretically with problems that reflect such extremes can—and often do—change the course of their students' lives for the better. In doing so, they add to their personal strength as the professionals they are, and they also strengthen the society in which we are all active participants.

I hope you will read and react to this book, but I hope even more fervently that *Classroom Encounters* is a book you will continue to refer to through the years, either by rereading parts of it or by recalling at crucial moments something from the book that will ease you through your classroom crises—and you are all bound to have a few of these!

Teachers and their students are our nation's greatest hope. Perhaps this book will help in some small way to make our nation's schools stronger and more effective than they now are. We live in a rapidly changing society. This book should provide you with coping mechanisms to meet the situations these changes impose upon all of us.

—R. Baird Shuman
Champaign, Illinois
18 February 1989

1. ON BEING A TEACHER: ENCOUNTERS OF INTERNS/HELP FROM THE EXPERIENCED TEACHER

The reasons people decide to become teachers are as varied as the people who enter the profession. Some opt for teacher training out of dedication, some out of desperation. Regardless of the initial motivation, however, it is hard to generalize on who is likely to become an effective teacher and who is not.

Some history majors have anxious parents who, concerned that their son or daughter has not been trained in college for a specific vocation such as accounting or engineering or hotel management, insist that their children get a teaching certificate as an insurance policy against future unemployment. It is not unusual for some students in this situation to discover during their teaching internships that teaching is the profession about which they are the most excited and in which they find their greatest fulfillment.

On the other hand, some people who have wanted to teach from the day they had their first happy encounter with a sympathetic and effective primary school teacher enter the profession with unrealistic expectations about who and what should be taught in today's schools and quickly turn their backs on the profession when they are faced with the day-to-day realities of the classroom during their teaching internships.

The staffs of institutions that train teachers and send interns into the classroom for their first exposure to teaching know that not all their students are the stuff of which teachers are made. They learn quickly, however, not to prejudge their students but rather to impress upon them that regardless of why they are in teacher training, they owe it to the schools that provide their internships—and, more particularly, to the students in those schools—to be the most conscientious teaching interns they are capable of being.

Trainers of teachers feel this way because they know it is their responsibility to assure the schools with which they work that their interns will not learn to be teachers at the expense of or to the detriment of the students in the classes they teach. A school's first responsibility is to its students. The school that has a negative experience with even one teaching intern may, quite understandably, be unwilling to cooperate with teacher training programs in the future.

But trainers of teachers also realize that they have a responsibility to the students they are teaching and supervising in internships, and it is largely their realization of this responsibility that compels them to demand that their teaching interns work at their highest possible levels. These seasoned professionals know that even those of their students who have virtually no thought of becoming career teachers must, for the sake of their own peace of mind and self-respect, do the best job they can during their internships. They also know that many an intern who did not at first have the most desirable motivation for entering the teaching profession has turned out to be a fine teacher who, sometimes because of a positive internship experience, has become eager to continue teaching.

CASE STUDY 1.1
Intern Distressed About Assignment

Judy M. is twenty years old and will be graduated from her college with a bachelor's degree in Latin in about seven months, two weeks after her twenty-first birthday. Judy finished high school just after her seventeenth birthday, having skipped a year in elementary school, and has always been in the top of her class. Her real hope is that she can go to graduate school to continue her study of classical languages and of art history, a combination that would be useful to her in archaeology, which is her first love.

Judy's hopes of gong directly from college to graduate school were dashed six months ago, however, when her father's business failed, leaving the family with significantly reduced financial resources. It appears that Judy will have to work for a few years at least immediately upon completing her degree. Faced with this stark necessity, Judy immediately began to take the block of education courses that will qualify her to do student teaching and to be eligible for teacher certification in Latin, her major, as well as in social studies, in which she has done substantial work.

Judy has just received her student teaching assignment, and she is distressed for a number of reasons. To begin with, she has been assigned to a school so far from campus that she will have to live in the community, where, fortunately, she has grandparents who have invited her to stay in their home. But living off campus will prevent her from registering for a seminar on Greek artifacts in northwestern Sicily that she had particularly wished to take with a noted visiting professor who will be teaching at her college for only one semester. The local high school and those in the surrounding area do not offer Latin, so she is limited in where she can go for her internship.

To make the situation worse, Judy has recently finished two days of observation at the school in which she will be teaching, and she has learned that for most of the internship she will be able to teach only one Latin class, an elementary one, and that she will be teaching one section of sociology and one of consumer economics to students in the general and business curricula. Only in the last week of her internship will she be permitted to teach her cooperating teacher's Latin 2 and Latin 3 classes. These three are the only Latin classes the school offers.

Judy is so disheartened that she is thinking of withdrawing from the teacher training program and just taking her chances of getting a job outside teaching when she leaves school in May. Her parents, with whom she has discussed the situation, do not want her to abandon the teacher education program because, although jobs are scarce in their area, the local high school wants to reestablish Latin as a foreign language and has expressed a willingness to hire Judy as soon as she is certified. Judy must reach a decision soon because it is time to register for her student-teaching semester, during which she will spend the first eight weeks on campus taking education courses and the second eight weeks off campus in her internship.

Questions

1. Do you think that Judy has a mature view of what teaching entails? What specific facts in her case study help you to formulate your answer?

2. Would Judy be better off to ask for a local placement in which she would teach only social studies? She has had enough courses in history, sociology, economics, psychology, and anthropology to qualify for social studies certification.

3. Should Judy have to do some student teaching in Latin in order to be certified in it? Does your state require that teachers must do student teaching in every field in which they seek certification? How many class hours of student teaching does your state require for teacher certification?

4. Do you think that college students should be permitted to decide at the last minute that they want to work toward teacher certification and qualify for certification merely by accumulating a set number of courses, observations, and internship hours during their last year of college? Do other professions permit entry on such a basis? What would be gained if prospective teachers were required to begin teacher training in the freshman or sophomore year of college? What would be lost?

11

Possible Solutions

1. Judy could talk frankly with her teacher training advisor, explaining that she needs teacher certification only to meet a temporary need and that she does not anticipate spending a lifetime as a secondary school teacher. She could gamble on her advisor's understanding her point of view and trying to help get her another placement—possibly a social studies internship—locally that would enable her to register for the archaeology course she wants so badly to take while she is student teaching.

2. Judy might request that the person in charge of placing students in internships ask the cooperating teacher whether Judy might be scheduled to teach all three of her Latin classes and pick up her sociology and consumer economics classes toward the end of the internship. Judy would be comfortable with this arrangement and would be willing to enter the internship under such an arrangement.

3. Given the total situation, Judy might decide that teaching away from campus in a situation that will permit her to deal with students of widely different interests and capabilities is a rare opportunity that she should make the most of. She might approach the professor who is offering the seminar on Greek artifacts in northwestern Sicily and ask whether she might take the seminar for credit, attending classes regularly for the first eight weeks and completing her work in the course as an independent study.

4. Judy could talk with her advisors in the Classics and Art History Departments to see whether they know of any teaching assistantships for which she might apply if she decides not to go into secondary teaching next year but rather to continue her university studies in the fields of her two major interests with the intention of going to graduate school next year. She might also ask whether they can suggest any stopgap jobs she might, with her qualifications upon graduation, reasonably apply for so that she could work and save money to continue her studies in the near future.

Thought Questions

Which of these solutions do you think is the most professionally responsible? Defend your answer. With which solution do your personally feel most comfortable? Why? What risks do you see in any two of the possible solutions offered? If you were Judy's teacher training advisor, would you encourage her to continue in the teacher training program? If you were Judy's academic advisor, what do you think

12

you would encourage her to do? In what order would you rank the desirability of these possible solutions, using 1 as the most desirable and 4 as the least desirable? Defend your rankings.

Consider This

Often we are forced to make difficult decisions in life. As we grow to adulthood, some of these decisions may trouble or disappoint the people who mean the most to us. Still, we cannot always live our lives according to the expectations other people have for us. Sometimes we are so convinced that one course of action suits us better than another that we embark on it regardless of the advice we receive and the people we disappoint. Judy has to decide whether she will follow her heart and immediately continue her studies in subjects that will perhaps lead her to a graduate degree and possibly to a career in archaeology or whether she will face the realities of her family situation and defer her own plans until such time as that situation is under better control.

Problems like Judy's do not lend themselves to easy or even happy solutions. What Judy has to do is assess what she most wants in life and determine how she can attain her goals within the realistic context of her own situation. Regardless of which decision she makes, she needs to work enthusiastically and positively to implement that decision. In arriving at her decision, she also needs to ask herself what compromise solutions are available to her. Often a compromise will meet needs, either permanently or temporarily, that appear to be in conflict with each other. People who have difficult decisions to make sometimes reach satisfactory solutions if they explore carefully various options and discuss them with those who can provide them with the most informed advice.

PROFILE OF A TEACHER

Attempts to describe teachers in terms of age, gender, appearance, or other such surface characteristics are bound to fail. Teachers, however, *can* be described in terms of some of the ideal qualities parents might hope to find in the people who are charged with educating their children or students might hope to find in the teachers with whom they work. Although the characteristics that follow are important, not every good teacher has all of these qualities in the same degree. For our purposes,

13

though, we can say that most effective teachers generally rank high in most of these characteristics:

- They have self-respect.
- They like to work with young people.
- They are dependable.
- They strive continually to be fair and consistent.
- They plan what they are doing on both a day-to-day and a long-term basis.
- They are eager to learn.
- They are flexible.
- They are sensitive to the feelings of others.
- They cultivate their imaginations.
- They can laugh at themselves.

CASE STUDY 1.2
Teacher Deals with Fighting Students

Gilda L. has taught fifth grade at Lowell Middle School for the past three years, having taught a combined third and fourth grade before that in a small school in a rural area. Gilda has thoroughly enjoyed her students in both schools, but her days, like those of most teachers, are not entirely trouble-free. Although she was an experienced teacher when she came to Lowell, some of her students put her through a testing process.

On one occasion during her second week at Lowell, the situation almost got out of hand as two students, angry with each other about the loss of one of the students' lunch money, began screaming at each other, and the larger of the two appeared ready to pounce on the smaller. Gilda got into the middle of the fray, put her hand on the shoulder of the larger boy, who seemed to be losing control, and said quietly, "Jeff, students in this class must control themselves. You are getting out of control. Go outside and wait for me in the hall." Jeff began to bicker, and Gilda interrupted him softly but sternly and said, "The hall, Jeff. The hall. Right now." "But it's not fair," Jeff continued. "The hall, Jeff. Right now," Gilda said as she tightened her grip on his shoulder and turned him toward the door.

A few minutes later, when Gilda went outside to talk with Jeff, she began by saying, "I am sorry that I seemed unfair to you, Jeff, but you know that I cannot allow people to fight in my classroom. When things start to get out of control, people are not always treated fairly. Now let's forget that this happened. You come back into class as soon as you think you have cooled off enough to work on your fractions."

14

Questions

1. Which of the qualities listed as being desirable in a teacher did Gilda demonstrate in her encounter with Jeff? Did she display any other qualities? If you think she did, identify them.

2. Was it all right for Gilda to touch Jeff and to tighten her grip on him? Might the situation be handled differently if Gilda were a male teacher and if the two combatants were girls? Does your state or your school district have specific rules that govern whether teachers can touch students?

3. Was it inconsistent for Gilda to refuse to respond to Jeff's accusation of unfairness in the classroom and then, on going out to see him in the hall, to tell him she is sorry he felt she was unfair? Why do you think she acted as she did in both situations?

4. Why do you think Gilda did not scold Jeff when she talked with him in the hall? Was it wise for her to tell him he could come back into the room when he felt like it, or should she have scolded him soundly and then brought him back into the room with her? Do you think Jeff will conclude that Gilda is a weak person and will take advantage of this perceived weakness of her in the future? Why or why not?

Possible Solutions

1. On realizing that a physical encounter was likely, Gilda might have stayed away from the center of it, so that she would not be hurt if any fisticuffs erupted. She might have remained in the front of the room and yelled at the two boys loudly enough so that they would be sure to hear her over the din. She might have threatened them with after-school detentions or with being sent to the principal's office.

2. Knowing that a fight was about to take place in her classroom, Gilda might have asked some of the bigger boys in the class to restrain the two boys who were angry with each other. With the bigger boys holding them, she could then try to find out what had become of the lunch money they were arguing about by grilling first one boy, then the other or by asking other students what they knew about the missing lunch money.

3. Gilda could have separated both boys and let them get their complaint out in the open before the entire class. That would have been a democratic way of handling this difficult and threatening situation. Gilda handled the situation pretty well up to the point that Jeff accused her of being unfair. Instead of discussing the situation with him, do you think she reacted unreasonably, asserting her authority

15

and giving him no opportunity to tell his side of the story? Then, apparently after realizing how wrong she had been, did she undermine her own authority by coming just short of apologizing to him?

4. Realizing that fifth-grade students are not going to be on their best behavior all the time, Gilda could have let the two boys fight with each other and be done with it. After the fight, she could have sent both boys to the principal or vice-principal, who is used to dealing with such situations. She also might have telephoned each boy's parents to complain about their behavior in her class the day of the fight.

Thought Questions

What must a teacher's first concern be in dealing with a situation like the one Gilda was confronted by? Do you think a more lasting solution to the problem would have been achieved had Gilda used one or more of the possible solutions above rather than the one she actually used? How do you defend your answer? Does consistent treatment of students mean that each student will be treated in exactly the same way in every situation? Is utter consistency in the classroom always desirable?

Consider This

Teachers always feel threatened when physical violence is about to erupt in their classrooms. They cannot allow behavior problems to interfere with the learning environment in the classroom. Nevertheless, effective teachers turn such inevitable events into learning experiences for as many students as possible. They realize that overt conflicts like the one described above can be symptomatic of problems students might be having outside the classroom, although such is not always the case. The main thing teachers must try to bear in mind when they are forced to think on their feet in order to respond effectively to the unexpected is that they are involved in a transaction with their students. They should not bring outsiders into the less pleasant aspects of that transaction unless there is absolutely no other way to deal with the situation or unless the negative behavior is so threatening as to put others in jeopardy. Once a crisis has passed, it is best not to revive the memory of that crisis but rather to go on to other things, minimizing the disruptive event and allowing the participants in it to resume their participation in the positive aspects of what the class is doing.

HOW SMART DO TEACHERS HAVE TO BE?

The response to this question is probably another question: "Smart in what?" Some people who are smart in mathematics or science or literary analysis or history run into terrible difficulty when they try to teach others the subjects they excel in. This situation can arise among teachers who are so naturally gifted in a given subject that they cannot understand or anticipate the learning problems of those less gifted than they who try to learn the subject. Teachers like this sometimes complain that they cannot reach some of the students in their classes because the students do not have enough background to learn the material to be covered.

The best teachers often turn out to be those who have themselves had problems learning the subjects they are now teaching. Such people may not qualify as geniuses in their fields, but they may be so perceptive about people, so people-smart, that they can help their students overcome the obstacles that block their learning. Good teachers have to be smart about *something* if they are to succeed. That something, however, is not always reflected in their grade-point averages or in their own school performances, although people are expected to have basic competency in the fields in which they teach.

CASE STUDY 1.3
Star Basketball Player as Teaching Intern

George T. is not sure he wants to teach. He has been a star college basketball player and harbors some hope of becoming a professional player after he is graduated next month. His eight-week student-teaching internship is in a middle school that serves a rural community, which has recently become a bedroom community for people who work in the computer industry that has developed in this area. The middle school now serves a combination of students whose formal educations will likely end when they leave high school and an increasing number of students who will continue their educations at the college level.

In his internship, George is teaching social studies and health education. He is responsible for teaching three of his cooperating teacher's five classes. Two of these classes, one in civics and the other in health education, enroll virtually the same students, most of whom do not anticipate going to college. They knew George by reputation before he came to their school because of the publicity his prowess in basketball gave him. They regard him as an idol, so he has no trouble teaching these classes.

17

George's third class, however, focuses on the U.S. Constitution. The students in it are among the best in the school. Nearly every day some of the students in this class ask George unexpected questions that he cannot answer. They also catch him occasionally in factual inaccuracies.

George has good rapport with the students in this class, and despite the problems that George thinks exist, students appear to respect him and to respond well to his teaching. George is so unnerved by having to teach this class, however, that he finds it difficult to face coming to school every morning. Most nights he has disturbing dreams in which hundreds of students fire specific questions at him that he cannot answer. These dreams wake him up. He tosses and turns for hours afterwards, too disturbed to sleep. He does not know how he can complete his teaching internship, although his cooperating teacher and his college supervisor have found no fault with his teaching and have consistently complemented him on how well he is doing.

Questions

1. What does George's reaction to his problem tell you about him? Do you think he can eventually become an effective teacher for students in classes like the one that is bothering him? Defend your answer.

2. Why do you suppose George has failed to discuss his problem either with his cooperating teacher or with his college supervisor? What would you do in George's situation? Can you think of anyone else whom he might turn to for help?

3. If you were in George's place, would you ask to be relieved of the class that is causing you problems? Why or why not?

4. If you were George's cooperating teacher and he asked you to be relieved of the problem class, how would you respond? Defend your answer.

Possible Solutions

1. George could structure his problem class more tightly so that students would have less opportunity to ask questions. If George decides on this solution, he must realize that he may discourage open inquiry and that his students may be reluctant to participate in discussions later on. This solution could alleviate George's immediate problem, but it could create new problems for him and his students in the future.

2. George needs to find out whether this class frequently asks

18

their regular teacher questions that she cannot answer. Certainly this is a question George can ask in an offhanded way without casting himself in a bad light, which apparently is what he most fears. The chances are that any teacher fortunate enough to teach bright students will find that such students often ask questions he or she cannot anticipate or immediately answer. One way to handle such a situation is simply to admit that you don't know and suggest ways to find answers.

3. George might level with his class, congratulating them on the depth of the questions they ask and asking them if it bothers them that he cannot answer all of their questions. The chances are that they are used to asking questions that teachers cannot answer and that they were not aware that a problem exists.

Thought Questions

Which of the solutions listed above are you most comfortable with? Why? What alternate solution(s) to George's problem can you think of? Do you consider George's problem typically a problem of a beginning teacher, or is it a problem that experienced teachers sometimes have to face as well?

Consider This

During any typical year of teaching, we are all likely to have in our classes some students who are brighter than we are. If this were not so, the future of humankind would be bleak indeed. To say that some of our students have more inherent brain power than we have is not the same as saying that we have nothing to offer these students. Most of us are superior to most of them in age, training, and experience. We need to do all we can to help bright students develop their full potentials, rejoicing in their intelligence rather than being threatened by it. Most of our students are eager to learn from us, and all else being equal, we can also learn from them. Some of the most effective learning occurs when the learning experience becomes a two-way street.

DEMONSTRATING RESPONSIBILITY

Not all teachers relish the idea of turning their classes over to teaching interns, particularly if they have worked hard to bring their classes up to the point they are when an intern would logically take over. The colleges and universities that place their teacher trainees in internships strive al-

19

ways to make the placements they think are most likely to succeed. They try to cultivate a solid interrelationship between their institutions and the schools they work with. Therefore, it is incumbent upon those who go out into internships to do all they can to inspire their cooperating teachers' confidence and to work steadily and consistently to build that confidence throughout the period of the internship.

Every cooperating teacher deals differently with interns. Some require extensive lesson plans, which become the bases for daily conferences with the teaching intern. Others trust their interns to prepare well and presume that if they run into trouble in their teaching, they will seek guidance from the cooperating teacher.

Some cooperating teachers turn classes over to their interns and leave the room. Others never leave the room while the intern is teaching. Some school districts forbid cooperating teachers to leave the room because they are legally responsible for what goes on in it whether they or the intern is teaching. If your cooperating teacher stays in the room while you are teaching, do not leap immediately to the conclusion that he or she does not trust you. It may be that this teacher is under a mandate to stay there, or it may be that he or she has no place to go at that particular time.

If the cooperating teacher sits in the back of the room writing furiously while you are teaching, do not conclude immediately that you are doomed because he or she is making copious notes about your teaching performance. It is just as likely that the cooperating teacher is catching up on a report that has to be on the principal's desk before the three-thirty bell and that all the writing has nothing at all to do with you. When we are in situations in which we are being judged by outsiders, it is quite natural to experience a mild paranoia, but to let this paranoia get out of control is to sell yourself short. If you are well prepared and have confidence in what you are doing, you likely have nothing to worry about.

CASE STUDY 1.4
Intern Observes Supervising Teacher

Todd U. comes from a family of teachers. He has always wanted to teach, and now he is fulfilling his dream. He has himself been an excellent student, and he loves going to school. He went through school in a small town where everyone knew each other. The atmosphere in all three schools he attended before college was warm, friendly, and informal.

Todd had the opportunity to return to his old junior high school for his teaching internship in mathematics and science, but he thought that would be a bad idea because he knew everyone at the school, students and faculty alike, and because his sister is teaching French there. Instead, Todd has requested and received placement at Hoover Senior High School in a large industrial city about a hundred miles from his home and thirty miles from his college.

Todd visited the site of his internship for two days of observation before his eleven-week teaching quarter began. He met his supervising teacher, Mr. K., who had prepared a packet of materials for him to orient him to what was going on in the classes he would be observing. Todd sat in on Mr. K.'s classes. Mr. K. introduced him to a number of other teachers and members of the school's administration. He gave Todd the textbooks he would need to prepare for his teaching and discussed with him which of his classes Todd would most like to teach at first. Todd was pleased that Mr. K. introduced him to each class as a teacher who would soon be sharing the teaching of some of Mr. K.'s classes. During Todd's two days of observation, Mr. K. invited Todd to work with some students who were engaged in small-group activities. He also gave Todd seating charts so that he could get to know the names of the students in the classes he would be taking over.

Before it was time for him to leave, Todd thanked his cooperating teacher for making him feel so welcome and for involving him in some classroom activities. He said that he was eager to begin to work on his lesson plans for the first two weeks of his internship and asked Mr. K. whether the school had any particular form it followed for lesson plans. Mr. K. gave Todd a supply of lesson plan forms the school district used and told him that each teacher was asked to complete brief lesson plans for each class every week and to leave these lesson plans in the top drawer of the desk every Monday morning so they would be available to a substitute teacher in case the regular teacher had to be absent.

Todd volunteered to send his first week's lesson plans to Mr. K. so that he could look them over and give Todd any input he felt would be helpful to him before he began his actual teaching.

Questions

1. Did Todd show good judgment in requesting that he serve his internship in a school in which he was not known and in which he knew no one? What advantages might he have had had he accepted an internship in his old junior high school? What counterbalancing advantages is his present placement likely to have over the one he decided against?

2. What are the major purposes of having teacher trainees observe in the school and with the teacher they will be working with during the internship? What should the intern expect to accomplish during those days?

3. If interns find during the days of observation that their cooperating teacher has made no plans for their arrival, does not have extra copies of the books from which they will be teaching, or totally ignores them as they sit in the classroom observing, should the interns take any action? What can interns who find themselves in such situations do in their interaction with the cooperating teacher? With the college supervisor or with the placement office for teaching interns?

4. How did Mr. K. make Todd feel welcome in the classroom? How did Todd work to make Mr. K. feel that he has a professional outlook, that he is serious about his work, and that he is dependable?

Possibilities To Consider

1. Todd rode over to Hoover Senior High School from the college with two classmates who would be serving their internships there at the same time Todd would. They were all eager to find out as much as they could about the school and to compare their experiences during this observation period. They agreed to meet for lunch the first day, so they could talk things over. Just before the lunch hour, Mr. K. says to Todd, "I hope you can join me for lunch. The math-science coordinator is having lunch with me, and I think you should get to know her." At this point, Todd might say that he has lunch plans but that he would be pleased to have lunch with Mr. K. and the math-science coordinator the next day. He might, on the other hand, forget about having lunch with his friends and do as Mr. K. has suggested. A third course would be for him to tell Mr. K. that he had made plans but that he can easily change them because he really wants to meet the math-science coordinator. He could say to Mr. K., "I'll see my friends for a minute or two right at the beginning of the lunch hour, but I will be pleased to join you in the Teachers' Lunch Room."

2. Mr. K. gives his first-period class some instructions and then has them divide into groups, each of which has a problem to work on cooperatively. Mr. K. circulates among the groups but does not suggest that Todd do so. Should Todd just sit still and watch, or should he involve himself with the students? If Todd is just sitting and watching the group activity and a student from one group asks him, "Do you know how to read this chart we're using?" should Todd just begin to work spontaneously with that group, or should he ask Mr. K. if he would like him to work with it?

3. The fourth-period class has just adjourned, and the next period is Mr. K.'s lunch hour. Mr. K. has not asked Todd to have lunch with him. Should Todd suggest that they go to lunch together? Would it be better for him to ask Mr. K. something like, "What time would you like me to be back here?" or "Do you have anything you would like me to do for you during the lunch period?"

Thought Questions

What specific things can cooperating teachers do to help make interns feel comfortable during their first exposure to the school and to the actual classes they will be teaching? In what specific ways can interns establish that they are approaching the internship in a professional manner? Should interns expect cooperating teachers to ask them which of the available classes they would prefer to teach at the beginning of the internship? If a cooperating teacher does not do this, what might the reasons be? Is it ever legitimate for interns to say that they do not feel equipped to teach a given class that their cooperating teachers normally teach? If so, should they approach the cooperating teacher directly or through the college supervisor?

Consider This

The prospect of the teaching internship can be unsettling and intimidating both for the interns who are about to teach for the first time and for the cooperating teachers with whom they are assigned to work. Most interns want to do well, but they may find themselves paired with cooperating teachers whose methods are so different from those the interns feel comfortable with that problems seem inevitable. Still worse, interns are sometimes placed with teachers who are so popular and so dynamic in the classroom that students resent having to give up their teachers to be taught by people who are still finding their ways quite tentatively, perhaps stumbling occasionally in the process of learning how to teach.

One way to ease the transition from regular teachers to teaching interns may be for cooperating teachers to involve interns in teaching parts of classes rather than whole classes at the beginning of the internship. It is also desirable for cooperating teachers to let their interns know that there is no single "right" way to teach. Every teacher teaches in his or her own way. What works for some teachers will not work for others. Interns should be assured that if they are conscientious and consistently well prepared, they are free to adopt teaching

23

styles different from those of their cooperating teachers. Interns must also be ready to make some concessions to their cooperating teachers. They, after all, have been working with the students in their classes every day for quite a while by the time the interns arrive, and they will resume working with these students full time when the interns leave. In fairness to the students involved, transitions from regular teacher to teaching intern and back again must be as smooth as possible. The cooperating teacher's first responsibility is to the students in his or her charge. This fact cannot be ignored.

DEALING WITH THE UNEXPECTED

It is difficult to anticipate everything that may happen to interns during the early days of their internships, but one should expect the unexpected. It is impossible to plan in detail how to handle unanticipated events, but common sense tempered by patience and understanding should prevail when such events occur. Interns may feel quite threatened by something that is basically not threatening at all.

For example, suppose that the first day an intern is teaching, a student in the class directs a question like, "May I get a drink of water?" to the cooperating teacher, who is sitting in the back of the classroom. The cooperating teacher may, without thinking, answer, "You can wait. It is only five minutes until the bell rings." A more appropriate response would certainly be, "Mr. U. is your teacher. Ask him." Responding to a student question, however, is frequently a spontaneous act on the part of a teacher, and interns should not feel that their authority is being undermined if their cooperating teachers occasionally forget that they are now observers in rather than teachers of the classes assigned to the intern.

Sometimes more significant problems arise, such as the one outlined in the case study below. Interns faced with problems like this one must approach them with understanding, tact, and patience. These, after all, are qualities that an internship should help one to cultivate along with the more obvious teaching skills that interns learn. Interns who have legitimate complaints should remember that whenever it is possible, it is more professional for them to make those complaints to the college supervisor directly rather than to anyone in the school.

Interns must realize, as well, that not all legitimate complaints can be dealt with effectively. Sometimes interns just have to grit their teeth and live with problems during the internship. It is less likely, however, that they will have to do this if they act professionally and responsibly at all times. Such actions often beget similar actions from those with whom one has a professional relationship.

24

Substitute Asks Intern To Teach Full Load

When Todd U. arrived at Hoover Senior High School to begin his internship, he was enthusiastic and optimistic. He had begun preparing for the classes he would begin to teach when the marking period was over on Friday. Meanwhile, he observed in the classes of Mr. K., his cooperating teacher, trying to learn the names of the students he would be teaching and to learn something about their interests and abilities.

Everything went well for the first three days of Todd's observations. When he arrived at school on Thursday, however, he learned that Mr. K. had had a sudden death in his immediate family and would have to miss school until the following Tuesday. A substitute teacher was scurrying around the room when Todd arrived. He introduced himself to her, and she promptly said, "I don't know anything about math and science. I'm taking an M.A. in Cinema Studies. As long as you know these kids and what they're doing, why don't you teach the classes?"

Todd was perplexed because he did not want his first teaching experience with these students to be spur-of-the-moment. He really was not specifically prepared to teach the material they were scheduled to cover today, and he was not sure whether he should do something else with them. He was reluctant to refuse to teach, but he wondered why the district was paying a substitute teacher if the substitute was not going to teach. Further, he was not prepared to teach all five of his cooperating teacher's classes.

Todd felt cornered, so he did the best thing he could to extricate himself: he took the classes for that day and told them the history of how the concept of zero had come into mathematics. He demonstrated what a convenient concept zero is by having his students try to multiply and divide with Roman numerals. The lesson was popular enough that Todd was able to save face, but he now had to reach a decision about Friday and Monday.

Questions

1. Should Todd have expected Mr. K. to telephone him and forewarn him that he would be out of school for three days? Should Todd get in touch with Mr. K., and if he does, what should be the purpose of his call?

2. Was the substitute teacher being reasonable when she suggested that Todd take over the classes? Why do you think the principal

did not call Todd before school and suggest that he take over the classes, perhaps even that he be paid for those three days, rather than hire a substitute who was not trained in mathematics and science to handle the situation? Would that not have been a reasonable solution to the problem?

3. Do you think Todd did the right thing in agreeing to teach all of his cooperating teacher's classes on Thursday? What should he do about Friday and Monday? If you were in Todd's situation, do you think it would be best to discuss the matter after school on Thursday with the principal, your college supervisor, or, if you can reach him or her, your cooperating teacher?

4. Should Todd suggest to the principal that he can take the classes over on Friday and Monday and that the substitute need not be employed for those days? In your state, would it be legal for Todd to take those classes over for two days with no supervision from a certified teacher?

Possible Solutions

1. When the substitute teacher suggested that Todd take over the classes, Todd might have sought some sort of compromise, such as having the students break into small review groups, some of which he would handle and some of which the substitute teacher would handle. He might justify this compromise by saying that he had worked with these students in small-group situations before, but that he wanted his first regular lessons to them to be well planned and he really was not yet ready to teach them in any formal sense.

2. Todd is better qualified by training to teach these students than the substitute teacher who has been employed to cover the classes. He knows this, and the substitute teacher realizes it. The district, however, has hired a substitute because its substitutes have been screened and are drawn from an approved list of people in the community who meet the legal requirements to be substitute teachers. Todd, therefore, might simply refuse to do what the substitute teacher has asked him to, saying that it is not his job to do this. The substitute teacher could hardly refute such an argument.

3. Startled by the suggestion that he begin teaching immediately, Todd could excuse himself politely, going directly to the school principal to explain the situation. The principal certainly engaged the substitute teacher with the expectation that this teacher would teach. The principal would have to back Todd in this conflict, but Todd must also consider what messages he would be sending to the principal by dumping the problem in his or her lap.

4. Knowing that he has one interesting lesson that is good for a full day of teaching, Todd could tell the substitute that he will be willing to give that lesson so that the substitute will have time to prepare for the next two days, but that he does not feel ready or able to take over all five classes for the entire three days his cooperating teacher will be away from school. To make sure he will not be called upon to teach on Friday and Monday, might Todd simply call in and say that he is sick and cannot come to school on those two days?

Thought Questions

Would it be fair for Todd to call his cooperating teacher at a difficult time in that teacher's life in the hope that the teacher could resolve the problem? Which of the solutions given above do you think is the most professional one to use in dealing with this situation? If the substitute teacher were to agree to Possible Solution 4 above, do you think Todd should call in sick on Friday and Monday? If not, what might he do in school on those days? Should he seek suggestions from anyone about how to occupy himself on those days?

Consider This

First impressions are often hard to dispel. For this reason, teachers should make sure that their initial classes are carefully planned and well thought out. It is usually desirable, especially for beginning teachers, to plan more activities for the first days of teaching than they really think they can get to. Having extra activities to fall back on will help the beginning teacher build confidence. The best classes are usually those that have three or four different kinds of activities scheduled for the class hour, which, depending on where you teach, runs anywhere from forty-five to fifty-five minutes. If you find yourself in an emergency situation like Todd's, be polite but firm in declining to do anything that you feel you cannot do well. You will be working with these students for your entire internship. The substitute teacher will not, so a second-rate performance by a substitute teacher, while unfortunate, will not have the damaging effects that an initial, second-rate performance by a teaching intern might have.

WHEN THE GREMLINS CONSPIRE

No matter how well-intentioned and well-organized teaching interns are, they are sometimes at the mercy of forces outside their control. Some of these forces are less likely to plague them when they are regular teachers, but for now they seem to have no way of dealing with some of the problems that face them.

No matter how prompt a person is, if that person is dependent on someone else for a ride to school in the morning, it is the driver's punctuality that will determine the punctuality of everyone riding in the car. Interns are not always in a position to buy themselves cars or to take taxicabs to school in an emergency, especially if the school is twenty-five or thirty miles away. Interns must realize, nevertheless, that a great many judgments that are made about them will be based upon their dependability, punctuality, and sense of responsibility. For better or worse, this is a fact of life that interns cannot ignore.

If you think such judgments are unfair, think of them in terms of something related to your own life. Suppose you schedule an eight-o'clock appointment with your dentist, knowing that you have to be at work at nine. You get to the dentist's office shortly before 8:00, and at 8:45 you are still waiting. The dentist arrives, saying breathlessly, "Sorry to be late. My radiator boiled over on the way here."

The excuse is valid, but you have your life to live. You do not want excuses. You want a dentist who can be depended on to keep his or her appointments. You are now forced to make a decision that you should not have to make: whether to be late for work or whether to forget about having your dental work done that day.

You may excuse your dentist once for a lapse of this sort, but if it happens a second time, rather than risk having such a situation occur again in the future, you might decide to change dentists. People do not want excuses from professionals; they expect and demand reliable performance. Such are the hard facts of life!

A FINAL THOUGHT

No one expects teaching interns to be superhuman. Those who work with them, however, have a reasonable right to expect that they will pay close attention to the following:

- They will make an effort to be responsible at all times.
- They will prepare for their classes.
- They will prepare written lesson plans.
- They will keep their cooperating teachers informed of what they are doing.
- They will abide by the rules of the school.
- They will be punctual both in arriving at school and in meeting their responsibilities.
- They will make a conscious effort not to disrupt the atmosphere the regular teacher has established.

2. STARTING THE JOB: INTERNS, FIRST-YEAR TEACHERS, EXPERIENCED TEACHERS IN NEW SCHOOLS

In this chapter, we will consider the early days of a teaching experience. Teachers new to their schools need to give serious thought to how they will prepare for their first two or three weeks of teaching because the tone they set in these early days determines in many ways the ease or difficulty with which they will fit into their new situations.

Among teachers new to a school are teaching interns, first-year teachers, and experienced teachers who have taught elsewhere but are moving into a new school. Understandably, all of these teachers will experience some apprehension as they approach their new tasks. Change can be threatening! A teacher who has taught for twenty years in one place and then moves to another may feel as much like a rookie as twenty-one-year-old college students who are having their first teaching experiences. Apprehension sometimes is strongest in those who will turn out to be the very best teachers. Good teachers have high expectations for themselves and are not always 100-percent convinced that they can meet these expectations, although most of them not only meet but far exceed them.

Although lack of self-confidence can be crippling in its extreme stages, in most cases it serves as a good control upon us. Because we want to do well and because we are not sure that we will, we recognize the need to prepare carefully and to anticipate situations that may arise. If we have at least tentative plans for dealing with the unexpected, then the unexpected will frighten us less than it would if we had never given any thought to how we might cope with it.

WHAT MIGHT HAPPEN?

On the teaching level, it is not unusual for beginning teachers to think that they do not know their subject matter well enough to teach it. Many of those who have recently been graduated from college have studied with professors who know a great deal about the subjects they teach. To the beginning teacher, a professor's mastery of his or her subject material may seem encyclopedic. These same beginning teachers might find that their teaching schedules include classes in subjects in which they feel only minimally competent.

Typically, for example, secondary school English teachers will have had more training in literature than in grammar and rhetoric, yet they will probably find that the systemwide study guide that mandates what they teach emphasizes grammar and writing at the expense of literature. Even the literature taught in many high schools may not emphasize the Chaucer, Milton, and Shakespeare that most English majors get ample doses of in college but may focus instead upon adolescent literature, folk literature, or science fiction.

Elementary school teachers, even those who barely passed their mathematics courses in college, can count on finding themselves called upon to teach mathematics if they teach in grades one through five or six. The mathematics that gave them so much trouble in college, however, is quite different from the level of arithmetic they will likely be teaching in the lower grades, and they *will* be able to function in the elementary school setting. Likely they will also discover that their textbooks are carefully designed to meet the learning needs of young students and that they offer as well detailed teachers' guides that suggest valid and appropriate ways of presenting the material being covered and of testing students on that material. Subject matter supervisors and colleagues can be extremely helpful to teachers who need to have their confidence boosted—but they cannot help unless they know there is a problem.

No teacher knows everything. If your college has sponsored you as a student teacher or if the state has certified you as a teacher at a given level and/or in a given subject, it is because you are considered qualified for the job. You may or may not function as well in your first year as you will in your tenth or twentieth, but a combination of standard criteria has indicated that you have met certain prescribed standards of competence. Everyone has to begin somewhere.

It is important for all teachers, experienced as well as inexperienced, to know where and how to get help when they need it and to realize that advance planning will shield them from many problems. They must also realize that asking for help and guidance is not an admission or indication of weakness. Instead, reasonable requests for help are usually viewed as evidence of conscientious professionalism.

CASE STUDY 2.1
New Teacher Volunteers for Open Classroom

Rosemarie L. has always worked well with preadolescent children. She had done volunteer work with them in her church. She has spent three summers working with eight- to ten-year-olds in camp. She recently completed her B.S. in Education at a small private college with a strong reputation, and now she has taken a big step. She has taken a job teaching in an elementary school in a school district over two thousand miles from home. She chose to teach in this district because it has gained national attention for its innovative approach to education. She has volunteered to teach in an open classroom situation.

Rosemarie read and wrote a critical review of Herbert Kohl's book *The Open Classroom* for her class in Foundations of Education, but she has never seen the concept in operation. She took her teaching internship in a traditional elementary school, where she was assigned to a cooperating teacher, Ms. W., who taught fifth grade. Rosemarie got along well in her internship. Ms. W. was particularly pleased to have an intern whose presence in the school for ten weeks enabled this dedicated, experienced teacher to work individually with some of the slower students while Rosemarie assumed responsibility for a great deal of the regular teaching.

When they were initially dividing their teaching responsibilities, Rosemarie and Ms. W. each assumed major responsibility for teaching some of what had to be taught, with Rosemarie gladly taking the lion's share. Without making any great show of not wanting to teach English grammar, in which Rosemarie felt totally inadequate, she quickly volunteered to teach the things she felt fairly confident about—fractions and decimals, social studies, and literature. Seeing nothing wrong with this arrangement, Ms. W., who had taught grammar for years, acceded to it enthusiastically.

Rosemarie was so successful in her internship that, as soon as it ended, the school district where she interned hired her as a substitute teacher for a fourth-grade class whose teacher had taken maternity leave for the remaining four weeks of the school year. The experience was a good one, although during it Rosemarie scrupulously avoided teaching things she was not sure of.

Now, about to begin her new teaching assignment, Rosemarie is petrified because the school in which she is teaching has just announced that it will give special attention to teaching the English language throughout the district this school year, thereby attempting to meet community criticism that the English curriculum is not meeting the needs of its students. Rosemarie is particularly apprehensive because she knows that she will be teaching in open space where her fellow teachers can hear and see what she is doing with her students. The only enclosed spaces in her school are the restrooms, the kitchen, and the principal's office—and even the principal's office has no door.

Questions

1. Do you think Rosemarie will be attempting to adjust to too many new things in her first teaching experience? If you were in her place

and had a choice, would you volunteer for the open classroom situation, or would you begin in a more traditional setting? Why or why not?

2. What are some advantages of going far away to teach in one's first full-time teaching job? What disadvantages do you see in making such a drastic move?

3. Do you think Rosemarie really has made a realistic decision regarding where and in what setting she will teach? Do you see any evidence that she might be giving in to a passing enthusiasm? Is it always bad to give in to passing enthusiasms?

4. Do you think that other teachers in the new school are going to pay much attention to what Rosemarie is teaching and to how she is teaching it? What will they pay the greatest attention to?

5. What major differences do you see between teaching in an open space environment and in a more typical classroom? Would you expect students in the open classroom to be more or less involved in learning activities than their counterparts in more usual settings? Defend your answer.

Possible Solutions

1. Rosemarie is obviously a resourceful and independent person. She is not afraid to tackle new experiences, although she has certain insecurities about some of the things she does. She might, given the distance she will be from family and friends, decide that she ought to teach in a regular classroom for her first year or two of teaching. Her only fear is that if she does not try this new experience, she might be reluctant to try it in the future after she has gained confidence in her ability to teach in the more conventional setting.

2. Knowing that she wants a complete change of scene when she finishes her teacher training, Rosemarie might try to find a job in a distant place she would like to try living in but might persuade a friend from college to get a job in the same place so that she would have some sort of support system when she needs it.

3. Rosemarie thinks it will benefit her to teach in a part of the country she wants to know more about, and she thinks that as long as she is making one change, she should make another, that of teaching in a nontraditional setting. She realizes, however, that she will need to make friends in her new setting, so that she will have people to turn to when she has a down day, as she knows she likely will. She works through the superintendent's office in the new district to find another new teacher with whom she can share an apartment. She also is determined to get there a few weeks early, so that she

can get used to the community and so that she can find a glee club to sing in because she loves music and she knows she can meet people with similar enthusiasms in a glee club.

4. Rosemarie might follow the course of least resistance and take a teaching job in her hometown, perhaps in the school in which she was a student a decade or so earlier. It would be much easier for her to live with her parents, to get back to her old room, and to have someone who would get her dinner on the table after a hard day. This solution seems extremely appealing to many young teachers— until they realize that they might wake up one day and find that they are approaching retirement and have never really lived!

Thought Questions

Who have your most stimulating teachers been? What has made them stimulating? Some people can spend their lives in one constricted area and still grow intellectually. Try to determine whether you are one of these by asking such questions as (1) Am I easily bored? (2) If I have two weeks free, would I rather go away or stay home? (3) When I plan a vacation, do I like to go back to someplace I know, or do I prefer to head to someplace I have never been before?

Consider This

No two people are exactly alike. Some people remain alive, fresh, and intellectually vital no matter how geographically limited they are. Others can wander eternally over the face of the earth and never really benefit from new experiences because they are not receptive to new people and to new ways of doing things.

Rosemarie obviously is in the class of people one might call venturesome, and that is a strength that should help her to build her confidence in all areas of her life. One of the advantages people like Rosemarie have is that when conditions change, they are adaptable enough to deal with change. If the school in their hometown has a sharp decrease in enrollment, they are willing to pick up and go where the jobs are. If their school district adopts a new way of teaching, such as writing and/or reading across the curriculum, they are willing to give the new method their best efforts.

If you are something like Rosemarie, you should venture into new areas and seek out new experiences. If, on the other hand, you know yourself well enough to realize that striking out as Rosemarie has would terrify you or disorient you, avoid drastically new places and experiences. Don't close your mind to change; rather, approach it gradually. Instead of going two thousand miles away to teach, teach closer to home, but take a summer course somewhere far away, maybe even abroad. Don't volunteer to teach the experimental class in your first year of teaching; instead, find a more traditional setting, but try new tactics as often as you can to teach your students in this setting.

Trying group work or a field trip or switching classes with another teacher for one day does not commit you the way Rosemarie's decision commits her, but it affords you an opportunity to take the first plunge toward being more flexible than you seem naturally to be.

Do not look down on yourself if you are not venturesome. Remember that Immanuel Kant, one of the most revered German philosophers, spent his entire life within forty miles of his home, but he had a mind that encompassed the universe, and this mind made him the exciting person he was. On the other hand, it would be hard to think of Ernest Hemingway spending his whole lifetime in one place.

WHAT MIGHT YOU BE EXPECTED TO TEACH?

Teachers are not always aware that they may legitimately be asked to teach outside their fields of formal preparation. In most states, school principals are authorized to meet curricular needs by assigning to teach the classes their schools must offer those teachers who, in their eyes, are best qualified to teach them. On the surface this does seem unreasonable, but in practice, particularly in small, isolated school districts, some unexpected assignments are made, and in most cases, they are not in violation of the laws of the state or the rules of the district.

Every principal wants to have the best school possible. Let us say, however, that School X has, despite valiant efforts, been unable to find the science teacher it needs for the upcoming school year. If the school year is about to begin and that position has not been filled, then the principal has to examine the transcripts of the teachers who are available. If the transcripts show that Mr. J., who teaches social studies, is the only person on the school's faculty—aside from the science and mathematics teachers already in place for next year—who has had college courses in chemistry, physics, biology, and calculus, even though Mr. J. may have received grades of "C–" or "D+" in all of these subjects, the principal might have to assign Mr. J. to teach general science or beginning algebra as part of his teaching load.

Social studies teachers are usually easier to find than science and mathematics teachers. Therefore, the only solution available in a situation like the one described here might be to hire a social studies teacher who can take some of Mr. J.'s social studies classes and to assign Mr. J. to teach two or three science classes. Reasonable principals would not follow such a course unless no other options were available to them. When the school year is about to begin, however, principals sometimes must accept extreme solutions to desperate problems.

Most principals who are forced to seek such desperate remedies to their staffing problems do so with the full hope and expectation of resolving the problem as well and as quickly as they can. Teachers forced to teach out of field should expect timely relief from their situations, as well as considerable help from their colleagues and from district personnel while they are meeting an emergency staffing situation.

CASE STUDY 2.2
New Teacher Asked To Teach Out of Field

George B. has been hired to teach physical education and coach basketball at Snavley Senior High School in a large southern industrial city. He completed the work for his teaching certificate four years ago but has not taught since. He has been working as an account executive for a brokerage firm, but an unexpected economic downturn has resulted in his being relieved of his duties with two weeks' notice and with two months' separation pay, hardly enough to support him and his wife, who quit her job when their baby was born five months ago.

George is well known and respected in his community, and the school district had tried earlier to interest him in coming to it as a teacher and coach. George's teaching certificate is in health and physical education and in social studies. Although he is glad to have a job that seems a little more secure than his last one, George is worried about beginning a new career.

When he was hired, George was told that he would teach seven sections of physical education, each meeting twice a week, and two of health education, each meeting five times a week. The two health education classes use the same textbook and cover identical material. Each enrolls students of mixed ability.

Wanting to make a good first impression, George has prepared a tentative outline for the first month of teaching his health education classes. He also knows essentially what he wants to do with his physical education classes for the whole term. He will do his coaching after school, and he will receive a supplement for his night and weekend work with the basketball team during the season.

The school year opens with three teacher preparation days, and George looks forward to having time to organize his teaching further before classes begin. On the afternoon of the second preparation day, the principal, Dr. R., asks George to come to his office. When George gets there, he learns from Dr. R. that one of his colleagues in mathematics is in the hospital terminally ill. She might be able to return to school for brief periods during the term, but this is doubtful. Dr. R. says to George, "I didn't want to ask you to teach math because you are not certified in it and have not had many math courses." George breathed a sigh of relief!

"But," Dr. R. continues, "it has been devilishly hard to work things out this late in the hiring season, and the only solution I can come up with is to have Ms. C. cover the math classes, hire a long-term substitute in social studies, and get several regular teachers to divide Ms. C.'s consumer education classes among themselves. It is not an ideal solution, I know, but," Dr. R. says, shoving a yellow legal pad toward George, "you can see what I am up against and what problems I had coming up with even this imperfect way to cover the classes."

"I take it that you want me to pick up one or two of the classes that need to be covered," George says. "Oh, yes," he continues, looking at Dr. R.'s scribblings, "I see my name here. Consumer econ."

"Yes," Dr. R. replies. "I am going to have to ask you to give up two of your physical education classes and replace them with one consumer econ class. I hate to do this to you, but I can't see any way around it. I am taking Ms. C.'s other consumer econ class myself. I used to teach the course way back when. I'll be glad to share anything I can with you and to work together with you in preparing to teach the course. Your work at the brokerage house should give you a good background to take this course on."

George leaves the interview downhearted, troubled, and pessimistic.

Questions

1. What might happen if George just outrightly refused to do as he has been asked? Would he have a valid argument if he simply told Dr. R. that he was not hired to teach consumer economics and that it is in violation of his contract to ask him to do so?

2. Have you ever tried to teach someone something you knew little about? Do you think that a good learning experience can result when people, including the teacher, are learning new things together? Do you think a really good teacher can teach almost anything?

3. Do you think Dr. R.'s solution to the problem he has to deal with is reasonable? Do you think Dr. R. is a kind of principal you would be comfortable dealing with? Why or why not?

4. Consider whether George and Dr. R. both have acted profes-

sionally thus far in the scenario given above. Can you think of any available solution to the problem that has not occurred to Dr. R.?

Possible Solutions

1. George leaves Dr. R.'s office, goes through the rest of the school day in a depressive funk, and then goes home. After he talks the situation over with his wife, he decides that he has no recourse but to tell Dr. R. that he cannot teach consumer economics and that if he is forced to, he will have to resign. He has checked with his father, who owns a lumberyard, and he can work there at minimum wage if he has to until he can find something better.

2. George is shocked by the news of the change that Dr. R. has had to make, but as he thinks it over, he realizes that teaching consumer economics might be a worthwhile challenge. There is nothing wrong with learning something new, and Dr. R. will be brushing up on the subject to do his own teaching. Probably they can swap notes and handouts for a while and maybe arrange to have lunch together twice a week or to meet occasionally in the morning to plot strategy.

3. George frankly has no faith in his ability to teach consumer economics well, but he realizes that the existing situation will not go away and that he has a professional responsibility either to do what he has been asked or to propose a more reasonable solution to the problem. One of the economists who was terminated at the brokerage house at about the time George was has been looking for a job, but is presently away for a month doing a short-term, free-lance accounting job in Canada. Although this economist is not a certified teacher, she has had all the education courses except student teaching. After her first week of student teaching, she decided not to be a teacher and withdrew from the program. George thinks she might be wooed back into teaching on an emergency certificate for this one difficult year—and who knows? If she is treated well and has a good experience, she might end up realizing that teaching has its rewards. He decides to tell Dr. R. that he will teach consumer economics until a better arrangement can be made and to put him on the trail of his friend.

Consider This

We often know more about some things than we realize. Given normal intelligence and a slight background in some fields, many people can turn into effective teachers as long as they are conscientious and well organized, and as long as they have a good support system in their school. In an ideal situation, everyone teaching in a

37

field will have been trained extensively in that field. School principals would be the last people to deny this statement.

The stark realities of actual teaching situations sometimes demand a kind of juggling that requires a degree of compromise on the parts of teachers and administrators. Teachers who have the experience of teaching something for which they are minimally prepared sometimes find that the classes involved become their best classes because they are sharing learning problems with their students. A situation like George's is not hopeless as long as the teacher involved has an optimistic outlook, a sympathetic understanding of the problem, a valid assurance that the situation will be remedied as soon as it can be, and a willingness to spend a little extra time preparing classes.

WHAT KINDS OF PLANS DO THE MOST GOOD?

Beginning teachers usually have a struggle just to survive from day to day. To begin school every Monday with detailed lesson plans for a whole week is not always possible at the beginning of one's teaching career. To have a complete sequential, pedagogical, and philosophical overview of a semester's—or even a month's—work is a cherished dream rather than a reality for all but the rarest of beginning teachers or teaching interns. The pressures ease with each year one continues in teaching. The second year is usually worlds easier than the first.

Veteran teachers have all sorts of worksheets, lesson plans, computer disks, and old examinations squirreled away. But the first year is at times disheartening, especially to the most conscientious beginning teachers, because teachers living through the first year in the classroom may be painfully aware of how much better they could be performing if they just had more time and a little better background. Of course, the very best teachers have nagging doubts about their performances even in the year before they retire. They are the best teachers because they never assume they have arrived, and they are, even in their last month of teaching, trying to find better ways of teaching their students.

The first and most important step in eliminating teaching deficiencies is for us to recognize and admit those deficiencies without allowing such realizations to paralyze us. The second step is seeking to get control over our most troublesome deficiencies—to work on them one at a time and always to acknowledge the realities and limitations of the context within which we work.

If you are under incredible pressure early in your teaching experience, you may have to get by with sketchy lesson plans, but adopt the form of lesson plan your district uses or try to find a form of lesson plan that works for you. Then make sure that you have plans, no matter how fragmentary, for every class you teach for at least one day in advance. If you have not been present for the initial teacher workdays most districts hold at the beginning of the school year, you may have to settle for badly fragmented plans, but make sure that you have *some* plans and that they are in writing.

Make sure as well that each lesson contains at least three kinds of activities. You may, in reality, not use all of these activities, but it is comforting to know that if class discussion or group revision of papers is waning, you have another activity related to the lesson for the day that you can fall back on.

CASE STUDY 2.3
New Teacher Gets Job at Last Minute

Although she was newly certified to teach in elementary school, Lois B. feared she would not get a job in Toledo, the town in which she had to live because of a family situation. The school year began, and she was still unemployed, although she had made the best of a bad situation by placing her name on the district's list of substitute teachers. The sixth day of the school year, however, Lois's luck changed. She was invited to become a third-grade teacher at Lowell Elementary School on the other side of town. She was to begin the next day and was put on the payroll the instant she accepted the job, so that she could spend half of that day in her school getting materials and information about what she would be teaching.

Lois arrived home swamped with materials, totally bewildered and confused. Tomorrow—only sixteen hours from now—she would be facing the students she was to teach for the next year. She knew that tomorrow would be an important day for her and for her students; what happened tomorrow could in a quite real way determine the course of the coming months and could very much affect the success Lois's students would have in her class.

Lois looked at the schedule she had been given; then she began to think of the things she had to teach in the course of the school day, the container within which all of the contents of the curriculum were to be arranged. Lois remembered having heard in her teacher training courses that good elementary school teachers interrelate a great deal that goes on in the classroom. Certainly the cooperating teacher Lois worked with in her teaching internship made her classes interesting and effective by the interrelations she made among the subjects she taught. But for now, Lois can think only of getting through tomorrow, then of surviving her first week of real, full-time

39

teaching. For a while, she will not have time to think about making the kinds of interrelations that she knows are possible and in which she firmly believes.

Questions

1. Lois is at home with her armload of materials. What do you think she should do with them? How might she best prepare to meet her students tomorrow?

2. Lois learns that the students she will be teaching have been studying with a teacher who has been promoted to the building principal in another school. Would it be appropriate to telephone that teacher at home to find out something about what the students have been doing?

3. Should Lois apply herself to studying all the materials she has, staying up all night to get through them if she has to? Tomorrow is Thursday, so she has to get through only two days this week; then she can catch up on her sleep.

4. Do you have any strategy that you might use with students at the level you are teaching or are preparing to teach that will permit you to gain a little preparation time if you are suddenly thrust into a situation for which you are not well prepared? If not, try to figure out something that might help to carry you through such a situation.

Possible Solutions

1. Inasmuch as the school district is hiring Lois to teach for the whole year, she might ask whether a substitute teacher could be hired for two days so that she would have four days to work through the materials she has and be well prepared for school on Monday. She has, after all, missed the teacher workdays during which the other teachers had time to make preparation and for which they were paid.

2. Lois looks at the daunting packet of materials she has been given and decides that the best thing she can do is spend two or three hours looking through them, during which she will decide what to emphasize tomorrow, and then get a good night's sleep. She realizes that the worst thing she can do is to go into class exhausted on her first day; first days can be exhausting enough.

3. Lois decides that she will not try to accomplish much in terms of subject matter during the first two days she is with her classes. She will ask all her students to write brief stories about themselves, and she will write along with them. She will use these stories as a basis for discussion and will, meanwhile, ask her principal whether the district

40

supervisor might come by and talk with her so that she can decide what direction she should be moving in. She will volunteer to stay after school or go to the supervisor's office after school if that is the only way the two of them can get together.

Consider This

It is difficult to teach third-grade students before you get to know them and let them get to know you. At this point in Lois's teaching, she should not worry as much about teaching subject matter as about building rapport with her students. The weekend will be her salvation, and she will have to use it well to plan her first full week of classroom work.

Lois should get to school early Thursday and talk with her principal to find out whether the art teacher, who is scheduled for next Tuesday morning, might be able to shift his schedule and come in for half a day on either Thursday or Friday. If such an arrangement can be made, Lois will have time to learn her students' names and to think of activities she can use with them to get them through the week.

The first two days will be Lois's greatest problem, but once she has a week's worth of plans before her, she will gain confidence and so will her students. The main thing to do in a situation like this is not to panic and to think of activities that will help the teacher learn something about the students.

WHAT GOES INTO A LESSON PLAN?

Although a lesson plan can consist of a few words jotted on the back of an old envelope, teachers usually feel more secure about their teaching if they devise some sort of standard form to use as they plan their lessons. Because planning constitutes about 90 percent of good teaching, the author will devote most of the remainder of this chapter to discussing lesson plans and how to compose them.

Effective planning is essential to all professions. Teaching particularly requires planning for each day's activities. Teachers who try to wing it rather than planning efficiently quickly lose the confidence of both their students and their colleagues.

Daily lesson plans usually grow out of a unit topic designed to last anywhere from a week to a month or, in some cases, longer. As unit topics are planned, long-term goals begin to emerge, giving students and teachers alike a gratifying sense of direction in their work. Lesson plans permit teachers to break down their long-term goals into specific parts that can be covered day by day and that lead to the fulfillment of the goals for the overall unit plan.

Lesson plans can follow a number of formats. It is best to follow a format that meets your own teaching needs as you perceive them or one that is required by your school and school district. Good lesson plans usually include all—or a least most of—the following:

- The title of the unit of study and the specific lesson
- The date for which the lesson is planned
- Objectives of this lesson—general, specific, and behavioral
- Specific procedures to promote the stated objectives
- Leading questions to stimulate discussion
- A list of books, films, or filmstrips to be used, along with page numbers for the books
- A list of materials to be used during the class
- Alternative activities to fall back on if one activity doesn't work well
- A statement of how student progress will be evaluated for the lesson
- A brief and objective evaluation of how the class went.

HOW DETAILED MUST LESSON PLANS BE?

The best lesson plans are brief but inclusive. They are stated directly. They are for the teacher's guidance and that of a substitute should the regular teacher have to be absent. Not everything in the lesson plan need necessarily be stated in complete sentences. Not everything stated in the lesson plan will necessarily be accomplished. Overplanning will protect you from running out of material before the class hour is over.

Because a substitute teacher may have to depend upon your plans, full titles of books, filmstrips, and other media should be included in lesson plans. When you cite books, page numbers should also be provided.

The longer you stay in teaching, the more likely it is that you will use some of this year's lesson plans to prepare for next year's classes. Because this is the case, the little time it takes you to jot down a self-evaluation of each class is time well spent. Next year, you might want to use three-quarters of a given lesson plan, but if interest lagged in the discussion period, you should make note of that and change your lead questions for next year or add an activity that would stimulate discussion better.

Teaching year after year from the exact same lesson plans would be deadly dull. Teachers should always update their lesson plans and add new materials to them. Entering each new year of teaching with the accumulation of ideas that well-constructed lesson plans contain can, however, provide teachers with a solid base from which to work as they shape their classes for each new school year. Working from this field-tested base should also increase their self-assurance.

SAMPLE LESSON PLAN FORMAT

Name: _____   Unit Title: _____

Approximate   Lesson
Date To Be Used: _____   Title: _____

Class Period(s): _____

OBJECTIVES:
  General:

  Specific:

  Behavioral
  Outcomes:

PROCEDURES:

ALTERNATE
PROCEDURE(S):

LEAD
QUESTIONS:

MATERIALS
REQUIRED:

BOOK(S) TO BE
USED AND PAGE
NUMBERS:

WAYS TO EVALUATE
STUDENT PROGRESS:

AFTER-CLASS EVALUATION
OF EFFECTIVENESS:

Lesson plans are simply a guide, a sequential development allowing you to visualize procedures toward the achievement of your goals. Lesson plans are not meant to be strict plans of action; rather, they should be flexible enough to adapt to student interest and input where feasible. It is important that you, as teacher, use the lesson plan and not let the lesson plan use you. In preparing lesson plans for each class, consider student needs (individual and collective). Fit each lesson plan to the students, not the students to the lesson plan; i.e., the lesson plan should be for students and should include their participation in a variety of ways, making them a focal point while involving them actively in learning. When teachers try to dominate the activities in the lesson plan, the student-learning situation may be unsuccessful.

What are some values of lesson plans? Written lesson plans—

1. Give direction to teacher and student efforts, thereby permitting the teacher better preparation for the specifics of the lesson being taught and allowing the teacher a better position for actuating the lesson;
2. Bring more clearly into focus both sequence and continuity of the learning to be achieved during any given lesson;
3. Provide a reference point for the teacher; and
4. Provide a record for the teacher.

Lesson plans have additional value in that they provide needed information to substitute teachers who may replace an absent teacher for one or more days. They are also of value to supervisors, principals, or others who come to observe in the classroom.

Often both beginning and experienced teachers question the necessity of writing lesson plans. There is little doubt that lesson plans take time and effort if they are to be prepared correctly, but planning is an important aspect of teaching. Professionals are expected to plan well. It is important that plans be current. Your classes change each year. Your respective students' needs change as well. The same lesson plans cannot and should not be used year after year. Lesson plans must be reviewed and updated. Material should be added to or deleted from the lesson plan according to the needs of students. This process is a vital means by which teachers teach effectively and students learn effectively.

CASE STUDY 2.4
Teacher Asked To Cover Unruly Class

Karry C. is a first-year teacher at Maplewood Elementary School, an inner-city school with an enrollment of about one thousand students. Mr. M., an authoritarian-type principal, expects strict discipline and always seems to be in full control of his school. Karry has a group of lively third graders. She works hard and plans diligently for each school day. The children have accepted her quite well.

Karry was three months into her teaching year and just beginning to feel comfortable and secure with her class when suddenly one morning the class was interrupted by the intercom and Mr. M.'s voice: "Attention, teachers! I need someone to cover Ms. F.'s sixth-grade class from two o'clock until the end of school. Those of you who have a free period, please let me know." Karry knew she would have the art teacher with her for that last hour, so she informed Mr. M. that she would be available.

Because Karry's day was busy, she had no opportunity to discuss lesson plans with Ms. F.; neither did she have time to prepare any lessons of her own, nor was she familiar with the sixth-grade students with whom she was to work.

As she hastened toward Ms. F.'s room, Karry was somewhat apprehensive about the assignment. Upon arriving at the door, she panicked even more. The scene was chaotic—students were scattered everywhere about the room. The teacher was trying to read a story to the class, but few students were listening. As Karry hesitatingly entered the room, Ms. F. stopped reading and boisterously scolded the unruly class. When this tactic failed to work, she slammed a yardstick against the board to gain their attention. Karry, not accustomed to this sort of situation, contemplated leaving, but before she had the chance, Ms. F. saw her and beckoned her into the room. "Wow, am I glad you are here! They are really wild today," she said. Ms. F. then handed Karry the book from which she was reading as she grabbed her things and headed out the door, saying, "Try to finish the story, and thanks. Good luck!"

Questions

1. Should Ms. F. have talked with Karry prior to her taking over the class? What should they have discussed?
2. Is it fair to put another teacher in this type of situation? Explain.
3. How might written lesson plans have eased the problem for Karry? For the students?
4. If you were left with a similar situation, what would you do?

Possible Solutions

1. Karry is not technically free just because the art teacher is in her class. If she is to integrate art and music into the other elements of her teaching, she needs to know what is done when the art and music specialists are with her two hours each week. Because she is not technically free, she is foolish to volunteer for the extra duty.

2. Karry is naturally a good citizen, and this quality is highly regarded within the school community. She has volunteered for extra duty because she thinks her services are legitimately needed, and that conclusion is probably not in doubt. The principal has agreed to let Ms. F. leave school early, presumably for a valid reason. Perhaps the situation would have been better had Karry found at least two or three minutes during her lunch hour to talk with Ms. F. As it is, when Karry saw the situation in Ms. F.'s class, she followed her out into the hall and called after her, "You will have to come back. I cannot handle this! You need to get them under control and introduce me."

3. Karry is shocked by the disorder she notices in Ms. F.'s class. Ms. F. fortunately has left her a seating chart, and Karry walks down to the noisiest student. She has matched him with the name on the seating chart. She calls him by that name, Lynn. Everyone laughs. It turns out that Lynn is a girl who is not sitting in her assigned seat. The noise persists. Karry goes over to the light switch and flicks the lights on and off. She needs to get the students' attention, but she does not want to add to the already high noise level to do it. Her tactic quiets them down. She faces them and says to the girl who turns out to be Lynn, "Lynn, would you please tell me about the story Ms. F. was reading to you? I am not sure I know that story, and I would like us to read it together."

Consider This

Substituting in someone else's class, whether for a full day as a paid substitute or for an hour or two while some other teacher is for some reason unable to teach, is never easy. Students try to take advantage of substitutes. Minimally, those who substitute should expect to have seating charts and lesson plans available to them. Ideally, the substitute will be able to talk with the regular teacher to find out a little about the class, but this luxury is not always possible. If a teacher is substituting in a situation such as Karry found herself in, the major effort is to keep the class orderly and in control. If the substitute can cover material the regular teacher has been teaching, it is all to the good. Little teaching can take place, however, in a chaotic classroom, so teachers must give the highest priority to establishing a teaching environment.

3. EARNING A PROFESSIONAL REPUTATION

Think back to your own school days. Which of your teachers leaps immediately to mind when you think of your school experience? Now consider why that teacher—or those teachers—leapt immediately to mind when you thought back. What salient characteristics make teachers memorable to their students?

If you list these characteristics, you are likely to come up with two lists. One list will contain positive characteristics associated with teachers you liked and remembered favorably. It will help you to think of specific positive characteristics if you complete the sentence, "I liked this teacher because he or she . . . ." Among your responses might be some of the following:

- made me feel as though I mattered.
- made sure that students understood what went on in class.
- treated me with respect.
- could admit not knowing something, but could always find answers when it was necessary.
- encouraged me to stretch my mind.
- had reasonable rules that students understood.
- did not play favorites.
- communicated clearly.
- knew my name by the second day.
- never compared me to my brother who was in her class two years ago and was much smarter than I am.

Exercise 3.1

1. Make your own list of characteristics you appreciated in your teachers.
2. Jot down specific behaviors by which your teachers communicated to you two virtues noted on the list above or on your own list.

Most of us remember quite clearly some teachers we did not like. In some cases, these teachers, perhaps unknowingly, did something that at the time seemed so humiliating to us that we will never forget our humiliation. It is important to know precisely what these teachers did to us that we remember so well and to make sure that we never do the same thing or anything like it to any of our students. On the next list, you might complete the sentence, "I disliked this teacher because he or she . . ." with some of the following:

- scolded me before the whole class.
- accused me of cheating when I did not cheat.
- asked questions and interrupted before we had time to answer them.
- was sarcastic to me in front of other students.
- never seemed to have time for me.
- made assignments and then did not grade and return them.
- made us get our work in on time and then handed it back weeks later with hardly any comments.
- never made assignments long enough in advance to allow me to budget my time.
- made assignments and then forgot having made them.
- often came to class unprepared.

Exercise 3.2

1. Make your own list of characteristics you objected to in your teachers.
2. Jot down specific behaviors by which your teachers communicated to you two characteristics noted on the list above or on your own list.

The more you think about it, the more you will be able to expand on both of these suggested lists. You should make the effort to do so because the way you teach is, in a very real way, determined by the way you have been taught. For better or worse, no matter how much educational theory we study, we all begin our teaching with an image—a Platonic idea, really—of what constitutes good teaching. That image is shaped largely by what we have experienced as students. Educational reform often begins when individual teachers analyze teacher behaviors they resented when they were students and make a conscious effort not to repeat those behaviors in their own classrooms with their own students.

When you make the two lists suggested above and reflect on them thoughtfully, you will probably be on your way to becoming an effective teacher. You will realize consciously what your actions in certain situations imply if you reflect analytically upon your own school experience.

BUILDING YOUR REPUTATION

Teachers begin to build their reputations, good or bad, the first day they set foot in the classrooms in which they teach. This does not mean that you can never outlive the errors of your early days of teaching—we all make them, and we all find ways of overcoming them. Your life will

49

be simpler, however, if you do not have to live down a bad reputation earned in the early days of the school year.

The best way to begin your teaching is to communicate to your students certain reasonable expectations you have for them and to establish a simple set of rules that will govern your classes. Sometimes it is best to allow students to have a hand in establishing class rules. When they have decided upon their rules, it is best to put these rules into effect for a specific period, perhaps a month, after which the class will review the rules they made and amend them if that seems desirable.

What are some of the rules you and your students might decide upon? One group of fifth-grade students came up with the following rules, which for them began as a list of "DON'Ts" until a few students decided it would be better to state the rules in terms of "DOs." They made two posters on which they wrote these rules, and they posted them in the front and back of their classroom. Their initial list, which they altered at specific periods during the school year, was as follows:

- Students will be in their seats when school starts.
- Except in real emergencies, students will leave the classroom only during recess periods.
- Students will eat and drink only in the proper areas and at the proper times.
- Students who want to speak will raise their hands for recognition.
- If the teacher blinks the lights on and off, the whole class will become quiet and will come to attention, waiting for an announcement.
- When students are not in the classroom, they will remember they are still members of this class and will act in ways that bring credit to it.
- Students who have not been able to complete their homework assignments will tell the teacher at the beginning of class.
- After group work, all students will return their chairs and tables to the positions they were in originally.

This beginning list of rules worked well. The teacher, Ms. J., might have added some things to the list if she had made it up herself, but her students, with her subtle guidance, touched on most of the matters she thought were important. Ms. J. was also wise enough to realize that students are much more likely to obey rules that originate with them than rules that are imposed on them.

Exercise 3.3

1. What difference does it make to state rules in terms of "DOs" rather than "DON'Ts"? Do you prefer one of these ways over the other? Why?

2. Add to the above list any rules you would like to make for your students.
3. Justify at least two of the rules from your own list.

Perhaps the simplest way for teachers to succeed is to remind themselves frequently of the golden rule, "Do unto others as you would have them do unto you," or of Immanuel Kant's categorical imperative, "So act that you would wish your actions to become universal modes of behavior." Always try to understand how your students feel about things, to understand their hopes and expectations. Once you have done this, you will be in a position to meet their needs and to be for them the best teacher they have ever had.

CASE STUDY 3.1
Teacher Has a Retiring Personality

Greta H. is a sensitive, intelligent person. She is low-key, teaching often from the back of the room rather than the front; she is good at orchestrating activities, at having her students do rewarding group work. She sometimes wonders what has made her the sort of non-directive teacher she is. When she has these thoughts, her mind inevitably races back to the day in her eleventh year when she went to a lecture with her mother. The lecturer was riveting, and Greta finally screwed up the courage to raise her hand during the question-answer part of the presentation.

After Greta asked her question, the lecturer offhandedly said, "The answer to that question is so obvious that I won't waste our time addressing it," and called on someone else. Greta felt two inches high. She knew her face had turned red in embarrassment, and she sat beside her mother looking down at the floor and knowing that every eye in that large lecture hall must be on her.

Even though Greta is now over thirty years old and has bachelor's and master's degrees from two selective universities, she has never been able to ask questions or engage in discussions in public. Whenever she hears a speaker and has something to ask, she thinks back to the horrible day when she was put down publicly, and she feels diminished. She can't even remember what her question was on that fateful day, but she knows precisely the day her life was changed.

Questions

1. Has anyone ever embarrassed you in public? Think back to that incident, and try to determine whether it has had an effect upon your future life.

51

2. Has anyone done anything specific that enhanced your self-confidence? How did you feel as a result?

3. When you were a student, did you feel able to contribute to class discussions freely? If you were in a class or a public lecture and the teacher or the speaker brought up something that you considered factually incorrect, would you say something about it or just let it go?

4. How would you react if, for example, you asked your students to try to figure out how many consonants exist in the original dialect of the Polynesian language used by many native Hawaiians, and they came up with the seven consonants (*h, k, l, m, n, p, w*) in the language from their knowledge of Hawaiian words and place names, only to have one student ask, "Why not *t*? *Tiki* is a Hawaiian word, isn't it?" Would a question like that make you feel threatened? How would you respond?

Possibilities To Consider

1. Although Greta is an effective teacher, she feels she could be more effective if she developed more self-confidence in public situations. She vows to work toward making herself more assertive by consciously making at least one contribution or asking at least one question in every public lecture she attends and in every faculty meeting. She realizes that she cannot change her basic personality, but she can make certain adjustments in some of its manifestations, and she is working calculatedly in that direction.

2. In Greta's class is one student whose hand is always up and who always asks questions either that are much off target or the answers to which are obvious. Greta does not want to waste class time, and she sometimes wonders whether this student is making contributions and asking questions sincerely or whether this is just a time-wasting tactic. She has to decide on some course of action, and, thinking back to her early experience recounted in the case study, she decides that she will handle the situation by answering seriously and politely every question the student asks. She reasons that if the student is asking the questions sincerely, it is appropriate to answer them no matter how naive they are. If the student is asking the questions to waste time, her treating the student with dignity will soon make that student treat her with greater dignity, thereby controlling the situation.

3. The situation is the same as in Possibility 2 above. One day, Greta takes time to answer five questions the student has asked. Other students become restless during this exchange, and a few giggle

softly. She thinks something must be done, so the next day she announces to the class, "Most days I hear four or five times from some of you and not once from others. Let's try something, so that I will be able to hear from more of you. For the next week, if you have a question to ask, write it down first. Then raise your hand when you think it is the best time to ask it or give it to me after class. But for this week only, everyone will be expected to ask at least one question or make at least one oral contribution to the class every day, and until we have heard from everyone, no one may ask a second question or make a second contribution. Let's see how this works."

Consider This

We are all made differently. Some of us are naturally reticent, others naturally talkative. Teachers must respect these individual differences, but they need also to provide students with situations that will help them to develop their self-images and their self-confidence. Quiet students are not necessarily unprepared or unintelligent students. They sometimes are students who think that what they have to contribute will not add anything to the discussion or that other students will think they are dumb. Teachers can encourage reticent students by

- calling on them occasionally by just asking casually, "What do you think, Mary?" or "Do you agree, John?"
- referring to something quiet students have said in some of their written work, mentioning it in a positive light and asking, "Could you tell us a little more about that?"
- taking seriously every question they ask or comment they make, making an encouraging comment even if they ask something obvious or say something not terribly relevant, while simultaneously trying to move back to more relevant material.
- involving students in small-group work because many students who will not respond in front of thirty other students will contribute freely in a group of four or five.
- making a point of talking with the more reticent students informally whenever the opportunity arises.

WHAT ABOUT CHEATING?

Idealistic teachers sometimes have their idealism put to a bitter test when they first become aware that one or more students in their classes seem to be cheating. It is well to be prepared to meet this exigency, but it is better still to devise ways that will make it impossible for students to cheat. In order to understand cheating and to arrive at ways to handle it, try to assess the reasons that people cheat. The following are among the most common:

- The desire to do well at any cost
- Fear of failure
- Undue pressure from parents
- Lack of self-confidence
- Laziness
- Lack of interest in the material being taught
- Failure to see the relevancy in what is being taught.

Exercise 3.4

1. Add to the list above any other reasons for cheating you can think of.
2. Have you ever cheated or been tempted to cheat? If so, why do you think you were in that situation?

As a teacher, you cannot condone cheating, but it is your duty to understand its causes. It is also your duty to limit the possibility of cheating in your classroom in any way you can. Among the preventive measures you can take, the following are some of the most useful:

- Set up test rooms so that seats are as far apart as possible.
- Whenever possible, have more than one form of any objective test you are giving.
- To whatever extent you can, give students essay-type examinations and allow them to work from notes.
- Do not require students to memorize meaningless facts that, although they may be easy to test, really have little relevance to what your students need to know.
- Early in the school year, explain clearly to students what plagiarism is and what the penalties for it will be in your classes.
- At the beginning of the school year, distribute to your students a sheet entitled something like "Examination Policies."

Of all the measures noted above, perhaps the last is the most important. If you let your students know the testing policies you will enforce *before* any problems occur, your students will know that you mean business and that you anticipate a professional attitude from them. The following statement of examination policies was designed for use in a specific situation that might be quite different from yours. Your own situation will dictate the kinds of policies you set.

Examination Policies

1. Only in extraordinary situations can examinations be made up if you are absent on the scheduled day. In the case of absentees who have a legitimate excuse, the examination should be made up during the scheduled makeup period, which is routinely held in Room 231 for one hour after school every Thursday.

2. The instructor will set up the room for the examination as soon as the preceding class has vacated it. Please do not enter the class-room until you have been told it is ready for you.

3. Before you begin the examination, check the chalkboard for announcements. Also check it periodically during the examination to see how much time you have left.

4. Unless you are told that you may use notes or books, your desk should be completely cleared of everything except the examination and your supply of pens or pencils. **To ensure the integrity of the examination, you may not use earphones connected to radios or tape recorders during it. You may not use calculators or other electronic devices.**

5. You probably will do best on the examination if you read through it first. When you have done this, answer all the questions you are sure of. Then go back to the questions you are less sure of, and try to reason them out.

6. Before you leave the examination room, try to read through the examination again, making sure on this reading that you have answered every question.

7. If you think more than one correct answer is possible for any objective item, write your explanation beside that item or on the back of the sheet.

8. Remember that credit can be given only for answers recorded in the space provided on the left-hand margin of your paper.

9. It is best to complete your examination in pencil so that you can erase and alter answers about which you change your mind.

10. Please do not ask to leave the room for any reason during the course of the examination. If you absolutely must leave the room during the examination, you will not be permitted to complete your paper, and you will either have to accept the grade for the questions you have answered or have to take a makeup examination at the next scheduled administration, in which case a ten-point penalty will be assessed.

1. Make up a list of examination policies you think would work well for you.
2. Justify any two of your examination policies.

CASE STUDY 3.2
Adult Education Teacher Suspects Cheating

Don H. is a mathematics teacher in an adult education program connected with a large urban school. He teaches his geometry class from the standpoint of theorems and proofs, the method by which he was taught when he was in high school fifteen years ago. Don taught for two years immediately after leaving college. Then he became an insurance salesman, and he has been successful in this enterprise.

Don, however, always found a real satisfaction in teaching. When he was invited to teach evenings in the adult school, he eagerly accepted, and he has enjoyed the experience. His students are earnest and cooperative. All of them work during the day and are making a real effort to complete their high school educations. The age range in his geometry class is from eighteen to sixty-seven.

Don has given two examinations and is about to administer his third. He has been disturbed because one of his students, a man of about his own age, has asked to go to the men's room in the middle of both examinations. This man has never asked to be excused during a regular class session to go to the men's room. When he made his request to leave the room during the first examination, Don didn't think much of it. The man left the room and returned within three or four minutes. He scored a high "C" on the examination.

When the same man needed to leave the room during the second examination, Don immediately suspected that he might be cheating, but he certainly could not prove anything, and he hardly wanted to tell a grown man that he could not go to the men's room. This student scored a "B" on the second examination.

Now that Don is about to administer the third examination, he feels that he should take some action to prevent the kind of cheating he suspects. He has a bad feeling in the pit of his stomach about the whole thing and is wrestling with a solution to the problem.

Questions

1. In a situation like the one depicted in the case study, does it make a difference that the student is an older student? Would you deal the same way with a fourth-grade student or a high school junior

who are nine and seventeen years old respectively? Defend your answer.

2. Students sometimes write on their hands or arms, or they bring small notes to class, perhaps hidden in their shoes or socks. If you catch a student using such notes during the course of an examination, what would you do? Would you immediately take the student out into the hall and have a confrontation? Why or why not?

3. If a student of yours has done failing or almost failing work on two or three tests and suddenly gets an "A" on the fourth test, would you be convinced the student had cheated? Why or why not? How would you deal with the situation?

4. Make a list of some things you can do as a teacher to make your students want to be honest in doing their work. Punitive measures can control some cheating, but the best control is the kind students develop within themselves. How can you best encourage them to develop this control?

Possible Solutions

1. Don decides he has to control the situation he suspects. He gets to class a little early on the night of the examination and asks the student he suspects to step out into the hall. He tells him that if he needs to use the restroom, he should do so now because he will not be able to excuse anyone while the examination is in progress.

2. Don does not want to risk an individual confrontation. He goes into class the night of the examination and says, "Tonight's examination is quite long. If anyone needs to use the facilities, I will give you five minutes now while I am setting up the room. I will not be able to excuse anyone during the course of the examination."

3. Don decides to sidestep the issue somewhat. He goes into class on the night of the examination and announces, "The administration recently reminded the faculty of a policy some of us had forgotten. It is contrary to the rules for anyone to be excused from the room for any reason while an examination is being given. I have been asked to enforce that regulation stringently."

4. Don decides to try something risky. He goes into class after the second examination and says, "Someone has cheated on this examination, and I know who it is. It would be well for him or her to see me at the break and get the matter settled. I will have to deal harshly with the matter if you do not come forth voluntarily."

5. Don decides not to confront the matter unless it comes up. If the student in question again asks to be excused, he will simply tell him, "I am sorry, but it is not fair to the other students to let anyone leave the room during the examination. If you absolutely must leave, I

cannot allow you to go any further in the examination and will have to grade you on what you have done thus far."

Consider This

Your students come to you from a variety of ethical backgrounds. Some of them have never really seen honest and honorable behavior in the people closest to them. Many of them can learn positive lessons in school about the need for honesty in academic matters as well as in their lives. Some may never learn that lesson, but most teachers realize that society will be improved if students learn ethical behavior as they pass through the educational system.

You should also be aware that students from some ethnic backgrounds have been brought up to think that they should help their friends if their friends need help. Such students may offer help to another student in an examination without realizing that there is anything wrong with offering such help. Sometimes if they are merely informed that giving help during examinations is not acceptable behavior in your class, they will refrain from offering it. Teachers always have an easier time maintaining the integrity of examinations if the rules are spelled out before the first examination is given. A mimeographed set of examination policies distributed to students and discussed the day before the first examination will forestall many problems and will show students that the teacher is approaching examinations in the most professional way.

CAN WE EQUATE SUSPICION WITH GUILT?

When teachers suspect cheating, they obviously want to punish the person or people suspected of the infraction. They must, however, realize that they cannot make accusations unless they have proof. It is far better to let a cheat get away with cheating than to make a false accusation against an innocent student and to penalize that student unjustly. The best safeguard against cheating is to preplan test situations and other class work in such a way as to discourage dishonesty. No system of control is 100 percent effective, however, and teachers sometimes must deal with students who cheat. This is perhaps the most disheartening part of anyone's teaching experience.

CASE STUDY 3.3

[Author's note: *This case study will be presented from five points of view: those of a teacher who accuses a student of cheating, of the* student who has been accused, of the student's parents, of a close family friend who has known the student for over ten years, and of the school principal.]

CASE STUDY 3.3–A
Teacher Accuses Student of Cheating

Mr. T. has taught English in a senior high school for thirteen years. This year he is teaching two sections of eleventh-grade American literature to the top two groups of college preparatory students in his school. The first novel in the course is Nathaniel Hawthorne's *The Scarlet Letter*. Mr. T. has asked each student to write an interpretive paper not more than five pages long on the novel.

Gideon S. is a bright student, a sixteen-year-old who is responsive in class. Gideon is the son of a professor of biology at the state university and of a psychologist who has a private practice in town.

Mr. T. devotes the weekend after the *Scarlet Letter* papers come in to reading them. Most of them are quite similar. They begin something like this: "In the novel *The Scarlet Letter* that was written by Nathaniel Hawthorne over a hundred years ago...," and then they go on to give a plot summary. When Mr. T. comes to Gideon's paper, he is dismayed. It begins

Nathaniel Hawthorne's *The Scarlet Letter* (1850) is a novel of ironies, both surface and underlying. The most obvious of these ironies are that Hester Prynne has been condemned as an immoral woman although she is one of the most moral people in town and that Arthur Dimmesdale, who impregnates her out of wedlock, does not admit his deed and enjoys a glowing reputation in town as a much-respected clergyman. These are the fundamental surface ironies.

However, no scholar to date—not Newton Arvin or Richard Brodhead or Frederick Crews or Arlin Turner or Hyatt Waggoner or even Nina Baym—has probed beyond these surface ironies to the even more startling verbal ironies that are a part of nearly every Hawthorne paragraph.

This is as far as Mr. T. reads. He assigns the paper a grade of "F" and writes at the end of it, "Plagiarism is a VERY serious offense. It is a form of stealing, and it can even result in legal action against the plagiarist. Before I refer your plagiarism to Mr. J. [the school principal] for disciplinary action, we need to talk about this. See me after class." His only other comment on the paper occurs in the margin beside the names of the Hawthorne scholars Gideon has mentioned. Mr. T. has written "Name Dropping!!!" beside that list.

Questions

1. In a situation like the one described in the case study, identify at least three important things the teacher needs to weigh before assigning the paper a grade.

2. If a teacher is highly suspicious of a paper like the one described, need a grade be assigned to it before the teacher has had the opportunity to talk with the student who wrote it?

3. Has anyone ever accused you or anyone you know of cheating without being able to substantiate the charge fully? If so, tell about it; if not, tell how you think you would react.

4. Was Gideon jeopardizing himself when he wrote such a sophisticated, thoughtful paper as this one? Would it have been smarter for him to have written a more superficial paper? He is a good writer and would probably have gotten an "A" or, at least, a "B+" had his paper been more like those of the other students. Some very second-rate papers receive high grades. Consider the implications of your answer.

Possible Solutions

1. Having read Gideon's paper, Mr. T. tries to recall Gideon's classroom contributions. He remembers that Gideon has had some remarkable insights; still, he cannot quite accept as credible the idea that a high school junior could approach Hawthorne with the sophistication this paper reveals. He talks with Gideon's English teacher from the last year, and she tells him that Gideon really has a deep appreciation for and understanding of literature. She reads Gideon's paper at Mr. T.'s urging and agrees that it is extremely precocious, but her parting words are, "I am not convinced that he would be incapable of writing such a paper on his own." Mr. T. decides to withhold the grade and to have Gideon excused from homeroom for a conference with him. He will ask Gideon very specific questions about Hawthorne, each of which is addressed in the paper. If Gideon can answer the questions articulately, he will accept the paper as Gideon's own work and will assign it the grade it deserves.

2. Mr. T., convinced that the paper in question is not Gideon's own work, thinks it is best if he not deal with the problem directly. He turns the paper over to the vice-principal, who regularly handles cases of academic dishonesty. If Gideon is not guilty, the vice-principal will find that out. If he has cheated, the vice-principal will handle the problem as it should be handled. "After all, teachers are not police," Mr. T. tells himself. When Gideon comes into his class the next

day, Mr. T. tells him to report to the vice-principal's office and writes a hall pass for him.

3. Knowing that Gideon's parents are education people and that they are much concerned about their son's progress in school, Mr. T. telephones them right after he reads the suspicious paper. As luck would have it, Gideon answers the telephone and recognizes Mr. T.'s voice. Mr. T.'s embarrassment shows in his voice. Gideon puts his mother on the telephone, and Mr. T. tells her that he thinks her son has unquestionably cheated.

Consider This

The United States is a nation based on law. Our system involves due process, and it presumes that no one is guilty who has not been proved guilty beyond reasonable doubt. This is a guarantee that must apply to everyone in our country—not just to some people. Schools and those who work in them do little to demonstrate citizenship to students if they do not observe the tenets of the American judicial system, even though, in actuality, many school infractions are dealt with in violation of due process.

Mr. T.'s suspicions are understandable, but if he presumes guilt, he is dealing unjustly with a student in violation of that student's civil rights, and this is no small infraction of the law. Mr. T. is also dealing quite freely with a gifted student's reputation when he shares his suspicions with another teacher and with the student's mother, especially if he has not first attempted to obtain more information from the student himself.

Even if Gideon had plagiarized, he should know what he is being accused of, who is accusing him, and what evidence his accuser has. Both fairness and concern for students' rights dictate that Mr. T. discuss the situation with Gideon before he shares it with anyone else.

CASE STUDY 3.3–B
Student Is Upset by Accusation

Gideon S. has always been intellectually advanced for his age. Even as a preschool child, he always chose intellectual over physical activity when a choice had to be made. He cannot remember ever being unable to read. He remembers well that his parents often read to him when he was very young, and his mother read to him from some books that particularly intrigued him. His favorite books, the ones he wanted his parents to read him again and again, were

Twice-Told Tales, *A Wonder-Book for Girls and Boys*, and *Tanglewood Tales for Girls and Boys*, all by Nathaniel Hawthorne, who became Gideon's favorite author.

By the time he was nine, Gideon had read *The Scarlet Letter* and had discussed it with Nina B., a colleague of his father at the university. Nina, a brilliant scholar with an international reputation in American literature, was amazed not only that a nine-year-old had read *The Scarlet Letter* voluntarily but also that Gideon had understood it at a relatively sophisticated level.

By the time he ws thirteen Gideon had read the book three or four more times, always finding something new and alluring in it, always pushing himself to new and deeper critical understandings of it. For his thirteenth birthday, Nina gave Gideon a copy of Arlin Turner's authoritative biography of Hawthorne, and Gideon devoured the book. It led him to read other books about Hawthorne, including some by the people he had listed in his essay.

Gideon, obviously crushed by what has happened, can hardly stand to stay in Mr. T.'s class through the period. He is so concerned and angry that he has no notion of what is going on in class. As soon as the bell rings, he approaches Mr. T.'s desk. Mr. T., in earshot of students who are leaving and entering the room, says, "If there is one thing I cannot stand, it's a cheat." Gideon blurts out, "I didn't cheat, damn it! I know more about Hawthorne than you ever will!" This is the first time Gideon has ever had to confront a teacher, and it certainly is the first time he has ever been moved to swear at one.

Questions

1. In the normal course of interrelationships among teachers and their students, it is relatively rare for students, particularly in classes for the gifted, to swear at their teachers. If you were Mr. T., what action would you take when Gideon swears at you? Defend your answer.

2. If a student approaches you in anger, how can you defuse that anger? On seeing that Gideon is approaching and knowing the situation, would you allow him to speak first, or would you speak first? Why would you do one or the other?

3. In a situation like this one, should the student's first inkling of the problem be when he or she gets the paper back with a failing grade and an accusation on it?

4. What would you do as a teacher if, on receiving a paper like the one Gideon has received, the student (a) broke down and cried or (b) got up and bolted from the classroom? Consider your responsibility to all the students in the class, not just to Gideon.

Possible Solutions

1. Mr. T., students clustered around his desk as Gideon approaches, fears that a confrontation is going to take place. He understands why. He stops talking to a student with whom he has been discussing tomorrow's group presentation, turns to Gideon, and says, "Gideon, we need to talk, but it would be better if we did it when we are a little less pressed for time. I'll give you a note to come to the library at the beginning of sixth period to see me. I will be at one of the tables in the reference room." Gideon mumbles, "All right," and takes the note from Mr. T.

2. As soon as Gideon swears at him, Mr. T. begins shouting. He says, "I won't put up with that kind of talk, young man. You get out of this room instantly. Go to Mr. J.'s office, and I will be there in five minutes. We are going to sort this out. You are in deep trouble." Gideon begins, "But, Mr. T. . . ." Mr. T. shouts, "Get out! Are you deaf? Get out before I lose it entirely." Gideon leaves the room as his classmates look on.

3. Knowing that Gideon's paper is going to be a source of difficulty, Mr. T. does not return it with the rest of the papers but rather says, "Gideon, please see me after class about your paper." At the end of the class, other students flock around Mr. T.'s desk. Gideon, who has been apprehensive throughout the period, finally says, quite politely, "Mr. T., I have my math class next, and I'll be late for it if I don't leave now." Mr. T. answers, "I'll be right with you. Don't worry about being late. I'll write you an excuse." Mr. T. finishes with the other students as quickly as he can. Once they are alone, he closes the classroom door and says, "I'm afraid I have some bad news about your paper, Gideon. It really isn't your own work, is it?"

Consider This

Most people prefer to avoid confrontation. When they see that confrontation is inevitable, however, they may overreact, as Mr. T. has in this case. His overreaction triggers a similar overreaction on the student's part. Although the student's reaction is ill-advised, the student cannot be considered wholly responsible for it; he has been goaded into it at a time when he is understandably tense and upset.

Mature people realize that when confrontation occurs, they can keep it at a civilized level if they take the initiative. Accusing a student of cheating within earshot of other students is always a mistake. Given this situation, the teacher should have told Gideon that he knows what they need to talk about and that he will be right with him or he can see him at some set time. This approach would not have provided Gideon with the opportunity to have the unfortunate outburst he did. Teachers should always remember that if students speak disrespectfully to them, the reason might be—although is not always—that they have not commanded respect. Civilized behavior often begets civilized behavior.

CASE STUDY 3.3–C
Student Tells Parents About Accusation

Gideon is the sort of student who has always kept his problems pretty much to himself. After his encounter with Mr. T., he says nothing to his parents, even though his situation at school has not been resolved. Mr. and Mrs. S. know that something is wrong. Gideon seems disheartened and distracted. At first they think it might be adolescent moodiness, but soon they know that something deeper than that must underlie Gideon's uncharacteristic behavior.

After considerable questioning, Gideon's mother gets him to tell her what the problem is. She is appalled, particularly because literature and school mean so much to Gideon, who is extremely honest, unusually dedicated, and very sensitive. He has few friends his own age and engages little in the activities usually associated with a sixteen-year-old.

After Mr. and Mrs. S. and Gideon have talked the situation over, Mr. S. decides that he has to go to school and talk with the principal. Gideon says, "I don't think that's fair, Dad. In the first place, this is my problem, not yours." His father interrupts, "I agree that it's your problem, but I am not going to sit back and allow you to be treated unfairly!"

Gideon says, "I appreciate that, Dad, but it's not fair for you to go over Mr. T.'s head. You owe it to Mr. T. to talk the situation out with him. If he doesn't give you any satisfaction, then you might have to go to the principal." Mrs. S. agrees that it is best for her husband to see Mr. T. first, and Mr. S., finding out from Gideon that Mr. T. is free second period, calls the teacher at home to set up an appointment with him for the next day.

Questions

1. Do you think Gideon's father should involve himself in this situation if Gideon does not ask him to become involved? Would it be better for him to take the attitude that this is Gideon's problem and that it will be a learning experience for him to handle it himself?

2. Assuming Mr. S. and Mr. J., the principal, meet to discuss the situation, should Mr. S. insist that Gideon be present? Why or why not? Should Mr. J. insist that Gideon be present? Why or why not? Should Gideon insist on being present? Why or why not? Should Mr. S. insist that his attorney be present? Why or why not?

3. How can Mr. T. best handle this situation so that it will not be confrontational as the classroom exchange with Gideon was? Should Mr. T. insist that another teacher or a school administrator be present during his talk with Mr. S.? Why or why not? Should he let his principal know that the meeting is going to take place?

4. What do you learn about Gideon from his reaction to his father's threatening to go to the principal? Does this give you any clue as to why he was so indignant in the first place and why he swore at Mr. T.? Does it help you to decide about whether he should be involved in the meeting between his father and Mr. T.?

Possible Solutions

1. Mr. and Mrs. S. decide that they should not at this point add fuel to a flammable situation. Their son is angry, and his teacher is angry. What they must do first is seek to help the two reach an understanding, and Mrs. S. thinks they can achieve this best by helping Gideon to decide what measures to take to get Mr. T. to realize that his work was honest. She suggests that Gideon schedule an appointment with Mr. T. the next morning half an hour before school begins. She urges Gideon to call Mr. T. at home to make the appointment, and Gideon does so. The next morning, the two meet in a conference room off the main office. Gideon takes the initiative by saying, "Good morning, Mr. T. I am really sorry I swore at you yesterday, but I lost my temper because you accused me of cheating, and I did not cheat." Reaching into his knapsack, he says, "Here are all my Hawthorne books. I have been reading about Hawthorne for years, and I know a lot about him."

2. A meeting has been arranged between Gideon and Mr. T., as in the solution above. Mr. T., who is in the conference room when Gideon arrives, is the first to speak: "Gideon, I have been thinking this situation over, and I don't want to do anything that might affect your standing in my class or in the school. I am going to forget this paper and allow you ten days to do another paper on another topic." Gideon responds, "I am sorry I lost my temper yesterday, Mr. T. I shouldn't have done that, but I was angry, and I am still angry. I DID NOT CHEAT! I have never cheated. I want my grade for this paper. I

worked hard for it, and I deserve it." Mr. T. answers, "Well, there's nothing I can do, then. I have given you a chance and you have blown it, boy. The 'F' stands." He gets up and leaves the conference room before Gideon has an opportunity to say anything more in his own defense.

3. Mr. S. comes to school, and it is agreed that he and Mr. T. will meet alone for ten minutes; then Gideon and the school principal, Mr. J., will join them. Mr. T., who is waiting when Mr. S. arrives, inquires, "Would you like some coffee?" Mr. S. declines and begins, "You know, I guess, that I teach at the university, so I know what a problem plagiarism can be and how carefully teachers have to guard against it. I think you and I are both trying to defend academic integrity, but I know a little bit about this situation that I probably should share with you." Mr. T. listens and is beginning to be convinced, but he then says, "Well, that may be the case, Mr. S., but there is still the matter of Gideon's insolence. If I let that pass, I will lose face with my students."

4. Mr. S. arrives at school with his attorney, his wife's brother. When they enter the conference room, Mr. S. introduces himself to Mr. T. and then says, "And this is Andrew M., my attorney." Mr. T. flushes visibly and says, "I am very sorry. I will not go through with this meeting with an attorney present. If you insist on having an attorney, I will have to insist that the school board's attorney also sit in on the meeting!" He walks out the door.

Consider This

Sometimes two parties in a dispute prevent reaching a reasonable solution of it by being stubborn or by blowing the situation out of proportion. In this instance, a student is falsely accused. Given the fact that Gideon's paper seems more professional than those his classmates have written, Mr. T. has cause for suspicion, and it is his duty to ferret out plagiarism if it exists. In this case, however, he has made a great leap from suspicion to conviction, omitting many necessary steps in the process. Had he proceeded gradually, step by step, he would soon have discovered that the paper was legitimate, and tempers would not have flared.

The first thing Mr. T. needs to do is have a conference with Gideon to talk with him about the substance of his paper. In such a conference, he would likely have come to the immediate realization that this student knows more about Hawthorne than he does, and he could have capitalized on this interest to the benefit of the whole class by inviting Gideon to tell the class how he became interested in this author and what he knows about him.

Gideon was injudicious to swear at Mr. T., but Mr. T. really asked for it, and he would be well advised to call Gideon aside as soon as possible and apologize to him for calling him a cheat in front of other students. It is not a sign of weakness for teachers to admit to being wrong when they really are wrong. By admitting that they have made a mistake, they often help students to see that they, too, are human, but that they try to be totally fair.

An apology from Mr. T., followed by further investigation to determine whether or not Gideon's paper was the result of an honest effort, will probably make Gideon realize that he has a teacher of high professional integrity as well as one who is fair in dealing with students. In teacher-student conflicts, teachers usually have an initial advantage. They must be sure to use this advantage judiciously if they are to gain the trust of the students they work with.

CASE STUDY 3.3–D
Friend of Family Hears About Accusation

As luck would have it, just after Gideon and his parents had talked about his problem, Nina B. drops by on her way home from the library. She knows at once that something is drastically wrong; the atmosphere is thick enough to cut with a knife. Nina, never afraid to be direct, quickly finds out what has happened and is so angry that she just about goes through the roof. She says passionately, "I've known Gid for ten years. He knows more about Hawthorne than many of the students in my graduate seminar. How can that idiot teacher treat him like this? I'm not going to put up with it!"

Mr. S. and Gideon both try to calm Nina down, but she is so angry that the veins in her neck stick out and her face is ashen. She leaves because it is getting late, but as she drives home, she gets angrier and angrier. Nina is a just person herself, and although she is quite tolerant of other people, she becomes righteously indignant when an injustice of this sort has been perpetrated.

She tells her husband, Zack, what has happened and says, "I'm going to call that teacher and tell him what I think of all this." Zack tries to dissuade Nina from making the call, but Nina, never one to shrink from confrontation, dials Mr. T. and begins her conversation by identifying herself and then saying, "I will not have Gideon S. treated the way you have treated him! It is disgraceful. Mark my words: heads will roll."

Questions

1. Was it a mistake for Gideon and his parents to share news of the conflict between Gideon and his teacher? Does it make a difference that Nina B. is an authority on Hawthorne?

2. If you were in Mr. T.'s place and someone claiming to be Nina B., whom you know by reputation as a Hawthorne scholar, called you up at your home in the evening, would you talk with her? Why or why not?

3. If you refused to discuss the situation with your caller, would you merely terminate the call by hanging up, or would you refer the caller to someone else? If so, to whom? Would you get in touch with this person first to fill him or her in on the situation?

4. Do you think Nina B.'s telephone call will help to remedy the situation between Mr. T. and Gideon or will make it more difficult for them to resolve the problem? Defend your answer.

Possible Solutions

1. Mr. T. answers his telephone and cannot believe what he hears on the other end. He tells the caller, "I am sorry, but the matter you are bringing up involves privileged information between me and one of my students. I cannot discuss it over the telephone with someone I don't know." The caller responds, "Don't give me that. I know what happened, and I am outraged!" Mr. T. says, "I am sorry. I cannot discuss the matter. If you wish to discuss it further, you will have to schedule an appointment with me at school through my principal's office. Would you like to have that number?" The caller takes the number down. Mr. T. immediately calls his principal, Mr. J., at home to tell him what has happened. Mr. J., who has already been informed of the basic situation, thanks Mr. T. for keeping him informed and agrees to deal with the caller if she calls.

2. As soon as Mr. T. hears Nina B.'s tirade, he shouts, "I don't know what you are talking about, lady," and he slams down the receiver. His telephone rings again, and he picks the receiver up and puts it right back to disconnect the call. He then takes it off the hook and puts it in a drawer in his kitchen. He tells no one of receiving this call.

3. Mr. T. listens patiently to Nina B.'s invective. When she has finished, he says, "I can understand your being upset if you are a friend of Gideon's family and have heard the story you have just related. I cannot discuss this matter with you over the telephone, as I am sure you understand. I would be most happy to meet with you at school with one of Gideon's parents and with Gideon present, as well

68

as with my vice-principal. May I have your telephone number so that I can get in touch with you if I need to?"

Consider This

The situation outlined here demonstrates how a simple classroom matter can escalate into a public cause if it is not dealt with intelligently, fairly, and quickly. This situation need never have come to a head had the teacher followed due process. As it is, tempers are strained and the matter could conceivably grow into a lawsuit. Given the fact that the matter has reached the proportions it has, Mr. T. would be wise to thank Nina B. for her interest without giving her any information about the matter. After all, it might be that the caller is not the person she purports to be.

Mr. T. must protect Gideon's reputation by refusing to give details about the suspected plagiarism to some faceless person on the other end of his telephone line or to anyone else. Mr. T. should also realize that possibly Nina B. will be extremely helpful to him as the expert who can discuss the validity of the paper in question. Possibly her expert information will enable him to exonerate his falsely accused student, so fairness dictates that he leave the door open to this possibility.

CASE STUDY 3.3–E
Principal and Teacher Confer About Accusation

Mr. J. has been a principal for sixteen years. His teachers like him because he usually supports them. He is open-minded and fair. He has acquired a degree of wisdom through his long administrative tenure. He has never forgotten what it is like to be a teacher. He taught social studies for nine years before he became an administrator. Once, when he had aroused some ire in the community by having some of his students read *The Communist Manifesto*, both his principal and his superintendent of schools had supported him, defending the pedagogical justifications Mr. J. gave for having made this controversial title a supplemental reading in his course in comparative government.

The Gideon situation has been pretty well resolved by now. Gideon has demonstrated that he did not plagiarize. Mr. T. has reread his paper and given it the "A" it deserved in the first place. But some animus still exists between Gideon and Mr. T., who, although he has reevaluated Gideon's work, has never really apologized to him. Mr. T. thinks that even though Gideon has been exonerated, he should be punished for having sworn at him in front of students and for having demeaned him. He has scheduled an appointment with Mr. J., during which he suggests that Gideon should not be permitted to get away with what Mr. T. calls his "insolence." He tells Mr. J. that if nothing is done, his authority as Gideon's teacher will be weakened and that this weakening might affect his teaching adversely.

Questions

1. Would you expect your principal to defend you even if you were wrong? Think of a situation in which you might make a mistake that a parent or group of parents brings to your principal's attention. How would you least like that principal to handle the matter? How would you be likely to handle it if you were the principal?

2. If you realize that you have done something in your teaching that might cause controversy or even a public outcry, is it best to let your administrators know at once, or is it best to keep quiet and hope that nothing will come of it? Defend your answer.

3. If you anticipate that something you feel you must legitimately do in class—such as teach the Darwinian view of evolution or put a controversial book on your reading list—will cause controversy, should you let your principal know before you do it, even if the principal has little knowledge about the subject you teach? What should you do if you inform your principal, who then says, "I would rather you not do that"?

4. Do you think a teacher should make a public apology to a student in a situation like Gideon's? Do you think Gideon should be expected to make a public apology to the teacher for having sworn at him? Discuss both questions fully.

Possible Solutions

1. Mr. T. tells Mr. J. that he will not consider the matter resolved until Gideon has made an apology to him in front of the class for swearing. Mr. J. says, "Look, John, that happened two days ago. We've won the State Championship in basketball since then, and I think your students are remembering that more than they are remembering that one of your students swore at you. Let's not make mountains out of molehills. You and Gideon come into the office at the beginning of lunch, and I'll tell him I am glad the problem has been worked out, but that I must caution him not to lose his temper with teachers." "Well, all right," Mr. T. allows, "but then he has to apologize to me here before you." Mr. J. replies, "Why don't we let him apologize if he wants to? But if he doesn't, we can assume that a boy

that bright has gotten the message and that he won't swear at you again. After all, John, you are the adult, he is the child. You are big enough to give a little, aren't you?" Mr. T. agrees.

2. The situation above takes a slightly different turn when Mr. T. refuses to agree with the principal. He knows that one thing Mr. J. resolutely will not do is meddle with a teacher's grades. Mr. T. tells Mr. J., "OK, I'll go along with that, but if he doesn't apologize, I am going to knock his paper down to a 'B' for his insolence, and his term grade will be affected."

3. Mr. J. is troubled after his meeting with Mr. T. His personal opinion is that the matter has been settled and should be dropped. Nevertheless, he does not want Mr. T. to think that he is refusing to support him, and he agrees that in most circumstances, students should not swear at their teachers. The next day, fifteen minutes before Mr. T. and Gideon both have their lunch breaks, he sends a message to each asking them to come to his office for ten minutes at the beginning of the lunch period. Neither knows that the other will be there. The two of them arrive at about the same time and greet each other coldly. When they get into Mr. J.'s office, he says to Gideon, "Look, Gid, it's a mistake for a student to cuss a teacher out, but I think we both understand why you were upset, and everything worked out all right, didn't it?" Gideon says, sort of reluctantly, "Well, I guess so." "Then," Mr. J. responds, "I want the two of you to shake hands here and now and to agree to let bygones be bygones. You have seven more months to work together, and neither of you will get much out of those seven months if you aren't pulling in the same direction." Mr. T. extends his hand, and Gideon shakes it. The worst seems over. The two leave together, and Mr. T. says, "Look, Gid, why don't we have lunch together in the student cafeteria? My treat."

Consider This

Schools are societies in miniature. Everything that happens in a typical town or state or nation probably happens on a smaller scale in most schools. Just as people must resolve legal conflicts and nations must resolve international conflicts, so must schools resolve conflicts—if possible in such a way that all parties in the conflict can save face and will emerge from the situation feeling they have been treated fairly.

Mr. J. is caught in the middle in this situation, trapped between an unwritten code that demands school administrators to defend their faculty to every reasonable extent and his personal feeling that one of his students has (1) been accused unjustly of cheating and (2) been provoked into exhibiting classroom behavior that is generally considered unacceptable. Mr. J.'s job is to bring the two warring factions together without seeming to take sides. If he is successful, both Mr. T. and Gideon will be victors. If he fails, one will be the victor, the other the defeated—and if students are defeated in situations like this, they sometimes lose faith completely in the educational system. Some of them may drop out of school over a matter of this sort. Others may decide that honesty doesn't pay and may begin for the first time to take the easy way out—and someone as clever as Gideon can find remarkable ways to cheat and not be caught!

If students, teachers, and administrators sincerely believe that they are all working for the same sorts of general social objectives, schools will run harmoniously. If they constantly seem to be working at cross purposes, the schools will be in chaos. The entire situation with Gideon could have been nipped in the bud instantly had Mr. T. followed due process, had he gathered the information that he eventually had to gather anyhow to convince him that a suspicious paper had, indeed, been well researched and honestly written.

If a principal can achieve an outcome like that in Possible Solution 3, both parties in the dispute will be able to begin building a more productive relationship than they had before, but such an outcome usually cannot be reached until both parties are brought to the point that they genuinely realize they are both working toward the same general ends.

TAKING A STAND WHEN THE WORLD SEEMS AGAINST YOU

At times we all find ourselves in the position of having to take an unpopular stand because we cannot ethically do otherwise. When we are forced into a position like this, we can end up feeling terribly alone, and we even ask ourselves whether the disdain we are suffering is worthwhile. We ask ourselves sometimes whether it would not have been easier to compromise, to go along with community sentiment even though we do not feel comfortable with it. But teachers, as leaders in their communities, must stand up for what they believe; if they refuse to, who will?

At times like this, teachers should always try to see both sides of the issue involved, but when they finally reach a reasoned and, to them, reasonable decision, they owe it to themselves and to society to stick with it and defend it.

72

CASE STUDY 3.4
Teacher Asked To Take AIDS Victim As Student

Helen H. teaches fourth grade in a fairly large elementary school in a quiet, conservative community of about thirty-five thousand people. Although the school has four fourth-grade classes, Helen is so well known and is so effective in teaching her students that parents struggle to see that their children are assigned to her class. Class assignment is random in this school. Gifted and talented children are taken from class and spend half a day every week at the education center working on special projects.

In her eighteen years of teaching, Helen has built a strong reputation as a superb teacher. Five years ago, she was named teacher-of-the-year in her state.

One afternoon shortly before the final bell, the principal asks Helen to come to the office for a few minutes after school. When she gets there, she is surprised to find the three other fourth-grade teachers there also. Ms. Y., the principal, loses no time in explaining to them the reason for meeting. She says, "We have a potential problem brewing. You have heard I am sure of the family that was driven out of a southern town because their children, all hemophiliacs, have contracted AIDS. It's been on the news night after night."

The teachers had all heard about this situation and deplored what had happened to the stricken family. The principal continued, "Well, they have rented a house here, and their son Jerry will be in fourth grade. The superintendent of schools has met with the Board of Education to discuss the matter. They conferred with public health officials and reached the decision to allow the boys to attend school as long as they are able. The other two boys will be in the middle school, but Jerry is all ours. I have called you together because I want to provide this student with the best learning environment we can offer, and that means assigning him to a fourth-grade teacher who is willing to work with him." There is an awkward pause. Finally, Ms. M., who has taught in the school for two years and has continuing discipline problems, says, "Well, I feel sorry for the poor boy, but I would worry myself to death if he were in my class. My students have short fuses. They fight sometimes, as you well know, Ms. Y. Suppose we had bloodshed, and someone caught this boy's infection?"

Ms. Y. says, "Well, I understand how you feel, Ms. M. How do you feel about it, Mr. L.?"

Mr. L. squirms and says, "I'm sympathetic, heaven knows, but Lori and I have a new baby. I am afraid to be exposed to anyone

73

with a disease like AIDS. No one knows for sure how people contract it. What would happen if I somehow infected my family?"

Helen breaks in and says, "I've read a great deal about AIDS. I am satisfied that it cannot be transmitted through casual contact. I will be glad to work with Jerry, but I will ask for a few concessions before I take on this assignment."

Ms. Y., relieved to have a volunteer, inquires, "What do you want us to do?"

Helen responds, "I don't want Jerry in my class until I have had an opportunity to prepare my students and their parents for his arrival. There is likely to be publicity, and those most affected have to be ready to handle the situation."

"I think that's a wonderful suggestion," Ms. Y. answers. "How do you think we should go about working with the students and their parents?"

Helen answers, "I know most of the parents involved, and I think they trust me. I suggest we invite them to an evening meeting as soon as we can arrange it and tell them what we are planning. I want to have a well-qualified doctor from the Department of Public Health there to make an informed presentation and to field questions. I also want to distribute handouts on AIDS. The next day, I want the same public health doctor to come to my class and talk to my students and answer their questions. They will have plenty to ask. I think these steps are vital."

"You are right on target, Helen," says the principal. "I will set the wheels in motion. Do you think that Jerry's parents should be invited to the parents' meeting?"

Ms. R., who has been silent up until now, interrupts. "I don't think you're being fair to the rest of us, Helen. It is dangerous to have an AIDS victim in our building. I won't have any peace of mind if I know he is here with the other children."

Questions

1. How much do you know about the transmission and treatment of AIDS? Do you know that you can receive free information about the disease by requesting it from the U.S. Surgeon General's Office in Washington, D.C., or from your local public health office? Free pamphlets are available in bulk quantities.

2. Do you think it is wise for Helen to let her students know that the new student has AIDS? Why or why not? What problems should she anticipate and be prepared to deal with?

3. Do you think Helen is asking for trouble by letting her students'

parents know about the situation? What problems might she anticipate from them, and how should she prepare herself to deal with them?

4. Besides seeing that her students and their parents are informed accurately about AIDS, what positive steps might Helen take to make sure Jerry's early days in a new school environment are as encouraging as possible for him?

5. Helen knows that a former teacher in the system has contracted AIDS from a blood transfusion she had three years ago. Her illness is presently in remission, and she has regularly spoken to religious and civic groups about the disease. Many of Helen's students and their parents know this former teacher. Do you think it would be a good idea for Helen to involve her in any way in this situation? In what specific ways might she be involved?

Possible Solutions

1. When Ms. R. raises her objection, Helen says to her, "Kate, we are placed in danger every time we cross the street. It is much more likely you or some of your students will be struck by a car than it is that someone here is going to get AIDS just because one child with the disease is in my class." Mr. L. says, "Well, I sympathize with the poor boy and his family. After all, it isn't *his* fault that he got AIDS. But I'm still not sure we know the whole truth about the disease." Helen responds, "I can understand how anyone would be apprehensive about this situation, but we have a professional responsibility, and I think we have to honor that responsibility. I also think that we need to have an after-school workshop for the entire faculty and staff of the school to make sure that everyone here knows precisely what the facts are about AIDS." Ms. Y., the principal, agrees that this is necessary and thinks that the superintendent of schools and members of the school board need to be involved in that meeting. She says that she considers the meeting top priority and will schedule it within the next three days. She also will request permission to shorten the school day by ninety minutes on the day of the meeting so that teachers who have already made after-school plans will not have to cancel them. She wants to be sure that everyone attends.

2. Plans are now afoot for the school to take responsibility for informing the public about its decision and about AIDS. The new family is to arrive in town the following Wednesday, and their children are scheduled to begin school the next Monday. Helen thinks that it would be well for her to meet Jerry and the rest of the family for the first time outside the school setting. Realizing that the family's tele-

phone might not be connected yet, she mails a note to them on Tuesday telling them that she will be Jerry's teacher and welcoming them to the community. She expresses her desire to meet them all if they can spare her a half hour over the weekend and gives them her telephone number. She ends her note by saying, "I know that things will still be unorganized in your house, but I can sit on an orange crate if I have to; I just want to get to know all of you and to extend a welcoming hand!"

3. Helen tries to mollify Ms. R. and Mr. L., both of whom are becoming more and more negative in their comments about accepting an AIDS child into the school. Finally, Ms. M., the other fourth-grade teacher, who has remained quite silent, says, "Well, I think we should put it to a vote of the faculty. If more than half think we should take this student, then we will just have to live with it." Ms. Y. reminds her that the rule of the majority is not applicable in this situation: "The Board of Education has made a decision, as has the superintendent. We do not have a vote to exercise." Helen joins in: "What we need to do is sleep on this. We need to try to put ourselves in the place of the family that faces losing three children to a disease for which no cure has been found. I think if we look at the whole situation rationally, remembering that one cannot be infected through casual contact, we will all want to do what we have been called upon to do." Ms. R. is furious and blurts out, "Well, I'm not putting my life on the line for some student I don't even know!"

Consider This

Situations like the one described here have faced a number of school districts, and the problem will not diminish in the immediate future. People panic when they feel threatened by the outbreak of a fatal disease for which there is no known cure, no matter how unlikely it is that the disease can be transmitted casually. It would be well to analyze the underlying sentiments in what each teacher has said in the case study and in the possible solutions. Mr. L.'s use of the word *fault* tells us something. Ms. M.'s seemingly fatalistic approach is probably not fatalistic at all because she has a fair notion of how the vote will turn out and will probably work to see that it does turn out that way.

A situation like this one does not lend itself to easy solutions. If you feel a sense of frustration after having read the case study and the possible solutions, you are not alone. The writer knows what he would do if faced with a situation like this one, but he cannot impose his solution upon you. You have to reach your informed conclusions on your own, but you must be sure that the conclusions you have reached are informed by scientific evidence rather than by emotion or by widespread condemnation of a group of people.

Project

Assume roles and improvise the question-and-answer period that takes place in the auditorium where parents have come to be given information about AIDS and to be told that an AIDS patient will enter Helen's fourth-grade classroom the following Monday.

Exercise 3.6

This chapter has dealt with a number of problems, but central to each of them is the question of how teachers build and earn their reputations. You might wish to summarize your feelings about the degree to which each of the teachers and administrators mentioned in the case studies strengthened their professional reputations by ranking them on the following chart, using a scale of 1 (low) to 10 (high). Be ready to defend your evaluations of each person listed below.

10 9   8   7   6   5   4   3   2   1
(High)   (Low)

Greta H.
(Case Study 3.1)   _____

Don H.
(Case Study 3.2)   _____

Mr. T.
(Case Studies
    3.3–A to 3.3–E)   _____

Mr. J.
(Case Study 3.3–E)   _____

Helen H.
(Case Study 3.4)   _____

Ms. Y.
(Case Study 3.4)   _____

	10 9 8 7 6 5 4 3 2 1
	(High) (Low)
Ms. M. (Case Study 3.4)	_____
Mr. L. (Case Study 3.4)	_____
Ms. R. (Case Study 3.4)	_____

4. AND I USED TO THINK I COULD GET ALONG WITH ANYONE!

Part I: Dealing with Students and Parents

Teachers, like most other people, play an assortment of roles every day. At one moment they are authority figures to the students they teach; at the next they are the people answerable to the administrators who run their schools or their school systems. Teachers work intermittently with supervisors or with helping teachers, as some school districts call them. They work closely with their colleagues and have a peer relationship with them. In some districts they work regularly with consultants who come to their schools as a part of in-service programs.

Teachers who do not quickly get to know the secretaries in their school offices and the staff in their media centers do themselves a great injustice. Teachers work indirectly as well with the maintenance staffs of their schools, although they may never see members of those staffs who work outside regular school hours. They also work with parents and people from the community.

Chapters 4 and 5 focus on the professional relationships teachers have with others. The emphasis of Chapter 4 is on how teachers deal with students and parents. Chapter 5 focuses on how teachers work with the other people who are a part of their professional lives.

YOU AND YOUR STUDENTS

Schools exist for students. Therefore, your most important professional relationships are those you have with them. In order to deal effectively with your students, you must come to know them, you must try to understand how they have to live their lives, and you must work to individualize your instruction to the point that you reach as many students as you possibly can in the course of your teaching.

CALLS FOR EDUCATIONAL REFORM

Some people who call for educational reform are actually calling for a return to the schools and standards of a different era. People like this recall with dewy eyes the time when all high school graduates could read and write well, and it is historically accurate to assert that high school graduates at the turn of the century were better equipped in the basics than today's average graduate is. Such will always be the case when only 10 percent of a nation's youth ever gets beyond seventh or eighth grade, and in 1900 that is the percentage that continued their educations beyond the elementary school.

We can look at a time closer to ours when schools were more orderly places than they are now, more no-nonsense institutions, safer institutions than those we find in many metropolitan areas today. But order was often bought at the cost of segregation, at the cost of denying opportunity to large elements of our supposedly egalitarian society, at the cost of perpetuating a type of conformity that few thinking people—indeed, that few people with a social conscience—can condone.

Even those who would condone it must inevitably face one stark reality: it is not possible to set back a social clock once it has begun to tick. If we dream of the effectiveness of such institutions as the one-room schoolhouse, we must realize that the obverse side of the coin—the nightmare scenario, if you will—shows a pre–Civil War school system that had few college-trained teachers and that in most areas functioned for only two or three months a year, the months in which young people were not needed as farmhands because the weather was not right for planting, cultivating, or harvesting.

INDUSTRIALISM AND EDUCATION

Industrial society long ago replaced the agrarian society of our great-great-grandparents. An information society that deals in knowledge more than it does in the kinds of products that used to come out of foundries and mills and factories is the society for which contemporary students are being prepared. When public schools were first instituted in England at the beginning of the Industrial Revolution, they had one major social end to achieve—that of transforming a society built on cottage industries into a society that was centered around factories.

The schools of late eighteenth- and early nineteenth-century Britain had to emphasize those qualities that people needed if they were to work successfully in factories. If the schools failed, the factories necessarily failed as well. The most important qualities for factory workers to develop were obedience, punctuality, dependability, and perseverance. These became the prime virtues of schools that were established to educate not the elite, but the emerging working class. A democratization of sorts was taking place in education, and the rise of the working class that culminated a century or more later in movements like the unionization of workers was creating a new type of citizen in much of the western world. Today's students need another orientation. They need to develop skills of reasoning and of problem solving if they are to serve well in the work place.

The smokestack industries that made American great from the post–Civil War era until the end of World War II required workers with the qualities our schools then instilled. They did not necessarily require high school graduates, but in a real way industry dictated in quite unsubtle ways what our educational system would be. When industry wanted to keep young people off the labor force, it supported the establishment of the junior high school, reasoning that if a decisive break came in education at the end of ninth grade in a 6–3–3 system rather than at the end of eighth grade in an 8–4 system, youngsters would stay in school a year longer and enter the job market one year more mature than the people who had previously entered it.

When industry wanted to control its flow of applicants even more, it began to demand a high school diploma of those seeking employment for many routine jobs that in actuality did not require a high school education for their effective execution. And so it has gone through the present century, with young people who do not stay in school for increasingly longer periods being denied access to fruitful employment.

Various problems have developed because of changes the work place has imposed upon education and upon society. As industry grew, cities sprang up where only a decade before small towns had served the needs of the small enclaves of people who lived near them on farms. As people moved into cities to find work in factories, schools became larger and larger. They also served a more diverse student body than they had ever been called upon to serve in the past, and new curricula, many of them not college preparatory, were devised to meet the needs of this diverse student body and of the work place that awaited its members.

Contemporary teachers will find themselves frustrated by today's schools and by the students who attend them if they fail to realize the historical development that has brought us to where we now find ourselves educationally in the United States. Most of the problems that bother teachers are, although admittedly distressing, understandable and were, indeed, predictable long before they surfaced full blown.

The major factor in educational change in our country during this century has been the industrialization of the United States, followed by its subsequent change from a society of heavy industry to one of information services. Each stage of this change has made it incumbent upon the emerging work force to stay in school longer. This has led to the development of a school population that is older and more sexually sophisticated than ever before. Whereas for most people in 1900 the onset of puberty was followed by marriage within two or three years, the onset of puberty in our society is inevitably followed for most students by anywhere from six to sixteen additional years of schooling. Rampaging hormones account for many discipline problems in our schools, and the release of sexual tensions leads to such other problems as promiscuity, unplanned pregnancies, the spread of sexually transmitted diseases, and that panoply of other disturbing manifestations of sexual coping often referred to broadly as a "moral breakdown."

Contributing to these problems are two more important factors: Because most United States households include either two working parents or a single parent, youngsters reaching puberty have much more unsupervised time at home than their counterparts did before World War II. Also, because of the very structure of contemporary society, it is increasingly necessary for teen-agers, plumb in the middle of puberty, to have cars. These cars give them an opportunity for increased sexual freedom and also place them under financial pressures that the sixteen-year-old bicycle rider of an earlier era did not face.

This brings us to yet another fact of contemporary life that teachers need to acknowledge—their teen-age students need more money than students ever have before, and they usually get it in one of three ways:

1. Their parents or guardians give it to them;
2. They earn it, sometimes working such long hours that their schoolwork suffers;
3. They find ways of making "easy money."

The first of the options above is the one that affects the smallest numbers of students in most modern schools. From sixteen on, most students work anywhere from five to forty hours a week to earn the money—or at least some of the money—they need. If they don't work, they don't ride, and that is something many of them are unwilling even to contemplate.

The third option brings us to another set of realities that many teachers would prefer to ignore or deny. Students who opt for easy money will usually get it either in one or in a combination of the following ways:

- Thievery, ranging from shoplifting to armed robbery
- Dealing in goods someone else has stolen
- Prostitution, both male and female
- Selling drugs.

If you teach fifty students in any school setting in any grade from three to twelve, probably at least *five* of these students, even in rural farming communities, have engaged—and perhaps are still engaging—in one or more of the activities listed above. Some of these students will have weekly incomes higher than your monthly salary—and these incomes are for the most part tax-free! Few such students will be regular in their school attendance or will keep up in their schoolwork, although notable exceptions to this generality exist.

What you have just read was not easy to write. You may deplore having had to read it. You may think that this view of the American youth culture is cynical. However, statistics bear out the disheartening facts just presented, and if our society faces any significant threat, that threat comes as much from within as it does from fear of foreign aggression. If any group of people can help to turn this situation around, that group is school people—well-informed, realistic, intelligent teachers and administrators. These people cannot turn this situation around unless they face the realities that surround them.

RELATIONSHIPS WITH STUDENTS

The early case studies in this section will confront some of the types of problems teachers have actually had that do not relate directly to learning activities but that have a great deal to do with how well students learn. A second group of case studies will deal more directly with typical learning situations teachers deal with on a daily basis.

CASE STUDY 4.1
Teacher Notices Personality Change in Student

Jason B. was a real find for his school district. He loves to teach adolescents and was willing to leave his senior high school teaching job to take on two sixth grades in a complex metropolitan neighborhood. He teaches English, social studies, and mathematics to one group of students in the morning and teaches English and mathematics to another group in the afternoon. He also has his morning students for homeroom.

Jason's morning group represents a staggering range of abilities, socioeconomic levels, and ethnic backgrounds. Jason knows his students well. Before he began to teach in this school, he took a walking tour of the neighborhood it serves and found that the school drew from three distinct districts—an affluent residential neighborhood near the river, a transition neighborhood to the south of the river where many of the large, old houses have been turned into apartments or rooming houses, and a high-crime neighborhood that many people would be afraid to go into at night.

Billy, one of Jason's students, is from the last of these three neighborhoods. He comes from a single-parent home. He, his mother, and three siblings live in a three-room apartment. The family is on welfare. Jason notices that Billy, whose attendance is sporadic, is never absent from school on a very cold day or on a rainy, damp day when the cold is penetrating even though the temperature is in the thirties. He soon realizes that school is the only place where Billy can keep warm. He always wears his hat and coat in class. Jason does not make an issue of this; he has more important things to do with Billy than argue with him about keeping his coat and hat on.

Billy is usually sullen. It is difficult to get him to respond to anything, and sometimes he falls asleep in class, often breathing so loudly that the other students laugh. Billy is a year older than Jason's typical twelve-year-old students. On one occasion Jason thinks he notices the smell of alcohol on Billy's breath, but he cannot be sure. Billy sleeps through most of class that morning.

One day Jason notices a change in Billy. He seems more alert. The other students seem to be more accepting of him. They joke with him, which they never did in the past. Jason is pleased to see this change. Billy looks better. He is wearing new clothes, and his new jogging shoes almost light up the floor around him.

One Wednesday, after a week of forewarning, Jason collects from each student a book that the class will no longer be using. Billy does not have his book and tells Jason he has lost it. Jason asks him, "Are you sure? Couldn't it just be under something."

"Nope," Billy replies. "I ain't had it for weeks. It's gone, vamoosed."

"Gee, Billy, I'm sorry, but I'll have to make you pay for it. It's going to cost you six dollars, but you can pay me any way you want to—a quarter a week or anything that's convenient."

"Man," Billy drawls, "I don't need to pay no quarter a week." At that, he reaches into his pocket and pulls out a roll of bills that makes Jason's eyes pop. He peels a bill off the top, hands it to Jason, and says, "Here. You got change for a fifty?" Jason notices that the bill below the fifty Billy peeled off is another fifty.

He asks Billy, quite dismayed, "Where did all that green come from, Billy?"

Billy smiles broadly, winks at Jason, and says, "I got me a part-time job, man, a part-time job. Dig?"

Questions

1. If you are to begin teaching in an area with which you are unfamiliar, what advantages can you see in making a survey of the neighborhood, as Jason did? What are some specific things you would look for in making such a survey?

2. In what specific ways do you think Jason's neighborhood survey helped to prepare him to deal with his teaching situation? Could it in any way have prejudiced his judgments?

3. Would you make an issue of the fact that a student in a situation like the one described wears his hat and coat in class? Defend your answer.

4. Nearly every teacher has to cope sometimes, as Jason did, with having a student fall asleep in class. List at least five specific things to which a student's frequently falling asleep in class might be attributed.

Possible Solutions

1. Jason hates to leap to conclusions, but Billy's sudden popularity, his dramatically improved wardrobe, and, most particularly, his unaccountable affluence indicate that he is obtaining significant sums of money from a part-time job that yields much more than the minimum wage he could command if he were old enough to work—and he is three years short of the age required for working papers. Students who never paid much attention to Billy before are suddenly seeking him out. Jason does not think he can or should handle the situation by talking directly with Billy, although that would be his natural preference. Given Billy's home situation, he does not think he should attempt to talk with Billy's mother, and he has little confidence that she will notice the situation and look into it. After a restless night, he decides that he needs to refer the matter to someone. He knows the counselors in his school try to emphasize academic problems in their counseling, so he goes to the vice-principal, who handles most disciplinary cases, and outlines a hypothetical situation to him, protecting Billy by not revealing his identity. The vice-principal listens, taking a few notes. When Jason has told him most of the story, he asks, "You're talking about Billy M., aren't you?" Jason is surprised and responds, "What makes you think that?"

2. Jason decides that the place to begin is with Billy's mother. He telephones her several times before he finally reaches her. He tells her that he would like to see her for fifteen or twenty minutes before or after school on a day that is convenient for her. She tells him that

she works every day until almost six, so she can't come to school to see him. He tells her it is important or he wouldn't have called her. She finally agrees to meet him at 7:30 at a public library just two blocks from her house where Jason knows the head librarian who will let him and Billy's mother use a conference room for their meeting. When the meeting takes place, Billy's mother shows her annoyance at having to take time to talk with a teacher. Jason mentions that Billy seems to have a great deal of money lately. The mother says, "What's wrong with that?" Jason answers, "Nothing, except that most kids his age don't pay for things with fifty-dollar bills." Her reaction is, "Back off, man. If you got proof of somethin', you show it to me, If you ain't, you jes' back off." She gets up and leaves without another word.

3. Jason meets the mother in the library as above. She is nervous and shows it. She drums her fingers on the table and then plays with her hair. Jason presents her with his concerns. All at once she puts her head down on the table, and great, heaving sobs erupt from her. Jason is not sure what to do. He pats her on the shoulder and says, "Come on, it can't be that bad. Tell me what you think the problem is, and we can work on it together." "Can't work on this problem," she sobs. "It's the same problem his brother had when he was six months younger than Billy. And when they was through wi' him, they knock him off." "What do you mean?" Jason asks. "They jes' knock him off, shoot him in the head." "Who did?" Jason persists. "You know who did," she continues. "The druggies done it 'n' they'll do the same thing to Billy." Jason is overwhelmed with anxiety.

Consider This

Students, especially at Billy's age (thirteen), sometimes arrive in class dressed up. Sometimes they sleep in class. One should not read too much into either of these things, although experienced teachers, when they detect patterns of changed behavior in their students, usually become vigilant, as is wholly appropriate. If a thirteen-year-old arrives in class with a wad of money and begins flashing twenty-, fifty-, or hundred-dollar bills around, something is badly awry. Immediate action is indicated, and the problem is serious enough that it should in most cases be channeled through the principal's office directly because other students in the school may be directly affected by what is going on. In no case should teachers talk with anyone outside the school about the situation, and in no case should teachers take it upon themselves to call the police into a situation like this. The principal will do that if the facts warrant police intervention. The principal—and the police, if they are called in—will be helped greatly if teachers have kept anecdotal records with dates and times that indicate the reasons for their suspicions. Often teachers will need to observe a student like Billy for a week or so to verify patterns of behavior, and an event like his flashing a wad of money would finally precipitate that teacher's taking the matter to an administrator.

CASE STUDY 4.2
Student Flashes Roll of $100 Bills

During the past three weeks, Billy, the student in the preceding case study, has begun to miss class often. Whenever he comes to class, his conspicuous consumption is obvious. When one of the students in class is hospitalized to have her appendix out, the home-room students ask Jason if they can chip in to send flowers to her in the hospital. Jason agrees to their suggestion and asks them how much they think each one should give. Then he says, "I am going to put in the first contribution. I'll give three dollars, but that's a lot more than you should give. I have a job and a salary."

The students decide that the flowers, along with tax and a get-well card, will cost about thirty dollars. With Jason's three dollars, that leaves twenty-seven dollars for them to raise among the thirty-two of them. They decide on a minimum contribution of fifty cents each, but some will give more than that. They should have no difficulty raising the twenty-seven dollars.

All at once, Billy, who has been dozing on and off, says, "Man, twenny-five bucks for flowers. You gonna send her stinkweeds or somethin'? Here. Get her something she'll like," and he puts two hundred-dollar bills on his desk, again taking them from a thick roll in his pocket. Billy, remember, is thirteen years old.

Within seconds of this munificent gesture on Billy's part, a strange sound comes from his person. Billy says, "Mr. B., that's my beeper. I have to go an' call in."

Jason is dismayed. "What do you mean your beeper? You know you can't leave class to make phone calls unless there's really an emergency. Sit down."

Billy is meticulously polite, but he keeps going toward the door, saying as he does, "I can't sit down, Mr. B. I got to make that phone call. It *is* a emergency. I could be in big trouble if I don't. There's a lot of money riding on it."

Questions

1. To your knowledge, do any students in the school in which you teach or in a school where you likely will be teaching wear beepers? Why might students wear beepers? List as many possibilities as you can—but stay within the realm of reason.

2. Does your school district have a policy about beepers? About students leaving class for any reason except at specified times?

3. Do you think the drug problem is largely one found in urban schools? Do you think it is largely confined to secondary schools in urban areas, particularly senior high schools?

4. Do you know some signs to look for in students who are taking drugs? To what extent is it your responsibility as a teacher to try to control the use of drugs among your students? Where might you obtain bulk quantities of pamphlets and other information about the hazards of drug addiction?

Possible Solutions

1. Billy moves to the front of the room to get out the door. Jason moves toward the door and stands blocking it. Billy tries unsuccessfully to outmaneuver Jason. He shouts at Jason, "Get outta my way, man. I don't wanna hurt you." Jason, deceptively calm, says firmly, "Back to your seat, Billy." "I'm tellin' you, I gotta make a phone call. Man, my butt is on the line." Jason repeats, "Back to your seat, Billy." Billy does not budge. Jason does not think he should touch Billy at this point. He stands his ground and says, "If you have made up your mind not to do what you are told, Billy, there's nothing I can do to stop you. It's not worth fighting about. But if you leave, you cannot come back into this room without a note from Mr. G. [the principal]." Billy bolts out the door, shouting as he bounds down the hall, "Man, I can make more with one phone call than you turkeys make in a month!"

2. When Billy's beeper goes off, the whole class giggles nervously. Billy starts for the door, and Jason tries to restrain him and get him to return to his seat. The other students are tense and talk among themselves. Nervous giggles continue to erupt here and there, triggering still more giggles. It is apparent that the students know more about this situation than Jason knows for sure. He decides it is better to let Billy go, close the door, and then get the class to tell him what they know about the situation. He begins by saying, "I want to know what's going on here. Someone tell me what this is all about." Total silence. "I know you know what's happening. You are going to sit

here until you tell me if it takes until midnight." Many students squirm. Finally Jason says, "All right, I don't want to hear a sound from any of you. I am going to Mr. G.'s office, and I want complete quiet in here until I get back. Got me?" He heads down the hall, leaving the door to the classroom open.

3. As in Possible Solution 2, Jason decides that he has a better chance of finding out details about this situation if Billy is not in the room. As soon as Billy leaves, he closes the classroom door and says, "We were going to have some free writing for twenty minutes later today, but I think we should do some writing now instead. Each of you please take out a sheet of paper. Do not put your name on it. You have just seen a dramatic encounter between a teacher and a student. I want you to write an account of what happened." Jason is not sure that this assignment will accomplish his ultimate end of gathering more information about Billy, but it will at least give him a little while to regain his equilibrium and to write an account of the event for the principal, something that he must do while the whole matter is fresh in his mind. He is also relatively sure that, given the anonymity he is allowing, some of his students will provide small scraps of information that he can piece together into something resembling a coherent account of what the problem is and of how widespread it might be. Jason knows that he is likely dealing with a highly explosive situation here, and he must handle it with deftness, being sure throughout to protect Billy's civil rights. He knows that Billy could charge him with defamation of character if he makes any accusations to other people about him, and he also knows that in a courtroom, Billy would look innocent and say something like, "I just wanted to leave the classroom for two minutes to make a telephone call to my mother who was home sick that day."

Consider This

The drug problem is pervasive in today's schools. The drugs most often pushed in schoolyards and used in schools are marijuana, crack, and cocaine, although other drugs also sometimes turn up. Drugs that can be smoked or sniffed are easier for students to take in school than drugs that must be injected, although some students "shoot up" in school washrooms, which is why faculty members should patrol washrooms during periods when students are changing classes. Drug barons get rich fast if they are not caught. They often dispense drugs free to the uninitiated, and once they have them hooked, they demand excessive amounts of money from them if they want their supplies continued. If students cannot come up with the money, the drug barons often turn them into pushers, who at an early age can make a thousand dollars a day quite easily—and who likely will eventually have to spend more than that on their habits. Fortunately the media have rendered a valuable service in advertising the "Just Say No" campaign and other such antidrug initiatives. Most schools teach about the harmful long-term effects of drugs and of the dangers of addiction in health education classes. Nevertheless, the drug problem is one that most teachers will have to face directly at one time or another in a typical teaching career.

It is important to know the telltale signs of drug use, which are often confused with adolescent moodiness. If you have students who frequently fall asleep in class, who are frequently incoherent, whose dispositions have changed drastically in a short time, and whose attention spans have diminished markedly, you may be dealing with students who are high on drugs. Most schools today have established policies for dealing with drug and alcohol problems. One of the first things you should know about any school in which you teach is what its policies and procedures are for preventing, detecting, reporting, and generally handling this problem. A starting point would be to obtain from your public health department materials on drug and alcohol use and abuse.

Keeping Confidences

Everyone needs someone in whom to confide. Students often turn to the teachers they like best as confidants. On the one hand, this is flattering and may seem to be in the students' best interests. However, teachers must be aware of the hazards involved. If a student asks to tell you something in complete confidence and you promise that the revelation will remain confidential, you have a responsibility to the student to keep it so. If you fail to do so, your credibility and honor are at stake. Yet, some matters revealed in confidence require attention that cannot be given without breaking the confidence. Therefore, if a student requests that you listen to a problem and keep it completely confidential, your most honest answer should be, "I cannot promise that without knowing what you want to tell me. I can only promise you this: I will not be shocked, I will not use my knowledge of what you are going to tell me to embarrass you, and I will do everything I can to help you with your problem." Students usually reveal deep confidences because they want help and do not know where to turn for it. The answer suggested offers precisely what they need and want, although they may not realize consciously that this is the case.

CASE STUDY 4.3
Student May Have Been Exposed to AIDS

Maureen K. is a lovable student. She has always kept up well in her work. She is always available to help fellow students who are having problems. She makes valuable contributions in her eleventh-grade classes at Edgar Potts Senior High School in a midwestern town of thirty thousand that has a small private college in it. She has been a cheerleader for two years, she had the lead role in the school play last year, she is active in student government, and she sings in the choir of her church, where she also teaches a Sunday school class at the primary level.

Maureen's family is working class. She will be the first member of it to go to college, and a substantial scholarship seems assured. Sometime in February everyone begins to notice that Maureen is different in undefinable ways. She seems lost in thought in her classes and almost never volunteers an answer. If she is called on, she always has to ask the teacher to repeat the question. Her eyes are often puffy, and she seems to have been crying. Her teachers hold her in high enough esteem that they make an effort to understand what is happening to her, but they are at a loss to explain it.

Her art teacher, Ms. D., who has always been one of Maureen's favorites, fears that perhaps her parents are thinking of a divorce or that there is some illness in the family that she doesn't know about. One day she keeps Maureen after class, closes the door, and asks her directly, "Is everything OK in your family, Maureen?"

Maureen looks surprised and says, "Sure, why wouldn't it be?"

Ms. D. presses her: "Something's the matter, love. I've known you for three years, and you just aren't the same old Maureen you were two months ago."

Maureen looks down at the floor and says, "No, everything's fine. I've just been a little . . ." That's as far as she gets. She begins to sob. Ms. D. puts her arms around her and says, "What is it, honey? You can tell me anything. We've been good friends for a long time, haven't we? You know you can trust me."

With that, Maureen says, "Promise you won't tell anyone."

Ms. D. says, "Of course I won't, Maureen. You know you can trust me."

Maureen lets loose. She has been needing to do this for some

91

time. She starts, "You remember back in October I told you I was going out with Jim C. from the college?"

"I can't say that I do remember that. Oh, yes. It was just before Halloween, wasn't it? What happened?"

"Well, we met downtown at the Cow for a shake and some fries. He had borrowed a friend's station wagon because he wanted to see a movie they were showing at the drive-in. So we went to the drive-in. But he didn't want to see a movie. He parked way in the back where we could hardly see, and as soon as he turned the engine off, he was all over me." She is crying uncontrollably now. "I always wanted to—you know—save myself," she said embarrassedly. "But he wouldn't let me. I told him I wouldn't do it because I didn't want to get pregnant. He said you can't get pregnant on the first try. Then he said something that has really worried me ever since. He said he had to make it with a girl. He never had before. He had made it with guys, and he had to prove to himself he was a man, and I could help him. He hauled me into the back of the station wagon and that was that."

"My God!" Ms. D. exclaimed. "But you aren't..., are you?"

"That's just it. I am. I've missed three periods, and I'm sick every morning. But what I'm worried about most isn't being pregnant— that's bad enough. But Jim's been having gay experiences—a lot of them, he told me. What if he gave me more than a baby?"

"Have you seen him recently?" Ms. D. asks.

"No. He never came back to school after Thanksgiving vacation. I heard he had pneumonia."

Questions

1. As a teacher, how might you best respond if one of your students who is about to share a confidence with you asks you to promise not to tell anyone? What are the implications of agreeing? What alternatives do you have to saying yes?

2. Assuming you find yourself in Ms. D.'s spot, do you think you have to honor your confidence? Would it be fair for Ms. D. to ask Maureen to release her from that confidence?

3. Do you think you would approach a student whose attitude seems to be changing, as Ms. D. approached Maureen, or would you wait for that student to come to you to discuss his or her situation? Does the fact that Ms. D. took the initiative place her under a greater obligation to Maureen than she would be under if Maureen simply came to her and volunteered the information?

4. Given the particular circumstances of this case study, would it alarm you to a degree to learn that the boy involved had come down with pneumonia and had left school? Discuss the possible implications of this.

Possible Solutions

1. Ms. D., an experienced teacher, is not particularly surprised to learn that Maureen is pregnant; what she was not prepared for was that Maureen's sexual partner was in a high-risk group for AIDS. Teen-age pregnancies are nothing new, but today's teen-agers face problems much greater than having unwanted pregnancies or contracting a venereal disease that is treatable. AIDS kills, and it is most frequently contracted through sexual contact and through sharing hypodermic needles. One of the symptoms of AIDS is pneumocystis pneumonia, a type of pneumonia frequent in AIDS sufferers as their immune systems deteriorate. Ms. D., realizing this, says to Maureen, "Honey, I know I said I wouldn't tell anyone, but we have to get you a blood test as soon as we can. I am not going to run to your parents with what I know, but I will take you down to Public Health or, if you prefer, to my own doctor for a blood test." Maureen says, "But I know I'm pregnant. What good will a blood test do?" Ms. D. explains, "The blood test is necessary not because of your pregnancy. You may have been exposed to someone who is carrying the AIDS virus. We have to make sure." Maureen, looking dejected and sounding despondent, replies, "I was afraid that was what you were thinking. I have been worried sick over the same thing."

2. Ms. D. says to Maureen, "Look, honey, you have to tell your parents exactly what you told me. You don't have any choice. If it would help you to tell them here in school and to have me with you when you do, I will ask them to come in for a conference, but you cannot keep this from them." Maureen flushes and says, "I just can't tell them. They'll blame me. They won't understand how it happened." Ms. D. reminds her, "They're going to find out before long anyway, love. You'll start to show. And my guess is that they have been noticing changes in you already and that they have their suspicions." Maureen responds, "I thought I would run away, and they wouldn't have to know." Ms. D. says, "That would be a lot worse for them than having you tell them the truth." Maureen consents reluctantly, saying, "Well, I guess you're right. I think it would be easier for me to tell them if you were there." Ms. D. sets up the conference for the following afternoon and also calls the public health office to see when she can bring Maureen in for a blood test.

93

3. Ms. D. is horrified by what she hears. She says to Maureen, "Well, I never thought it was anything this bad when I first noticed a change in you. I know I said I wouldn't tell anyone, but it would be against school policy for me not to tell the principal. I have to, Maureen. I hope you understand my position." Maureen quakes with sobs, between which she keeps muttering, "But you promised, you promised!"

Consider This

The problems raised in this case study cut in several directions. To begin with, a teacher is put in the position of knowing that in one way or another she is duty-bound to break a confidence—with or without the permission of the person to whom she made her promise. The questions of premarital sex and teen-age pregnancy are substantially complicated (1) because Maureen seems to come from a quite traditional home that would uphold traditional moral principles; (2) because Maureen might not only be pregnant but might also have contracted a disease that to date has been fatal to most people who have had it; (3) because Maureen, if she is infected, is highly likely to communicate this disease to her unborn child; and (4) because in essence Maureen has been the victim of date-rape, a common phenomenon that often goes unreported with the result that men who get away with it usually strike again.

Matters that deal with sex are extremely controversial in typical school settings. Some people stridently insist that every child should, in the early grades, be given explicit information about contraception. Equally vehement groups, sometimes backed by substantial religious organizations, argue against teaching such matters in the schools. Sincere and well-motivated people take stands at both extremes of questions like this, and the schools cannot deny these people the right to express what they conscientiously believe in.

On the other hand, public health matters affect everyone, and sometimes the will of one group has to prevail over the will of an opposing group, although the policy in most school districts is to allow compromise to whatever extent they can. School administrators realize that their schools serve large constituencies and that because school attendance is compelled by law, they should strive to meet the needs of every group represented in the community. Matters like sex education painfully split some school districts, but most administrators will try not to make unilateral decisions unless they have absolutely no other alternative. Teachers are entitled to hold personal opinions about sex education, abortion, and other such matters that are quite contrary to school policy. They are, however, expected to adhere to school policy in such matters, regardless of their personal predilections.

CASE STUDY 4.4
Students Tell Teacher of Seduction Attempt

Rona J. is in the middle of her third year of teaching science at Heath Senior High School, a typical small-town high school in a village of about thirty thousand people. Rona was raised in a similar place less than fifty miles from where she now lives. She did her student teaching at Heath when she was a senior at a nearby state college. She has good rapport with her students, although she is not chummy with them. Her colleagues and administrators, both in her building and in the district office, respect her. She expects to be recommended for tenure in April.

One Saturday morning, Rona, who lives with her husband, Ned, in a house about a mile from the school, is surprised to be summoned to the door by two of the students in her junior chemistry class, Molly and Peg, who are visibly upset. Peg has red blotches on her face and obviously has been crying. Rona invites the girls in but asks them to be quiet because Ned was late getting home from a business trip and is still sleeping. The girls talk nervously about a variety of things, but Rona knows that they are evading their real reason for having come to see her unannounced. She suggests that they drive to the local mall with her and walk around it a little.

As they head for the mall, Molly says, "Ms. J., we know we can trust you. Promise not to tell anyone what we need to talk to you about."

Slightly alarmed and caught off guard, Rona agrees. Then Molly asks, "Ms. J., how well do you know Mr. D.?" Rona is slightly taken aback. Mr. D., chair of the English Department, has taught at the school for almost fifteen years. His wife works in the local bank as an assistant vice-president. They have no children. Mr. D. went out of his way to be helpful and friendly to Rona when she was a student teacher at Heath. He had even invited her to come to dinner with him and his wife one Saturday night. When Rona got to his house at seven in the evening, she remembered, she found that Mr. D. was home alone. He laughed and said, "Stupid me! I forgot Deanna had to help her parents move this weekend. Never mind, though. I'm a good cook, and I've got some lamb chops you won't believe."

Rona had been uncomfortable in this situation, but she stayed and ate dinner. Mr. D. put on some records after they had eaten and suggested that they dance. Rona declined, saying that she had papers to grade and had better not stay much longer. Mr. D. reached out and grabbed both her arms, saying, "All work and no play makes teachers dull!" He drew her toward him, but Rona moved away and quickly said, "Thank you for dinner." She was out the door in two seconds. Mr. D. was always uncomfortable around her after that but showed no overt hostility.

These memories raced through Rona's mind as she responded, "Oh, I know him about as well as I know most of the other teachers outside my department. Why do you ask?"

Tears trickled down Peg's face. Molly, turning to her, asked, "Do you want to tell her, or should I?" Peg sobbed; then words poured out in a gush: "Well, you know I have a small part in the play we are doing for commencement weekend, and Molly has the lead."

"Yes," Rona replies, "I recall that you had to miss a class last week for a daytime rehearsal."

"Well, yesterday, just after English class, Mr. D. called me aside and told me that he thought he might have to make some shifts in the cast and that I seemed perfect to him for a bigger role. He said he wanted to have me audition for him, but that he had to go home right after school, so I couldn't audition then. Then he asked me if I could come by his house at eight last night to read some lines for him. I told him I could, and I didn't think much about it. I thought his wife would be home with him—but when I got there, he told me that she had gone out of town unexpectedly because her father had been taken ill.

"Mr. D. was drinking wine and poured a glass for me. I drank a little of it because I didn't want to offend him. Then he gave me a script of a play I had never seen before and told me to read the part of Jenny; he read the role of Brian. The play got real mushy, and the next thing I knew, I was in Mr. D.'s arms, and he was kissing me."

"How did this happen?" Rona inquired.

"It was in the script," Peg responded.

"What did you do then?" Rona asked.

"I told him I didn't think we should be kissing with his wife away and everything. Then he said, 'Don't worry about it. You like Ms. J., don't you? She has been here with me alone, and she let me kiss her. It didn't do her any harm, did it?' I didn't believe what I was hearing, and I started to cry. Then I zoomed out the front door. He stood on the porch, yelling, 'Don't run away, Peg. Come back. You want the role in the play, don't you?'"

Rona was mortified to hear what had happened. It reinforced her initial fears about Mr. D. Seeming more calm than she really was, she said to Peg, "Try not to be too upset, Peg. I know that things like this

96

are hard to take, but don't make a mountain out of a molehill. Just make sure you aren't alone with Mr. D. again."

Peg asked, "But how will I face him in class on Monday? How should I act when I see him?"

Molly volunteered, "I don't want to go to his class. I'll never feel safe around him again."

Questions

1. Is it ever justifiable for teachers to invite students of the opposite sex to their homes when no one else is at home with them? What alternative arrangements could Mr. D. have made had he legitimately needed to have Peg audition for a larger role in the play?

2. What should Rona's role be in this situation? Is this a matter she must reveal to someone else? If so, to whom should she reveal it? Should she write a report of what she has been told? If so, to whom should she give it?

3. Should Rona confront Mr. D. with what she has been told? Why or why not?

4. Should Rona advise Peg to tell her parents about this encounter? Why or why not?

5. Could Rona jeopardize herself legally by carrying Peg's story to her principal or to the superintendent of schools? Discuss what kind of evidence she has to substantiate her case.

Possible Solutions

1. As soon as Rona has taken Peg and Molly to Molly's house, she rushes home. Ned is just beginning to stir, and she excuses herself and says, "I have to write something up before I forget the details." She puts what she has heard on a computer disk and prints a copy. Ned asks her what this is all about, but she doesn't want to say anything to him because he has business dealings with Mr. D.'s wife. She reads through her account of Peg's encounter and then calls Wanda P., her own department head, who is her good friend, to ask if they can get together in an hour or so to discuss something she thinks can't wait until Monday. Wanda is home baking bread and says, "Sure. Come over and we can have fresh bread, cheese, and a salad for lunch." Rona arrives, and after she and Wanda have exchanged greetings, she says, "I want you to read this. I have left out all the names." Wanda reads it and says, "I know at least one of the participants in this mess." Rona asks her what she means, and Wanda tells her, "This is not the first time Don D. has done something like this. He's been warned about it, but he never seems to learn. If this

gets out, I'm afraid that's it for him in this school district! As the super-intendent told him the last time, 'Three strikes and you're out.' This is his third strike—at least the third that we know about." Rona is torn apart: "What do you think I should do? I don't want to ruin anyone's future." Wanda puts her hand on Rona's arm and tells her, "Honey, you won't be ruining anybody's future. Don D. has been ruining his own future for fifteen years. You have to think about the students he gets into these messes."

2. After Rona leaves the girls off at Molly's house, she comes home and tells Ned what has happened. Ned asks what proof the girls have that this ever happened. Rona, not wanting to tell Ned about her own encounter with Mr. D. before she ever knew her hus-band, says that she doesn't have any proof she could use in court, but that she knows the girls well enough to realize they are telling the truth. Ned advises her, "Don't get mixed up in it. It can only come to grief for a lot of people. Peg didn't ask you to tell anyone; in fact, she asked you not to. Stick to your promise. It will all work out eventual-ly." Rona knows there is some truth in what Ned tells her, but she is not sure she is going to follow his advice.

3. Rona thinks it would be a mistake for her to get mixed up in this situation, although she is furious that Mr. D. made it sound as though he had kissed her—she is still more furious that he lured an innocent teen-ager into his house and then tried to seduce her. She wants to put an end to his nefarious dealings with unsuspecting women, and the best way she can think of to achieve this end is to encourage Peg to share with her parents all the details Peg has just shared with her. Peg is reluctant, but Rona tells her that this is the only way to make sure Mr. D. will not do this to someone else.

4. As soon as Rona hears Peg's story, she tells her that there is only one way to handle this problem. She tells Peg to meet her in the school office at seven-thirty on Monday morning. She will set up a meeting with the principal so that Peg can tell him what happened. She also decides that this is the time to reveal to the principal what Mr. D. tried to do to her years earlier. Peg doesn't want to go along with this, but Rona asks her, "Do you want to go to Mr. D.'s class on Monday? Do you want to be in the play he's putting on? Do you want this to happen again, either to you or to some other student? You don't have a choice, Peg. You have to blow the whistle on Mr. D., or he'll go on like this forever."

Consider This

Few more difficult situations exist than encounters like the one de-picted in this case study. In dealing with as explosive a situation as this, all of the complaining parties must remember that they are dealing with someone else's reputation in such a way that they can and very well might ruin that person. Therefore, absolute honesty and truthfulness are necessary if a complaint is to be made. Some students might mistake a friendly pat on the back for a sexual overture, and it would be horrible to accuse a teacher of something that is basically quite innocent.

The facts of this case suggest that Mr. D. is far from an innocent victim. He has a problem that probably should preclude him from situations in which he has jurisdiction over teen-agers. He has been given a trust, and from all that is told here, he has violated that trust more than once. He needs professional help, and sometimes people fail to seek such help unless they are forced to seek it.

Because much of the evidence against Mr. D. is unverified, Rona might best be advised to tell her principal that she has a highly confidential matter related to a situation in the school that she is not free to discuss with anyone except the school district's lawyer and to ask that the principal or superintendent make an appointment for her. She should not reveal any of this matter directly to any other person at this point. Every school district employs counsel, and they do so in part to meet exigencies exactly like the one that is the subject of this case study.

Questions of Confidentiality

Sometimes teachers are taken completely aback when a student who has been the model of good citizenship displays a behavior that suggests a potentially dangerous pattern that seems completely out of character for that student. This sort of problem is intensified in small towns where everyone knows everyone else, especially if the student involved comes from a family that has considerable visibility in the community. One thing is certain: situations of this sort cannot be ignored.

CASE STUDY 4.5
Teacher's Home Is Vandalized

Ken D. loves the town he works in. It is away from the hustle and bustle of the big city. Crime is something one reads about in the newspapers. People here seldom lock their doors unless they plan to be away overnight. Ken, who teaches shop in the middle school, has gotten to think that the best security in all the world is not locks or burglar alarms, but living in a place where you *know* nothing terrible is going to happen.

Then one night Ken and his wife come home from a basketball game and discover that someone has entered their house and ransacked it. All kinds of things are missing: silver, phonograph records, jewelry, clothing, household tools, a .38-caliber pistol Ken inherited from his grandfather, and some initialed handkerchieves Ken's grandmother had hand-embroidered for him as a Christmas gift. The deputy sheriff comes out and is baffled. He shakes his head, commiserating with Ken. "What are things comin' to a fella can't go out for a couple of hours and not have somethin' like this happen?"

He fills out a report. Ken and his wife file a claim with the insurance company, and it is settled quickly. But they have lost something no sum of money can restore—their sense of security in a town they love.

One day six weeks after the robbery, Ken's students are cleaning up the shop before the bell rings. Mike J. has some lengths of wood under his arms. He turns quickly without looking, and the wood hits Fred S. in the face. Fred's nose begins to gush blood. Without thinking, Fred reaches into his pocket for a handkerchief. The one he pulls out has Ken's initials on it, the ones his grandmother lovingly stitched. Ken is dumbfounded. Fred is one of the most cooperative students he has taught. His father is a clergyman in town, and his mother is the clerk of the court.

Questions

1. Sometimes appearances deceive. Can you think of at least three explanations for Fred's having Ken's handkerchief in his pocket?
2. What might make a student from an upright family like Fred's commit crimes like housebreaking, vandalism, and theft, all of which seem to be involved in this situation?
3. What external pressures, aside from those encountered in the family, might lead any teen-ager to steal?
4. Does theft accompanied by vandalism tell you something about the intruder that theft alone does not suggest?

Possible Solutions

1. Upon seeing his handkerchief in Fred's possession, Ken grabs him by his arm and shouts, "You rotten little thief! You broke into my house, didn't you?" Fred breaks loose and runs out of the room,

dropping Ken's handkerchief as he does. Ken chases but does not catch him. He then returns to his shop where his students are busily at work, tells them to go on with their work, and goes to the principal's office to tell him of his suspicions.

2. Ken does a double take when he sees the handkerchief his grandmother had so lovingly initialed in Fred's possession, but he says nothing. He tells Fred that he had better run down to the nurse to see about his bleeding nose, and he writes him a hall pass. As Fred leaves, Ken says, "Come on back here as soon as you are finished with the nurse, even if the bell has rung. I want to make sure you're OK. I'll write you an excuse for your next class." He hopes Fred will not come back before next period because he is free then, and he wants to find out how Fred has come to be in possession of his stolen handkerchief.

3. Fred's pulling his handkerchief from his pocket was a spontaneous act. As soon as he has done it, he knows he has made a mistake. He looks at Ken, and their eyes meet. Ken says, "You get down to the nurse, Fred. Here's an excuse. We want to make sure Mike didn't break your nose or anything. Come back here as soon as you can. I think we have something to discuss, haven't we?" Fred cannot look Ken in the eye. He looks down at the floor sheepishly and says half-heartedly, "I don't think so. I'm not gonna sue ya. It was just an accident." Ken says, "I think you know what I'm talking about, Fred." He determines that when Fred comes back, he will begin by saying to him, "OK, Freddie boy, what do you have to tell me?"

Consider This

In a situation like this one, no matter what questions the discovery of the stolen handkerchief might bring up, the teacher must first be concerned with the physical welfare of the student who has accidentally been hit in the nose. Even if Fred does not seem badly injured, he must be sent to the nurse to verify that he is no more seriously injured than he appears to be. Sending Fred to the nurse also works to Ken's advantage because it provides him with time to decide how he is going to handle the problem that seems to be emerging.

Despite the circumstantial evidence, Fred could be completely innocent, and it would be terrible to accuse him of an act as serious as theft if he were. It could be that he bought the handkerchief at a flea market or that the real thief gave or lent him the handkerchief. All sorts of possibilities suggest themselves, although having the handkerchief turn up suggests that Ken soon may discover who did break into his house, even if it was not Fred.

If it turns out that Fred was, indeed, the thief, Ken then has to face a few more dilemmas. Does he deal with the situation without going public with it? If he decides it is best to do this, could his insurance company take some action against him if they learn what has happened? Ken has, after all, accepted their settlement for the theft.

If Ken goes public, Fred could end up in prison. Ken has to consider what he might be able to do to prevent this harsh punishment from being imposed on a student who is probably going through something that counseling might alleviate. He has no desire to ruin a student's life. This case study does not lend itself to any easy solution. By considering as many possibilities as you can, however, you can come to some insights that will lead you to an equitable solution.

Sometimes through vigilance, teachers can prevent problems in their schools. This vigilance, however, can land teachers right in the middle of situations that might prove threatening and that always prove distressing to them. Although such encounters are never easy, teachers who have given a little thought to how they might handle hypothetical situations will be better prepared to deal effectively with the unexpected than teachers who have never given any thought to such matters.

CASE STUDY 4.6
Teacher Catches Students Smoking Marijuana

Karen L. is a French teacher at Stevens Junior High School in a coal-mining community in the hills of Appalachia. She has lived there all her life and knows everyone in town. She has taught for fourteen years and is a highly regarded teacher. She takes her responsibilities seriously.

Karen's classroom is at the end of a long corridor. The media center extends for seventy-five feet south of her room and at the end of the hall, just north of her classroom, is a girls' lavatory. She routinely checks it between classes, and it is much cleaner than most of the student restrooms in the school, largely because of Karen's diligence. Although the school policy is that students are not to be excused to the restroom during class periods, girls sometimes come to this lavatory on their way to the media center when they have been excused from class to work on a project.

One Tuesday afternoon Karen looks out the window in her door and notices two students going into the girls' room. She is in the middle of giving her students directions about how to proceed on some exercises they are going to work on in class and does not want to interrupt her presentation, but as soon as her students begin to work on the exercises, she walks to the restroom. She hears giggling coming from inside it. She opens the door quickly and forcefully. The air is blue with smoke. The smell is more like burning leaves than cigarettes. It is obvious to Karen that the two girls, both of whom go to her church and live in her neighborhood, are smoking marijuana. One of the girls tosses her joint into the toilet and flushes it. The other girl tries to throw hers in but misses. Karen picks up the joint and snuffs it out. She wraps it in a paper towel.

Questions

1. Did the high school you attended have any policy about allowing students to leave the classroom during a class period? Does the school you teach in or plan to teach in have such a policy? Why do you think such policies have been adopted in many schools in recent years?

2. Among teachers' many duties is sometimes that of monitoring restrooms when classes are changing. Many teachers resent having to use their time this way. Why do you think schools consider it necessary to have them engage in this activity?

3. Do you think it would have been sensible for Karen simply to stay in her classroom and not check the situation when she saw the two girls enter the restroom near her classroom? Why or why not?

4. Having stumbled upon this situation, what must Karen's next step be? What consequences might the students face if Karen proceeds to report this matter.

Possible Solutions

1. Both girls are terrified. One of them has already been involved in one drug episode in the school, but the matter was handled internally. They begin to cry and to beg Karen not to turn them in. "You know we aren't hoodlums," one of the girls tells her. "You know us from church. Besides, this is only grass. It's not anything heavy. If you don't say anything, I promise you we will never smoke grass again." The other girl agrees to give up marijuana altogether if Karen lets them go. Karen says, "I know you're both good girls, but that doesn't change anything. You are in the restroom when you are not supposed to be and..." That's as far as she gets. The other girl says, "Just report us for that; don't lay a drug rap on us! This is the first time I ever smoked the stuff. I just did it because she wanted me to," she tells Karen, gesturing to the other girl, who says, "What do you mean? You gave the stuff to me. You made me smoke it." Karen

103

is adamant. "I am very sorry, girls, but I have to report you to the office. I have absolutely no choice—and if I did, I would still report you. This is a serious offense, and it has to be dealt with officially."

2. Just as Karen is wrapping the joint in the paper towel, the larger of the two girls charges her and tries to grab the evidence. Karen sidesteps her and backs off, saying, "Hold it right there. We are going to the office right now. Get moving." At that, the other girl says, "What's the big deal? Everyone smokes, and you know it. Half the teachers smoked grass when they were kids—I'll bet you did. Some of you still smoke it, don't you, Ms. L.?" Karen does not respond to this accusation but merely says, "To the office—NOW!" The larger girl says, "You turn us in and I'm going to tell Mr. F. [the principal] we came in here and caught you smoking the joint and you tried to pin it on us so we wouldn't be able to say anything." Karen intones, "To the office," takes the arm of the larger girl, and proceeds out the door with her, saying to the other, "You might as well come along. I'm going to report this incident whether you come with me or not."

3. Both girls are horrified, but no more so than Karen is. She knows these girls and their families. She went to college with the mother of one of them, who is now dead. The girls burst into tears and begin sobbing hysterically and begging Karen to let them go. She says, "You know I have to turn you in. This is a serious offense." Linda, the girl whose mother is dead, says, "But this is the first time we've ever tried grass. We aren't hooked or anything. It'll ruin us if you report us." Her friend says, "Yeah, it's just not fair. I found this stash in my desk in homeroom. I don't know where it came from." Karen asks, "Don't you think it's pretty dangerous to smoke something you just found? How do you know it's not contaminated?" Both girls chime in, "Yeah, it was dumb. I admit it. I didn't even like the stuff. I'll never do it again, I promise." Karen says, "OK, I'll forget it this one time, but I'm going to write it up and put my report in a safe place. If either of you ever steps out of line again, that will be it. I'll blow the whistle on you without a thought!"

Consider This

We are all human, and most of us who go into teaching like to have a positive view of our students and of people generally. This attitude can make it seem best for us sometimes to give our students the benefit of the doubt. Drug use in the school, however, is among the most serious infractions students can commit. The entire moral fiber of society is being weakened by the incursions that drug traffic has made upon people in every walk of life.

No conscientious teacher can ignore a drug problem as blatant as that depicted in the case study. Even if the girls are telling the truth when they say this is their first exposure to marijuana, they must be reported because someone in the school has supplied them. The story of finding a stash in a desk in homeroom lacks credibility, but even if it is so, the fact remains that someone is trafficking drugs to minors. The school administrators and the local police authorities must be told that such is the case, just as surely as public health officials would have to be told if someone in the school came down with scarlet fever. What is at stake here is more than the reputations of two students. The entire school population is at risk if drug trafficking is permitted to go on within the building.

Not only would Karen be morally culpable if she ignored what she has discovered; she would be legally culpable as well. Under no circumstances would it be appropriate for a teacher to allow this situation to go uninvestigated. She might eagerly serve as a character witness for the two girls, inasmuch as she knows them, but that is the only option available to her in a situation like this one.

Don't Tempt Students

Leaving a classroom full of students, although sometimes unavoidable, can led to problems. Teachers should never leave their classrooms unless they have absolutely no other recourse.

Be careful of your belongings. Purses and wallets that are not carried on your person should be stored in a locked closet or in a desk drawer, preferably locked. Other valuables and money collected for school lunches and the like should be kept in the most secure place possible. If temptation is not present, thefts will be minimized. It is unfair to students for teachers to leave money and valuables out where anyone can pick them up. One person may do the stealing, but the suspicion cast upon a whole class in such a situation is demoralizing and, if care is exercised, can be avoided.

Child Abuse

The question of child abuse, which has received considerable publicity, alarms educators and law enforcement agents. In the most loving of families, a recalcitrant or fractious child will sometimes be given a whack for some infraction. It is often difficult to identify child abuse and to decide what to do about it. Active children get banged around a great deal in the course of a typical week. They play rough games, they fight with

105

each other, they fall off their bicycles, they slip on the ice. All of these things can leave them battered, but the battering has occurred in the normal course of their daily existences, and no one is culpable. If you look closely at your own body right now, you will probably find that you have a bruise or two, perhaps from something like banging into a chair or knocking a suitcase against your leg as you rushed onto a train, bus, or plane.

On the other hand, some children—some of your students—may be bruised because they are constantly being hit at home. Some of them may actually be in severe danger, and if someone does not come to their rescue, they could end up badly injured or dead. If a child is being abused on a regular basis by a disturbed parent or by one who goes on regular drunks, it will do no good to ask the parent about the abuse. The child, too, may be quite reluctant to tell the truth about it, fearing that to reveal the abuse will be to threaten his or her home and family. The situation is a terribly important one to deal with, and a terribly delicate one to handle.

CASE STUDY 4.7
Teacher Fears Student Is Being Abused

Mark has been a student in Ed J.'s fourth grade for seven months. He does good work and is a dependable student. His parents have had two routine conferences with Ed. They impressed him favorably. They seem interested in knowing what Mark's assignments are, and they help him when he has trouble with his homework. They ask Ed to recommend some books they might buy him because he enjoys reading and talks of wanting to be a writer someday.

Shortly before Christmas, Mark limped into class one Monday. He was in obvious pain when he walked. He had a bruise and a scrape on the left side of his head. Ed asked him what had happened, and Mark said he had slipped on the ice and fallen. He pulled a hamstring and hit his head. His limp soon disappeared, and his bruise and scrape went away. Ed thought no more about it.

In late March, Mark came to school one day with a real shiner on his right eye, and the bridge of his nose had a cut on it and was slightly discolored. Ed asked Mark how that had happened, and Mark told him that he was shagging flies and a baseball had hit him in the face. "It'll go away in a day or two," he said cheerfully. "I'm always messin' up and hurtin' myself."

Ed probably would not have thought much about this second injury, but the weekend before, he had seen a special program on ETV about child abuse and about how often it goes undetected because

106

outward marks are attributed to routine accidents. Ed doesn't want to be a meddler, but he is beginning to have suspicions about Mark's repeated injuries.

Questions

1. What can happen to parents in your state if they are charged (not convicted, but merely charged) with child abuse?

2. To what agencies in your city and state are child abuse cases referred? If you suspect child abuse, what kinds of documentation do you start collecting? To whom do you first show it officially?

3. Where child abuse is suspected, should teachers make an effort to see the suspected abusers, usually parents, or not? What problems might be caused by a teacher's taking the initiative in that way?

4. Can teachers do anything unofficially with their school administrators when they suspect child abuse, or do all of their dealings at the administrative level have to be official dealings?

Possible Solutions

1. Ed is particularly cautious in proceeding with this matter because the program he saw that raised his consciousness of the problem also told about a family that was accused of child abuse and about what happened to them. The Department of Child Welfare immediately took their three children from them and put them in foster homes—each in a different one—where they remained for eight months, during which time the parents did not know where they were. When the case finally was adjudicated, the child whose injuries made his teacher suspicious gave a rational explanation of how he had been injured and expressed a fervent wish to be returned to his family. By this time the mother's nerves were so shattered that she was in no condition to look after her children. Her continued concern and nervousness had caused the dissolution of her marriage. Her children all had recurrent nightmares about being stolen from their homes. With this real-life scenario in mind, Ed realized that he probably should say nothing to anyone about his fears for Mark. After all, Mark had never shown any abnormal behavior in class, and he had explained his injuries. To be on the safe side, Ed kept a day-by-day account of Mark's injuries in case he should ever need it. He also made a point of seeing Mark one day after class and saying to him, "I hope you know, Mark, that if you ever have any problems you want to talk over, I am a good listener." Mark smiled and said, "I know you are, but right now I don't have a problem in the world. I just got a new bike!"

2. Thinking about how awful it would be for him not to recognize a *bona fide* case of child abuse that might endanger the life of one of his students, Ed approaches Marita McD., the building principal, and tells her that Mark seems to injure himself a great deal. He mentions Mark's recent black eye and the earlier injury. Without uttering a word about child abuse, he asks her whether it would be a good idea to have the district nurse come to look at Mark and to determine whether he has coordination problems. Ed hopes that if child abuse is present, the district nurse will be able to spot it. The nurse comes to the school the next afternoon. When Ed hears she is there, he considers sharing his suspicions with her, but decides not to. She examines Mark and verifies that his coordination is no better or worse than that of most ten-year-olds. Ed then asks her, "You don't think he could have gotten the injury from, well . . . you know, from having someone at home lose their temper with him, do you?" The nurse responds, "No. I always look for signs of abuse when I see kids this age. Mark just likes games so much that he'll probably go limping through adolescence. That's the way some kids are." Ed feels reassured.

3. The more Ed thinks about it, the more likely it seems to him that Mark is covering something up. He tries to test his theory by turning suddenly when he is near Mark's desk to see if the boy cringes like someone fearing he is about to be hit. Mark jumps slightly, but he doesn't actually cringe. Still, that nervous jump could have meant something. Ed asks Mark to stay in the classroom for a few minutes when the rest of the students have gone to the media center. He puts his hand on Mark's shoulder and asks him, "Mark, you aren't getting knocked around by anyone at home, are you?" Mark looks a little surprised; then he says, "No more than usual." Ed replies, "What does that mean?" "Well, I get a whack once in a while, but I guess I deserve it." Ed persists: "You didn't get that shiner from one of those whacks, did you?" Now Mark looks genuinely surprised: "Golly, no. If anyone at home hit me as hard as that baseball did, I'd take off and never come back!" Ed is pretty well satisfied that Mark is telling the truth. He feels a little annoyed at himself for having meddled, but he is also relieved.

Consider This

Because child abuse is a more pervasive problem than some of us realize, it is a good idea for schools to discuss the problem in faculty meetings and to have occasional workshops on it during professional enhancement days. The problem should also be broached in general methods courses that prospective teachers take.

Every school should have a policy regarding suspected child abuse because terrible things can happen to innocent parents and their children if false accusations get into official channels—there is no way to undo the harm that erroneous accusations can wreak upon a family. More than one family has been ruined by the suspicion of child abuse that has later been proved groundless, but the harm has been done.

The principal of a building or the superintendent of a district might wish to appoint someone trained in psychology—perhaps someone from the guidance and counseling office—to act as an impartial party where cases of child abuse are suspected. This person could listen, ask questions, and advise. Utter confidentiality would have to be assured. A major problem facing teachers when this situation arises is that they often need to talk it through but are, at the same time, understandably reluctant to make an official complaint on the basis of the kinds of circumstantial evidence most of them have been able to collect.

Project

Write a possible solution to this case study that results in Ed's actually discovering a *bona fide* case of child abuse.

Discipline

The only discipline that is worth anything is the discipline that comes from within that is based upon moral conviction. If someone does not run a red light because a police car is near, the control is only temporary. People who do not run red lights because they realize that society has, for the benefit and safety of the majority, made laws that prohibit them from doing so, will obey those laws whether or not anyone is watching. We can restrain students from doing things they should not do, but until they have been convinced that they must act according to certain precepts, prescriptions, and proscriptions of their society, their behavior is likely to be erratic.

Corporal punishment provides teachers with an immediate and direct way of dealing with infractions of rules by students. When it is used, however, the teacher is usually admitting defeat and is essentially saying, "I just can't think of any rational way to handle this situation." If the aim of disciplinary action is to alter student behavior over the long term, as certainly it should be, then acts of unacceptable behavior must be dealt with in such a way that students understand why a given action is unacceptable and undesirable. Corporal punishment, while it communicates dissatisfaction and disapproval, usually does not set students on a course of altering their behavior in such a way that they will not again commit the infraction for which they are being punished. The most persuasive argument against corporal punishment is inefficiency. It is used to achieve outcomes it seldom succeeds in achieving. If it serves any purpose, it is that of allowing a teacher to vent his or her aggressions on a student who is relatively defenseless. Mature people do not find it necessary to engage in such behavior.

Many professional organizations—the American Academy of Pediatrics, Defense for Children International, the National Education Association, the National Association of Social Workers, the American Public Health Association, and the International Reading Association—have taken a public stand against corporal punishment. A typical resolution regarding this matter is that of the International Reading Association, passed by its Delegate Assembly in 1988. It reads:

> Resolved, that the International Reading Association condemn cruel, degrading and humiliating treatment of students and call for an end of physical abuse and corporal punishment of all students in schools and other institutions where they are taught or cared for;
>
> that IRA urge its members not to participate in the administration of corporal punishment of students; and
>
> that IRA urge school districts and governing boards to provide in-service training in alternative and educationally sound classroom management and humane and just student discipline, and urge colleges of education to require pre-service education that includes the same.

CASE STUDY 4.8
Teacher Handles Bickering Student

May is not the easiest teaching month, particularly if one is teaching seniors. School is not on their minds; graduation is. Millie G., a science teacher at Jesse O. Wolfe Senior High School, dreaded meeting her anatomy class, forty percent of whose twenty-seven students were graduating seniors. Those who were going to college had been admitted. Those who were not going to college were job hunting. School was taking a back seat to other events in their lives, and their attitude was taking its toll among the sophomores and juniors in the class.

One of Millie's major problems was that students simply were not doing their homework assignments. She could not let the seniors get away with this practice and still hope to get work from the others. She felt that her class was falling apart. Finally, she decided to play her trump card in an effort to turn the situation around.

Mac S., one of the school's football heroes who had been sought after by a number of colleges and universities and had accepted admission to the state university, had not done his assignments for weeks and had received a failing grade on the last examination. Millie thought that she might turn the class around by making an example of Mac. When she called on him and he responded, "Ms. G., can I go down to the office and see if my class picture is ready yet? I'm supposed to take it and have it framed this afternoon," she pressed him by saying, "No, Mac. You may not leave the class. I want an answer to my question."

Mac persisted, "Aw, c'mon, Ms. G. Let me go and get my pictures."

"The question, Mac. The question. It was in the chapter that you read last night. If you look at the diagram you were asked to draw, the answer should be obvious."

"You're mean, Ms. G. Why are you buggin' me like this? You usta like me."

"May I see your diagram, Mac?" she asked.

"I forgot it. It's in my locker. Can I go and get it?" Mac responded.

"No, Mac. Instead you may report here at 3:10, and I will have a good two hours' work for you to do. You are going to make up your work or pay the penalty. You could fail this course, you know, and not be graduated."

Mac shouted, "I can't stay. I ride the school bus. I have to help my brother work on his car today."

"Three-ten, Mac. I will call your family and tell them to expect you home around five-thirty."

"Five-thirty! How will I get home? I'll have to hitchhike, and that's dangerous."

"Three-ten, Mac. I will drive you home." Millie then turned to the chalkboard and wrote, "Mac S., Detention, 3:10, May 9."

Questions

1. Bickering is a favorite student pastime. Lee Canter, a specialist in school discipline, warns, "Never argue with a kid. You'll lose—and they lose in the long run" (*Newsweek*, 10 July 1977, p. 69). Canter

suggests, instead of debate, that the "broken record" approach be employed—repeat the same thing ("Three-ten, Mac, three-ten") over and over again in a virtual monotone. Do you think Millie handled this situation in such a way that the bickering was minimized?

2. In a mixed class of sophomores, juniors, and seniors, should some special provision be made for the seniors during the last weeks of school? If so, what provision? Should each senior be required in some way to earn this special privilege?

3. Having carried the situation this far, should Millie have Mac serve his detention in her classroom or somewhere else? Defend your answer.

4. Should Millie have offered to drive Mac home? Why or why not? How else might she have handled the problem of seeing that Mac had a safe way to get home?

5. Was Millie wise to threaten Mac with failing the course? Could she carry through on this threat in the typical public high school? Discuss.

Possible Solutions

1. Knowing that Mac is probably going to be graduated no matter what she does, Millie finally decides to follow the lines of least resistance—it *is* May, and she is as tired as her students are. She calls Mac aside and tells him, "Let's not play games, Mac. We have always gotten along pretty well, haven't we?" Mac confirms that they have. "Well," she tells him, "we have two-and-a-half weeks left before the last day of classes. I won't hassle you if you don't hassle me. You turn something in every day—I don't care what. I just don't want the other students to think that you are getting away with doing no work." Mac agrees to go along with this arrangement, but he asks, "Gee, Ms. G., are you gonna make me sit here all period every day for two-and-a-half weeks?" Millie answers, "No, Mac, I am not. State compulsory attendance laws are what will make you sit here all period every day for two-and-a-half weeks. I have nothing to do with it except that I am paid to enforce those laws. They say you have to be here. Who am I to say you don't?" Mac seems to accept Millie's explanation.

2. Millie decides that the Mac situation will lead to an overall breakdown in discipline, so she sends for Mac during his free period. She tells him that she understands his position now that he has been accepted to college, but that she has to uphold the law and make him attend her class. "I can see, however, that although you are pretty capable, you are not getting much out of being here. Why don't

112

we make a deal? We will negotiate a contract for a certain amount of work from you between now and graduation. I will tell you precisely what you have to do to earn a 'C' or a 'B' or an 'A' for the marking period. You decide which grade you want to work for. I will set up an independent study for you that you'll be glad you were exposed to when you get into your basic biology course next fall. Remember, you're not going to have all the time in the world to do your work and play ball at the same time." Mac thinks this is a good idea, and he promises to cooperate.

3. Millie decides that Mac is just too cocky to cope with. He needs to have his sails trimmed a little, so she tells the school principal, Mr. W., exactly how Mac has been behaving. Mr. W. tells her, "Well, you know how students get when we're in the last couple of weeks of school, and the weather turns hot. I'll talk to him if you think it will do any good, but you know Mac. He's kind of got us where he wants us, and he knows it. He'll turn out all right in the long run, but he's a bit of a pain now, I agree." Millie feels defeated by Mr. W.'s attitude and is sorry she approached him because he does not seem willing to help.

Consider This

Mac appears not to be different from many students who are waiting around for commencement. Some schools allow seniors to serve in local internships or to do special field studies during their last marking periods; this arrangement takes some of the pressure off their teachers. If such arrangements are not available, however, teachers might do well to negotiate contracts with these students who, by the time they are seniors, should be responsible enough to work in this way.

Millie certainly did well in Possible Solution 1 to remind Mac that it is not her but rather state law that is keeping him in school for these final weeks of the school year. This is an explanation Mac can hardly refute. Consider whether Mr. W. shirked his responsibility when he was lukewarm to the suggestion that he involve himself in the matter in Possible Solution 3. He didn't say he wouldn't talk with Mac, but he certainly doesn't seem enthusiastic about doing so, and, with that attitude, Mac might come away from his conference with the principal more of a problem than he was when he went in. In order to think through Mr. W.'s response, you need to consider what pressures he is under at this time of year and what he thinks Millie's responsibility is in dealing with the matter she has now dumped in his lap.

113

Teachertalk

Students learn most and remember best what they have learned when they are actively and directly involved as contributing members in the learning process. Despite this fact, which has been well documented in reliable professional literature, extensive research has shown that teachertalk dominates most classrooms. Arno Bellack's landmark research on the subject of teachertalk indicates that teachers do over 80 percent of all speaking in the classroom [*The Language of the Classroom: Meanings Communicated in High School Teaching* (New York: Institute of Psychological Research, Teachers' College, Columbia University, 1965)]. Bellack classifies classroom talk into four major categories—soliciting, responding, structuring, and reacting. Of the teachertalk analyzed by Bellack and his associates, the largest amount (46.6 percent) was spent on soliciting, followed by reacting (39.2 percent), followed by structuring (7.7 percent) and responding (5.5 percent). Studenttalk, which constituted less than 20 percent of the total talk in class, was mostly in the form of responding (65.4 percent), with reacting (15.1 percent), soliciting (11.3 percent), and structuring (1.8 percent) trailing far behind.

Implicit in these research findings are two basic indications:

1. Although teachers appear to invite student participation through spending 46.6 percent of their time soliciting, they do not get much student response if students collectively talk less than 20 percent of the time;
2. Most studenttalk is quite passive (i.e., it is in response to questions). Structuring and soliciting, which require a considerable degree of initiative and action, are not frequent student activities in class. Structuring, which requires the greatest initiative (and can also lead to the most fruitful learning outcomes), is engaged in negligibly by the broad range of students in the Bellack sample.

Reasons for Reticence

Teachers who wish to increase student involvement in classroom activities should read Carl Rogers's *Freedom To Learn* (Columbus, Ohio: Charles E. Merrill Publishing Company, 1969), a book which makes cogent comments about the dynamics of classroom discussion and offers helpful suggestions on the art of inquiry. Other helpful resources are Mary Jane Aschner's essay, "The Analysis of Verbal Interaction in the Classroom," in *Theory and Research in Teaching*, edited by Arno A. Bellack (New York: Teachers' College, Columbia University, 1963); and "The Inquiry Process in Learning," which is Chapter 6 in John M. Lem-

114

bo's *Why Teachers Fail* (Columbus, Ohio: Charles E. Merrill Publishing Company, 1971).

If students are reluctant to participate actively in the classroom setting, teachers need to assess the reasons. A frequent one is that students are afraid they might say something foolish and be put down, thereby losing face with their peers. Peer approval is important to students—indeed, to most people—and educational researchers have determined that students around the fourth-grade level and again around the seventh-grade level are particularly vulnerable to peer pressures. [See Paul Torrance's comments on this subject in *Explorations in Creativity*, edited by Ross L. Mooney and Taher A. Razik (New York: Harper and Row, 1967), 187]. In these grades, students typically experience a marked decline in creativity, and Paul Torrance asserts this is because "... young people are more concerned about the evaluations of peers than of parents, teachers, and other authorities. ... Original ideas are common targets of peer pressures to conformity." Realizing this, remember to treat student contributions seriously and to show respect for the person making them.

Teachers sometimes forget that students can be surprisingly literally minded. Most of us were literally minded when we were younger, but we have forgotten that we were. I am reminded of being taken to the zoo by my parents in the summer before I began third grade. I was perhaps eight years old. When asked what I wanted most to see, my response was, "Gladly."

"Gladly?" my puzzled parents both asked simultaneously.

"Yes," I affirmed.

"What in heaven's name is Gladly?" my father pressed.

"Gladly," I persisted, "Gladly—the cross-eyed bear that we sing about in Sunday school!"

CASE STUDY 4.9
Teacher Ignores Student's Question

Fred T. taught social studies at Leonard Hall Middle School in an industrial town in a northeastern state. His seventh-grade class had been studying the founding of the United States and was well into a lesson about George Washington's presidency when Buddy P. raised his hand.

"Yes, Buddy, what is it?" Fred asked.

"Mr. T., why do you keep calling George Washington the father of his country? I have this book at home about the presidents and stuff like that that says George Washington didn't have any kids."

There were a couple of faint snickers, but Buddy did not smile.

Fred pretended not to hear the question and said to the class, "As I was saying, George Washington served two terms as President of the United States."

When the class was over ten minutes later, Buddy came up to Fred and said, "You didn't answer my question, Mr. T. Don't you know why George Washington was called the father of his country either?"

Fred stared down at Buddy and answered, "I didn't answer your question because it is a silly question. Case closed." Buddy began to say something, but before any words came out, Fred repeated, "Case closed, Buddy, case closed."

Questions

1. Buddy is twelve or thirteen. Do you think his question was designed to divert attention and block progress, or do you think he really wanted to know? If you were a teacher and were not sure, what would you assume? Why?

2. If Buddy really asked his question just to be a smart aleck and if Fred answered it briefly but accurately, do you think Fred would lose face with his students for seeming not to have realized what Buddy was doing?

3. Does the case study reveal any rudeness on Buddy's part? On Fred's? Do you think it is possible that a courteous response will elicit an equally courteous one from a person who might initially have been trying to get the teacher off track?

4. Do you think Fred missed a real teaching opportunity when he refused to answer Buddy's question? Defend your answer.

5. Might Fred capitalize in some way on knowing that Buddy has a book at home about the presidents? How might he make the most of this information?

Possible Solutions

1. When Buddy asks his question, a couple of students snicker. Fred turns to them and says, "Buddy asked a question that perhaps occurred to some of the rest of you." Then, pointing to one of the snickering students, he asks him, "Can you answer Buddy's question, Matthew? You seem to know why a man with no children could be called the father of his country." Matthew colors up a little, but then gets serious and says, "I guess it was because so many people looked to him like a father—sort of the way some people looked at President Reagan." Fred then asks Buddy if that helps him to under-

116

stand the use of the term and reminds him that sometimes words do not say exactly what they mean. He tells an anecdote of a woman who was throwing a bucket of wash water out a third-story window and yelled, "Look out!" Anyone who followed her advice exactly would have gotten wet.

2. When Buddy asks his question, Fred draws himself back in his chair and says to him, "That's the dumbest question I've heard in weeks. Everyone knows why Washington was called the father of his country. Don't you know anything?" A few of the students snickered when Buddy asked his question, but they weren't snickering now. Buddy has been humiliated in front of the class, and he is so near tears that he starts laughing loudly, presumably his only defense against breaking down completely in front of the other students. He is the only one laughing. Fred is not sure where to take things from here.

3. When Fred fails to answer Buddy after he has asked his question, Buddy asks it again. Fred turns to him and says, "I heard the first time, Buddy. If I had wanted to answer you, I would have. I am not going to allow you to ask idiotic questions that waste everyone's time. Is that understood?" Buddy says, "But I . . ." Fred interrupts him with, "No ifs, ands, or buts. We have work to do. Let's do it." Buddy vows to himself that he will never ask another question in public again.

Consider This

Even the brightest people sometimes ask questions that seem naive. They deserve the courtesy of legitimate answers delivered concisely, accurately, and without any comment about the quality of the question that evoked the answer. Even if the question was not asked legitimately, a legitimate response will allow the student who asked the question to save face and will make that student feel a little ashamed for having pulled a stunt like that. The chances are that there will not be a recurrence of such behavior.

If, on the other hand, a student legitimately wants to know something that everyone else in the class seems to understand, nothing is lost in conveying that information. A great deal can be lost if the teacher turns sarcastic or unresponsive. Students who evoke that sort of attitude may cease to have the kinds of inquiring minds that it is the purpose of education to encourage and cultivate.

Take every question seriously and, to whatever extent you are able, dignify it with a reasonable response. In the long run, your students will value you for your willingness to answer their questions and will value you for never putting them down in front of other people. Students who lose face are sometimes extremely hard to redeem.

Group Activities

Students may be unresponsive in class because they find it intimidating to say something in front of twenty or thirty other people. For some this might be almost as bad as making a speech, an activity many people equate with having root canal therapy. However, when a class of twenty-four students becomes a class of six discussion groups with four students in each or four discussion groups with six students in each, making individual contributions is easier. Therefore, it is desirable to involve students in group activity as a means of helping them (1) to overcome their reticence and (2) to focus on matters relevant to their class studies.

Initially, group work should be brief, and its focus should be clear. Each student in each group must appreciate that what the group is doing is directly related to the major concerns of the class as a whole. In initial group experiences, students are best assigned arbitrarily to their groups. The least confusion ensues if assignments are made according to where students sit: "OK, the four of you in the back—Millie, Jim, Anita, and Lou—you are group one. Move your chairs close together." Circulate from group to group during such activities, giving what help you can.

Early in the term, groups assignments should be in writing in order to minimize the repeated asking of questions when assignments are made orally. Place a time limit on group discussions either by monitoring the time yourself or by setting a kitchen timer (which is one of the teacher's best friends in the classroom) for ten or fifteen minutes. Accustom students to having group work followed by a smooth and orderly return to the full-class setting.

CASE STUDY 4.10
Teacher Replans Group Activity

Joanne W. had taught O. Henry's "The Gift of the Magi" to her fifth-grade students as a student teacher. She had always been fond of the story, but teaching it was not one of the striking successes in her student teaching experience. She asked her students to read it for a given day and began her class that day by asking, "How did you like 'The Gift of the Magi,' class?" Silence. "Oh, come on," she persisted. "You must have had some feelings about it. How many of you read it?" All but a few hands went up. "So, how did you like it?"

Timidly, one student responded, "I thought it was dumb." Then there was a chorus of "Yeah! Me, too. I think it's a dumb story. Why

118

can't we ever read anything good?" Joanne was crushed; however, she decided to try "The Gift of the Magi" again this year, her fifth year of teaching, with her fifth graders, but to approach it differently.

Joanne's class has twenty-five students. They are cooperative youngsters and can be depended upon to do their homework. Joanne assigned them "The Gift of the Magi," but not before telling them a little bit about O. Henry and a little bit about what they might expect to find in this very short tale. She also explained the title. She told them the story was short enough to be read in a few minutes.

The next day when two students were absent, Joanne made six groups from her twenty-three students attending. She passed out to the students a dittoed sheet with seven questions:

1. Does O. Henry plunge right into his story, or does he give you a great deal of background information? What effect does this have on his story?
2. When does the story take place, and why does the author select this time of year? Could the same story have been told at some other time of year? Why or why not?
3. Exactly what details do you know about the husband in the story? Write them down.
4. Exactly what details do you know about the wife in the story? Write them down.
5. Exactly what details can you list about how the husband and wife live? Write them down.
6. Who tells the story? What effect does this have on the way the story is told?

   If you finish discussing the question assigned to your group before the time is up, go to Question 7 and discuss it.

7. An *irony* is something that has an outcome the opposite of what is expected. For example, an unemployed man sells his car to buy food. The next day he is offered a good job selling insurance by a company that needs a salesman with his own car. What ironies can you find in "The Gift of the Magi"? How does the author use irony to develop his story?

After distributing the questions and assigning her students to groups, Joanne said, pointing to each group as she made her assignments, "Group 1, work on the first question; Group 2, work on the second question; and so on. I am setting the timer for ten minutes, so work fast."

The groups began their work as Joanne passed among them.

119

Questions

1. Think back to your own school days. What four expectations did you have of your teachers when you entered first, fourth, sixth, ninth, and twelfth grades? Some of these expectations might be identical for all five grades.

2. What expectations do you think your students have of you? Explain your answer.

3. In what specific ways does Joanne demonstrate that she is a more organized teacher than she was during her student teaching internship five years before?

4. In what specific ways does Joanne sharpen her students' focus as they read and later discuss the O. Henry story? Do you think they can transfer the methods of analysis they are learning now to their understanding of the more difficult and sophisticated literature they are likely to be reading in the future?

Possible Solutions

1. When Joanne's student said that he thought the O. Henry story is dumb, she was dismayed. She said, "But this is one of the most famous short stories ever written. It is a classic. You just don't appreciate it. What I want you to do now is read the story again. The second time you read it, you will get more out of it." They didn't. As Joanne thought back on the experience, she vowed not to let it happen again. She decided instead to begin with this lead question: "O. Henry's 'The Gift of the Magi' is considered one of the world's best short stories, but I am not convinced. What do you think?" After a few seconds of silence, one student said, "I think it was pretty clever, and I liked the way it moved. I knew what was happening right from the beginning." Another hand went up, and instead of responding to the first student, Joanne capitalized on the student enthusiasm she felt developing and asked the second, Bruce, to comment. "I agree with Mindy," said Bruce. "Sometimes when I read something, I am not sure what it is about. In this story, I always knew what was going on." It was Joanne's turn: "Did you guess how it was going to turn out?" she asked. "Well," said Louie, "I sort of did. I saw something like it on TV. It was about the Trumps. Donald sold his private 747 jet so he could buy Mrs. Trump the island that was blocking the view from her bedroom in their mansion in the Bahamas and have it blown up. But she sold their mansion in the Bahamas to buy him a new navigation system for his 747." Everyone laughed. Joanne said, "I guess some things never change!"

2. Joanne decided that the reason her lesson on "The Gift of the

Magi" failed the first time was that she did not demand enough of her students. This time, she assigns the reading four days in advance, tells her students that they should be sure they read it before then, and informs them that they had better know everything in the story because they will have a quiz on it. They ask her what kind of quiz it will be, and Joanne answers, "Identifications. Be sure you know names and details." Joanne is convinced that once she has found out whether her students have really read the story, she will be able to give them an interesting lesson about it.

3. Joanne decides to use the questions posed in the case study, but she thinks her students should have ample time to discuss them fully. She thinks that each group should take at least forty-five minutes to talk through the question assigned to it, and they do have the seventh question to fall back on if they run out of things to say about their primary question.

Consider This

No work of literature is a classic until it is a classic for someone. Shakespearean plays are not classics for people who cannot stand to read them or to see them performed. A work of literature becomes a classic for students when they arrive at the decision that something they are reading is worth reading again and worth encouraging their friends to read. Students in fifth grade will have different classics from students in twelfth grade or from adults or from teachers. The important thing to remember with fifth graders is that if they are beginning to develop an enthusiasm for reading, they will voluntarily read the classics some time.

Joanne has given her students a framework they can use to consider a piece of writing, and if she continues to follow this procedure through the school year, her students will be richer for her efforts and will have begun to develop good insights into literature, although their insights may not be her insights. She has also introduced an important term, *irony*, in a natural setting and in a way that permits students to take it or leave it. Irony has immense literary importance, but not every ten-year-old has to believe that such is the case. Students of this age have plenty of time left to become sophisticated, and childhood is not the worst state of being.

What Students Expect from Teachers

Remember that students have expectations about you. Among their expectations are the following:

- Teachers will offer leadership and guidance.
- Teachers will respect students sufficiently to demand that they do their best.
- Teachers will be fair and unbiased in their dealings with students.
- Teachers will be consistent.
- Teachers will be clear in stating what they expect of students.
- Teachers will show students that they care.

Teachers who remember these basic expectations will probably have good and rewarding relationships with their students in group work and will find immense satisfaction in these relationships.

RELATIONSHIPS WITH PARENTS

Parents can be a source of concern to teachers. The best school situations exist where teachers, administrators, and parents work together harmoniously with understanding and cooperation. Not all teachers are sure they have the ability to contribute to the sort of harmony that results in a productive teaching situation.

Children's First Teachers

By the time children reach school, they have had many teachers, and they have learned more than half of all they will ever know, no matter how extensive their formal educations are to be. They have learned from their siblings, but, more important, they have had prolonged and consistent teaching from their parents, or such surrogate parents as they may have been exposed to in their first three or four years of life. They have learned a variety of specific behaviors that are readily apparent: speaking, obeying, answering, counting, observing. They have also learned subtle lessons relating to moral codes, values systems, subconscious or unconscious reactions, and means by which to have their needs fulfilled and their desires satisfied.

Some students come to school reflecting the codes, principles, and language patterns of the dominant society because their role models—parents, surrogate parents, siblings—have been members of that society. Others come to school reflecting the codes, principles, and language patterns of societies foreign to their teachers and manifesting behaviors which their teachers find difficult to understand. When such is the case, it is easy for teachers, and particularly for teachers with minimal experience, to rush to judgments that can substantially color their attitudes toward some of their students and build barriers between them and the students they are trying to teach.

122

At this point it should be helpful to remember that the behaviors and values your students exhibit are usually learned within the family structure. To condemn these behaviors and values is to condemn the institution from which they have grown, the family. Whether students have had good or bad teaching within the family is really not a question to be debated. Students reach teachers at a given developmental stage. Teachers will succeed with students only if they strive to understand the developmental stage at which their students are and attempt to work intelligently and nonjudgmentally from that point.

Understanding Parents

Although few generalizations are 100-percent reliable, some generalizations can help you to understand situations involving parents. Two generalizations about parental attitudes toward children should spring to mind when teachers deal with parents, particularly when they deal, as they sometimes may, with hostile or highly critical parents:

1. Most parents regard their children as their most precious asset.
2. Most parents want their children to succeed, although their definition of success may be worlds apart from that of the individual teacher, the school, the community, and the dominant society.

Teachers at all levels will deal more effectively with parents if they remember that parents who come to school, whether in a spirit of cooperation or in a state of vitriolic displeasure, are, by their very presence, showing that they have an active interest in their children and in the education of these children. This is a base upon which you can try to build the bridges that must exist between teachers and parents if education is to work.

How To Handle Complaints and Questions

Angry parents are reacting protectively, possibly about something they do not fully understand or possibly about something that has been misrepresented to them. Your first job is to ascertain the parent's specific complaint or question and then in a calm and rational way to try to answer the complaint or question. The student involved should in some cases be present at well as the parents at parent-teacher meetings. If it is apparent that the parents have received a distorted version of something the teacher has said to the student or to the class, the student should be asked to retell his or her version to the parents with the teacher present. At this point, if the distortion persists, do not call in other students to substantiate what actually happened because this situation puts such stu-

123

dents in an awkward position. However, it may be that substantiation from other students should be given in private to a school administrator in your presence.

Administrators' Roles in Parent-Teacher Conferences

School administrators (principals, vice-principals, department heads) and support staff (counselors, subject matter supervisors, school psychologists, school nurses) can be a valuable asset to you during conferences with parents. Usually teachers should not be expected to have conferences with parents—except at times when all parents are invited to school to talk with teachers as part of a schoolwide activity—unless a principal, vice-principal, department chairperson, subject matter supervisor, counselor, or some other designated staff member is present. In many cases, the student involved should also be present unless the parent needs to reveal confidential information about the student to the teacher. For example, a parent might need to tell a teacher that a student is diabetic and should not be given sweets in class, or that a student has a heart murmur that might cause difficulties during strenuous physical activity. If the student is sensitive about such a condition, it would be best that he or she not be included in such a conference. Consider the following case study and think through or discuss with another teacher the questions that follow.

CASE STUDY 4.11
Parents Upset by Reading Assignment

Adele P. has been teaching English at Midway Senior High School for three years. She was asked one day to come to her vice-principal's office to meet with the parents of one of her eleventh-grade students. As soon as her third-period class was over, she went to the vice-principal's office because fourth period is her lunch break.

Mr. F., the vice-principal, met her at the door to the main office, asked her into his office, and told her, "Mr. and Mrs. M. are in the conference room waiting to talk with us. They are upset because Robin brought home a copy of *Catcher in the Rye* and said that she was reading it for an English assignment. I have just looked over the syllabus that you filed in the office and notice that you list *Catcher in the Rye* as one of six books that might be read in fulfillment of the requirement to read a novel during this marking period. Did Robin talk with you about her selection?"

Adele replied, "No, I don't recall that she talked with me specifically about the book, but I introduced each book on the list to the class.

I told my class that the language in two of the books, which I clearly identified, might be offensive to some students and that I expected them to exercise judgment in choosing a book that would be right for them. I specifically warned them about *Catcher in the Rye* because I know it has caused difficulties in other schools. But it is on our approved list of alternate readings for eleventh grade, isn't it?"

"Yes, Ms. P., it is on our alternate list, and you appear to have proceeded with good professional judgment in introducing the book. Also, you did file your syllabus, so, thankfully, we knew what you were teaching and were not taken completely by surprise," Mr. F. answered. He continued, "If you would like me to, I will handle the situation from here. But frankly, I would really like you to meet with the parents and try to explain the matter to them yourself."

"I am perfectly willing to do that," Adele replied, "but I would like you and Robin to be present."

"That's fine with me. I will send for Robin."

Questions

1. Did Adele show good professional judgment in deciding to meet with Robin's parents after Mr. F. gave her the opportunity to avoid the meeting? Why or why not?

2. What might be gained by having Robin attend the meeting? Do you think her presence might present some disadvantages?

3. Do you think schools have a right—or even a responsibility—to teach controversial books like *Catcher in the Rye* or controversial theories such as Darwin's theory of evolution? Discuss the pros and cons of teaching such materials in public schools.

4. Does the case study indicate that Adele approached the use of *Catcher in the Rye* with her students in a professionally responsible manner? Support your arguments in specific ways.

Possible Solutions

1. Knowing that *Catcher in the Rye* was on the district's approved list of alternate readings for senior high school, Adele saw no reason to discuss the matter with her principal prior to suggesting the book as one of six that her students might read to fulfill their assignment. When Robin's parents arrived in the school's main office, no one knew the circumstances under which the book had been assigned. The vice-principal was led to believe that this was the only book Robin could read to complete this assignment. Indeed, Robin had told her parents that the book was required and that she had to read it.

The vice-principal tried to quiet the parents down while he located Adele and got more information from her about the assignment she had made.

2. When Adele met the parents, she showed them the syllabus and said, "I am sorry you are upset over this reading assignment. Were you aware that Robin had to read just one of the six books on the list you have before you? You can read the assignment for yourself." Robin's father said, "Well, this isn't quite what Robin told us. We thought she *had* to read *Catcher in the Rye*. Now I'm not sure we have a complaint, even though I don't think any young people should be exposed to trash in school." Adele is not about to defend *Catcher* to these people because to do so would be to encourage confrontation that would likely lead to no desirable outcomes. Rather she tells the parents, "I am sure Robin can find a book on the list that will be more suitable for her." Just then Robin enters the room. Her father shouts, "Why did you make us think *Catcher in the Rye* was the only book you could read for this assignment when this syllabus clearly says that you have to read and report on one of the six books listed?" Robin is trembling, but she manages to say, "Because everyone has read *Catcher* and I want to. You're old-fashioned. You never let me do anything!" The father says, "We'll talk about this when you get home, young lady," apologizes to Adele, and with his wife leaves the office.

3. When Robin comes into the conference room, her father confronts her with the fact that he knows she had six books to choose from. Robin says, "Well, it looks that way, but I could tell by what Ms. P. was saying when she introduced the books that this is the one she wanted us to read. I was afraid if I didn't read it, she'd mark me down." Adele is shocked by this statement. She turns to Robin and says, "Robin, I think you have misunderstood me badly. It doesn't matter to me which book any student selects. Don't you think you should admit that this is the book you really wanted to read? I think you know me well enough to realize that I don't try to force my students into doing things that are contrary to their beliefs or those of their parents." Robin, who has always liked Ms. P., can hardly speak. Then she begins to cry and admits, "Yes, I wanted to read it. I'm sick of always being told what I can't do."

Consider This

Part of the wonderful appeal of the United States is that people of varying outlooks live harmoniously in it. Teachers must realize that it is not their job to tamper with their students' beliefs or to try to get them to question the beliefs of their parents—which many of them will do without their teachers' help.

It is unfair to students in your classes to try to force upon them anything they might find morally offensive. On the other hand, it is not fair to deprive all the students in a class of exposure to works or theories merely because some students in the class are offended by them. The best thing a teacher can do is

- Offer viable options for students whose religious faith or philosophical stand makes that seem desirable;
- Make sure that books you use are on the approved list of your school district if such a list exists;
- Make sure that controversial assignments are made in writing and that they clearly indicate the options students may choose; and
- File copies of your syllabi and other pertinent materials in your file in the main office.

Ambitious Parents

Many parents are ambitious for their children. They fret if the English teacher encourages free writing or creative dramatics rather than grammar drill or spelling. They feel that the social studies teacher who involves a class in playing games like Diplomacy or Tripoli is wasting precious time during which factual information—names, dates, treaty provisions—might be taught, losing sight of the fact that students, through playing games, might be learning concepts that will enable them to understand and apply the larger elements that motivate political and social development. In short, many parents—even the best educated—may not understand the inquiry method of teaching that has been used with considerable success since Socrates elicited from the slave boy Meno, through skillful questioning, an enunciation of the Pythagorean theorem.

Teachers dealing with apprehensive parents cannot very well suggest, without appearing condescending, that they go out and read the Platonic dialogue (*The Meno*) that recounts the lesson noted, although this is a dialogue teachers might well read and periodically reread. Rather, you need to understand and appreciate parental concerns and to be prepared to explain a teaching method that begins with student interest and enthusiasm and leads ultimately to a mastery of factual material as well as to the development of an ability to understand principles that will, once understood, enable students to cope with new sets of facts and with new complexes of situations. Put in rudimentary terms, if students in the pri-

127

mary grades are taught that two apples plus two apples equals four apples but cannot transfer that information to the abstract level (two of anything plus two of anything equals four of something), the learning experience is incomplete. Students who learn, let us say, the provisions of the Monroe Doctrine but are not encouraged to think of the Doctrine and its provisions in terms of the more recent Panama Canal agreement have not mastered any usable information, even though they may pass the test on the Monroe Doctrine. Students who have role-played the Panama Canal debates after having been exposed to the provisions of the Monroe Doctrine, even though they are engaged in a gamelike activity during class time, are being forced to use their information rather than merely to stockpile it. Most parents can be made to understand such learning, provided a patient teacher explains it lucidly and convincingly.

It may be useful in situations like this to invite parents to attend a class or two to see what is going on. However, before parents attend a class, it would be helpful to brief them on the substance of what is going on as well as on the philosophy of the learning experience. If you can work with a few parents in this sort of situation, these parents can become your greatest and staunchest allies when other parents misunderstand what is going on. The first function of teachers is that of helping people to understand things. *People* in this context does not mean only students, although it includes them; it means parents, other teachers, members of the community, administrators, and school staff as well.

CASE STUDY 4.12
Parents Want First Grader To Read

Muriel S. is a teacher at the Ashley E. Wolfe Elementary School where she teaches first-grade students. Late in January, the parents of Michael S. asked to see her after school one day at her convenience. A date was set, but not before Muriel ascertained that Michael's parents were concerned because their son was not yet able to read. Muriel's principal, who has a master's degree in reading, agreed to sit in on the conference which took place in Muriel's classroom at 3:15 in the afternoon.

After polite introductions, Michael's mother volunteered, "We don't like to complain, Ms. S.—in fact, we're not complaining. We are just worried. Michael has been in school since September, and he still can't read."

"I understand your concern," Ms. S. replied, "but I am sure you realize that children learn at different rates and that, even though Michael has not yet learned to read, he is showing above-average ability in other areas like drawing and music."

"But he won't be able to make a living at drawing and music," the mother retorted. "We want to see Michael make something of himself, go to college, and study for a profession. He can't use drawing and music for that, can he, dear?"

Mr. S. nodded and mumbled, "No, no. I guess he can't."

An uneasy silence ensued.

The principal interjected, "I am sure that Ms. S. does not mean to imply that drawing and music are all that Michael will be taught in the first grade, do you, Ms. S.?"

"Of course not. But right now Michael seems tense and nervous when he tries to read, and I think it is best to let him develop a little more self-confidence by working on things that he enjoys and can do well. Most of the children in Michael's room are reading, and I am sure that Michael will be reading very soon."

"But that is just the point," the mother responded. "The other children *are* reading, and Michael isn't. Why is this?"

"Not all the other children are reading; some of them, like Michael, are not ready yet. But every day they are making progress; and if they are not forced into reading before they are ready, they will learn to read more quickly once they start."

"Well, we don't care about the other children who can't read. Maybe they aren't going to college. But Michael is, and he has to learn to read."

Mr. S. nodded and remained silent.

"And he will," Ms. S. assured them. "In order that you understand some of the things we are doing, I wish that one or both of you could come and sit in on Michael's class when we have our Parents' Day, so that you can have a more complete picture of how the class operates and of the sorts of skills that every child is learning."

"I want to do that," Mrs. S. replied. "But couldn't I come sooner and observe for part of the day?"

The principal answered, "Before Ms. S. answers that request, perhaps we should consider whether it would make Michael feel awkward or embarrassed to have you attend the class when no other parents are there."

Mr. S. said, "That's a good point. We don't want to embarrass the boy. That would only make things worse."

Questions

1. Why do you think some children learn to read at an earlier age than other children do? How should primary school teachers deal

with their students who have not learned to read in their first three or four months in school?

2. Had the principal been unable to attend this conference, who else in the school might have been asked to attend it with Muriel?

3. If you have a conference with both parents and one parent does most of the talking, is it wise to try to bring the other parent into fuller participation? How might Muriel have done so in this situation? Might the principal have made an effort to involve Mr. S.?

4. If Mr. S. had been involved more fully in the conference, do you think its tone might have been somewhat different? Defend your answer.

5. Was Muriel's principal diplomatic and supportive of the teacher in this conference? Explain.

6. Was Muriel wise to encourage the parents to come to Parents' Day?

7. Having had this conference, do you think Muriel should put more pressure on Michael to get him to read? Discuss fully.

Possible Solutions

1. When Mr. S. says that he wants to attend Michael's class as Muriel suggests, Muriel turns to him and asks, "Are you as worried as your wife is about Michael's not being able to read yet?" Mr. S. replies, "Well, I know he has to learn how to read soon, or he'll be in trouble, but I think time will take care of it." The mother interrupts: "You always think time will take care of everything. Michael might go another year and not learn how to read if something isn't done about it!" Muriel asks, "Are you doing anything at home to help encourage Michael to read?" The mother says, "Well, I told him as soon as he can read, I will give him five dollars." Muriel replies, "Well, that *is* offering motivation, but are you doing anything else?" Mr. S. says, "I'm not sure what you mean. Michael sits in my lap every night before he goes to bed, and I read a story to him from his favorite book." "That's exactly what I mean," Muriel responds. "Sometimes we don't remember what it was like not to be able to read. If you read to Michael, he is developing broad reading skills through that. He is learning what to us seems obvious—that people read books from front to back, that they read pages from top to bottom and from left to right. I would recommend that you run your finger along the pages you read to Michael so that he can see the direction you are reading in." Mrs. S. says, "That's a good suggestion. I never thought of that, but you're right. Children have no way of knowing something like that unless they see it."

130

2. When Michael's parents complain that Michael can't make a living from drawing and music, Muriel reminds them, "Remember that drawing is the first step people take to learning how to write. Ancient people drew on cave walls and pieces of bark for centuries before they had an alphabet and before they could write in abstractions the way we do. The kind of drawing Michael is learning engages his muscles. As they get fine-tuned, he will be in a position to learn how to print and then how to write cursively." Michael's mother says, "I had never thought of that." She pauses, but then asks, "But what does that have to do with learning to read?" Muriel answers, "Oddly enough, some students actually learn to write before they learn to read, but once they have learned to write, they usually learn very quickly to read what they have written. You haven't anything to worry about with Michael. He is a bright, eager boy who's developing pretty normally. He'll be reading a couple of months from now. Trust me. I have seen it happen many times before."

3. As the interview proceeds, Muriel's principal, having taken reading courses and done research recently in reading, becomes involved in the discussion and says, "We are learning a great deal about reading that we didn't know before. People hear that John Stuart Mill could read Greek when he was three and think their children should at least be able to read English at an early age. What they sometimes fail to recognize is that muscular development is different in every child and that eyes are operated by muscles." He has a copy made of an article he read the night before [N. Roderick Underwood and David Zola, "The Span of Letter Recognition of Good and Poor Readers," *Reading Research Quarterly* 21 (1986): 6–19] and, telling them that the article is pretty technical, suggests that they at least read the conclusions that clearly show how a child whose eyes have not developed to a certain point cannot read words, but must focus arduously on single letters. He points out that in many children, the muscular development they need to read efficiently will come in as short a time as a month or so, but if they have been pushed into learning how to read before they are ready, they will develop bad reading habits that will affect their ability to read rapidly, and reading may forever be a chore for them rather than a pleasure.

Consider This

Children develop at their own rates, and although some generalizations can be made about six-year-olds or seven-year-olds, much generalizing of this sort is meaningless and, in some cases, downright harmful. To say "This six-year-old child cannot read" is less meaningful than to say "This 80-month-old child cannot read." Because of the rapidity with which children develop, the difference between 72 months and 83 months is huge.

Schools are increasingly placing children in ungraded primary classes. Rather than having a first, second, and possibly third grade, there is simply a group of students in the primary division. These children learn whatever they can learn at a particular stage of their own development, and if they are not developing in one area, like reading or writing, they are encouraged to work in the areas they can work in best. It has been found that in such configurations, most children achieve the skills they require in order to enter the later elementary grades and that if they have not been placed under pressure to learn, they are joyous and enthusiastic learners. Teachers in the primary grades realize one truth: young children want desperately to learn. It is best to teach them the things they want to learn *when they want to learn them*. If people around them are learning to read and write, they will put forth their best efforts to be like their classmates *if they are left to their own devices*.

Projects

1. List three learning skills you think students must learn before they can proceed to the first elementary grades after primary school.

2. List at least five social skills you think children learn in the primary grades.

CASE STUDY 4.13
Parents Complain About Teaching Method

Stewart B. teaches algebra and geometry at Technical High School. He knows the principles of the new mathematics and also has a good background in more traditional approaches. He himself learned geometry by memorizing theorems and their proofs. Often he did not really understand the theorems he had learned in any operational way, but with the theorems memorized and their proofs in mind, he could do well on his tests in the subject. Although he had received an "A" in his high school geometry course, it was not until he studied drafting, mechanics, and some basic architecture courses that he really began to understand how and why geometry works.

Therefore, as an enthusiastic, energetic teacher, Stewart has decided to teach geometry from an inquiry base; he has decided to work from actual problems to which students can relate in their daily lives rather than to use a textbook during the first three months of the course. He intends to introduce the textbook after the Thanksgiving holiday, by which time he expects his students to have learned inductively most of what they need to know about the relationships presented in the form of theorems in the geometry textbook.

Late in October, Stewart was called to his principal's office. The father of one of his students, Karen J., was present when Stewart arrived. After the two were introduced, the principal said, "Mr. B., Mr. J. has come to talk with me and to express his concern that you are nearly two months into the geometry course and have not yet used a textbook or taught any theorems or proofs. I don't know what to tell him. Our records show that you have been issued textbooks for the course. Do you have them in your possession?"

Stewart answered, "Yes, sir, I have them and I plan to issue them after the Thanksgiving vacation when the students have . . ."

"After the Thanksgiving vacation!" Mr. J. interjects. "That's the silliest thing I ever heard of. They'll be almost halfway through the course by then, and they won't know any geometry."

"Actually, Mr. J., Karen knows a great deal of geometry. In fact, she is one of my strongest students and seems to be headed for a solid 'A' in the course. She . . ."

"I don't care about the 'A' in the course!" Mr. J. retorted. "I want her to learn something. What kind of standards do you have?"

"I think I have quite high standards," Stewart protested. "I want my students to understand the workings of geometry before they begin to memorize theorems. Understandings are what I am trying to teach, not facts isolated from reality."

"Mr. B., please try to be calm," the principal intervened. "We will discuss this fully after Mr. J. leaves. Meanwhile, Mr. J., I promise you that Mr. B. will be using the books we have provided for him, beginning with tomorrow's class. I share your concern. I am no mathematician, but I will have high standards maintained in any school that I run or know the reason why. Thank you for calling this matter to my attention."

Questions

1. Did the principal show good judgment in calling Stewart to his office while the parent was sitting there?

2. Seeing the initial situation, could Stewart have acted differently from the way he did? Might he have done anything earlier to forestall the sort of situation which the meeting with Mr. J. became? If so, explain.

3. The principal served a judgmental rather than a mediating func-

tion in this scenario. How might he have been a mediator rather than a judge? Could Stewart have helped him to assume a mediating role? How?

4. Should Stewart have requested that the matter not be discussed on the spur of the moment but that a future conference be arranged? If so, who should attend the future conference? Why?

5. Did the principal have the right to make promises in Stewart's name? How would you have reacted to the principal's last portion of dialogue if you had been Stewart?

Possible Solutions

1. Most upset by the course the meeting has taken, Stewart turns to his principal and says, "With all due respect, sir, I would remind you that you are not a mathematician. I know what I am doing. If you think my teaching methods are irresponsible, I can get a job in industry. I don't need to teach, and I won't if people outside my field try to dictate to me how I will do it." The principal says, "I have a school to run and standards to maintain, Mr. B. We need to sit down and have a long talk about this." The parent is caught in the middle of this unpleasant exchange and adds weakly, "I must say, Mr. B., that Karen likes your class. This is the first time she has ever seemed to like mathematics; I'm just afraid she isn't learning anything." Stewart responds, "I appreciate your concern, but I can assure you that Karen is learning and that when we begin to do things more traditionally, she will learn much faster and better than she would have if we had started out traditionally. All I ask for is a little trust and patience on your part."

2. When Stewart is told the parent is waiting and is informed of the nature of the complaint, he tells his principal that he thinks it would be a mistake for him to meet with a parent until he has prepared for the meeting. He suggests that his principal talk with the parent, tell him that he will investigate the situation, and set up a time when the parent can meet with Stewart. Meanwhile, Stewart will prepare and mail to Karen's parents a summary of what he is doing in his geometry classes, indicating clearly how he will use the assigned textbook once the experimental, inductive part of the course is over. The course is a year long, so he has until late May to work with these students.

3. Having heard the parent's complaint, the principal says, "Thank you, Mr. J., for your concern and for bringing this situation to our attention. Mr. B. and I will talk the matter over, and I will get back to you." He and Stewart shake hands with Mr. J., and Stewart says to the parent, "Just trust me a little. I really do know what I am doing,

134

and I can assure you that my students know much more geometry now than students in my geometry classes last year knew at this point in the school year—even though they aren't doing theorems and proofs in the conventional way yet." The principal adds, "We have faith in our teachers, Mr. J., and I know that Mr. B. is one of our best. I go along with him in asking that you be patient and trust his judgment."

4. As soon as Mr. J. voices his objection, the principal says, "Well, I think Mr. B. and I need to talk this situation over. Why don't I take you to get a cup of coffee, and then we can resume our meeting in ten or fifteen minutes?" Mr. J. agrees and is shown to a teacher workroom where coffee is brewing. The principal returns to his office, turns to Stewart, and says, "What do you mean by not using the textbooks you were assigned? This is indefensible! I want an explanation, and it had better be good." Stewart responds, "If you are going to try to bully me, I'm afraid we won't accomplish much. I know what I am doing, and it's working. I'll try to explain it to you if you'll calm down."

Consider This

Many of life's crises result from inadequate communication. Teachers get into a teaching rut when they do the same things over and over again in the same ways. The best teachers constantly seek new ways to present material and to involve students so that they understand what they are doing by being participants in a process rather than recipients of isolated facts on which they will be tested—and which many of them may forget the day after the test!

The situation described in this case represents a breakdown in communication at two levels. What Stewart was trying to do with his classes is admirable. The problem is that apparently he alone—or perhaps he and his students—knew what he was trying to do. In not communicating this information to his administrators and to the parents of the students involved, he was asking for exactly the kind of trouble he got. An interview like this one can deteriorate into a nonproductive shouting match quite easily, as it did in two of the possible solutions. Nothing is gained—indeed, a great deal is lost—when this happens.

Perhaps you sympathize with Stewart; much can be said in his favor. But try to think of how a school principal feels when some busy morning he is working on a report that has to be in the central office by three o'clock and an angry parent comes in to complain about a curricular matter the principal does not know exists in his school. The principal is forced to drop what he is doing and immediately is dragged into the middle of a situation about which he has no detailed information. Of course he will be perturbed.

Had Stewart informed his principal in writing at the beginning of the term that he was planning to teach geometry from a new approach as outlined in his attached syllabus, the principal would not have been taken by surprise and would likely have been able to defend Stewart's teaching method without involving Stewart in the interview. Had Stewart been able to attach photocopies of articles or sections from textbooks in mathematics education that describe such an approach, these addenda would have given the principal additional materials to draw on when the complaining parent arrived. As it was, the principal was totally unprepared for the onslaught; he had no way to handle it in a satisfactory manner.

Stewart might also have written an open letter to the parents of his geometry students at the beginning of school, telling them of a new method he plans to use based upon something he learned in a workshop for mathematics educators at the state university during the summer. A copy of this letter should accompany the description of his course he submits to his principal.

A progress report from Stewart to his students' parents at the end of six weeks might also serve to keep them from being apprehensive about the new technique. Indeed, if administrators and parents know that something unique is being tried in the school, they often become boastful about the experiment and are publicly supportive of it. The only thing that can make them publicly supportive of something like this is information, and information requires clear, persuasive communication. The projects that follow will provide you with some practice in communicating with administrators and parents.

Projects

1. Write a brief note to your principal defending an unusual teaching method you hope to employ in a class you are teaching or are preparing to teach. Be sure to include information about the method, the anticipated outcome(s), the length of time you expect the experiment to take, and a clear rationale for its use.

2. Having decided to teach your course in an unusual way and having cleared this with your principal, write an open letter to the parents of your students that will inform them clearly and concisely of what you plan to do. Be sure to stress the anticipated advantages of this approach, the main reason(s) you are deviating from more traditional approaches with which they may be familiar, any expert opin-

136

ions you have to justify trying the new method, and a statement indicating that you have cleared your use of this technique with your administrators. Invite parental questions, comments, and prearranged visits to the classroom. You might also wish to remind parents that teachers are always pleased to have them volunteer as classroom aides.

Teacher-Initiated Conferences

Sometimes you will need to call one or both parents to school to discuss a student's behavior or academic progress. For such conferences, it is advisable that an appropriate administrator or staff member attend. In such conferences, specifics should be presented and concrete suggestions made to the parent(s), with possibly some of the suggestions in writing.

It is well to take into account the parents' work schedules and arrange the conference at the least possible inconvenience to the parents involved. Setting up the conference by telephone is a good idea. If the conference concerns a student of secondary school age (about thirteen or above), serious thought may be given to including the student in the meeting.

Summary

If teachers and parents fail to get along, often the problem is one of communication. Concerned parents are showing an interest in their children. You may want to explain what is going on in class and provide pertinent information for them.

Most distressed parents see school administrators before they see teachers. Therefore, school administrators need information about what is going on in the school. When such information is not available, administrators may be taken by surprise when a complaint is lodged and may have no rational basis on which to defend the teacher in question.

You can help to enlist the support of parents if you send them occasional mimeographed newsletters describing some of the class activities. Such messages will keep lines of communication open between teachers and parents. When practical, newsletters might be prepared every six to eight weeks and sent home with students. A copy of each newsletter should be on file in the main office so that school administrators have easy access to it.

Remember that anger in an interview situation accomplishes nothing. No matter how unreasonable a parent may seem, the only way to work toward understanding is through clear explanations of what is going on and through the presentation of valid professional justifications for the teaching techniques and materials employed.

Avoid, if possible, making vague accusations about students. "Johnny is disruptive in class" is not very descriptive. It is much more convincing to be able to present an anecdotal record that chronicles some of the disruptive things that Johnny has done:

9/7   Refused to work on homework. Bothered students around him so that they could not work.

9/18   Exploded a firecracker in his desk. Note sent to counselor.

9/19   Tore a page out of his social studies book when told he must do an assignment.

10/1   Threw another student's notebook out the window. Given a detention.

10/3   Failed to appear for detention.

5. AND I USED TO THINK I COULD GET ALONG WITH ANYONE!

Part Two: Dealing with School Personnel

Schools are microcosms, small images of the world outside them. In our bleaker moments, we sometimes view them as so bureaucratized that we think the only hope is, as Ivan Illich suggested, to banish them from society and begin all over with a clean slate. Then something happens, some unique satisfaction accrues to us in our teaching perhaps, that makes us realize how much schools mean to society and how intimately bound they are to every developed society's hope for its future.

When we stop to think of it, we soon realize that everyone connected with schools—from the superintendent of a district to the person who sweeps the floors and stokes the furnaces—contributes uniquely to the overall educational atmosphere of our society and of what society is likely to become. As teachers, we develop strategies for working within bureaucracies. The case studies in this chapter should help you to handle some types of encounters you might expect to deal with in the course of a typical teaching career. Each situation can be adapted to your own professional needs. These are generalized studies, but each is based upon actual occurrences in a broad variety of schools.

DEVELOPING A PROFESSIONAL ATTITUDE

Most teachers are good citizens who strive to get along with other people and to do their jobs well. They know they can succeed only if they work well with all the groups of people they deal with professionally. They do not necessarily like or even respect all of these people. If they are to have productive working relationships, however, they must find means of getting along with them. Teachers, like other professionals, must make a conscious effort to keep personal animosities out of their professional relationships.

They can do this best if they are patient, slow to anger, and willing to see situations from more than one point of view. It is naive, perhaps, to assume that everyone we work with has good basic motivations and intentions. It is disastrous, however, to assume that everyone who does not view life as we do has bad motivations and intentions. A world in which people never disagree is a totalitarian world that few of us would care to live in. The very fiber of our society, of the total structure of our legal

139

system, and of the varied emphases in most of our institutions is based on the fact that people have freedom of choice and the right to their own ideas and opinions as long as those ideas and opinions do not lead to acts that seriously threaten society or harm its members.

DEALING WITH COLLEAGUES

When a colleague in a faculty meeting punches holes in a proposal a teacher or a committee has made, one's first impulse, quite naturally, is to become defensive and/or angry. But before yielding to such an impulse, reasonable people stop to think carefully about whether the objector has pointed to a valid weakness in what has been proposed. Civilized discussion involves more than one point of view, and most of what we value in our lives has come about through civilized discussion among people whose views do not wholly coincide. Sometimes we leap to the conclusion that the opposition *totally* opposes what we are attempting to promote. The chances are that even the toughest objectors are no more than 70- or 80-percent opposed to our cherished ideas and can be made to see some value and validity in them if they have been well thought out before we present them. Frequently compromise is the oil that lubricates the wheels of professional progress.

CASE STUDY 5.1
Teachers Clash over Taking Students from Class

Lila J. is advisor to a special group in Puntarenas Senior High School, which serves the Latino area of a large southwestern city. If Lila has any mission in life, it is to work with youngsters who are potential dropouts and to help them find ways to continue their educations. She has been known to help some of her school's graduates with their tuition fees when they were admitted to colleges they could not afford to attend. She has canvassed the community on weekends to find part-time jobs for her students so that they would be able to make money to help their families survive while they continued in school. She has arranged special schedules so that students who were faced with the decision either of working or of continuing their educations were shown how they could do both.

So effective has Lila's work been that she has received district-wide recognition. As a result of this, her district superintendent has provided money for a regular guidance counselor to replace Lila, thereby enabling her to work full time with potential dropouts. On the

140

Sunday before school began, the local newspaper ran a profusely illustrated front-page article about Lila and her pioneering work.

At the first faculty meeting before regular classes begin, Lila announces her intention to have a half-hour conference with every new student in the school who has been labeled "at risk," a designation used to identify students whose academic and personal profiles suggest that they might drop out of school. Lila says that she will have to ask that these students be excused from their classes for this important interview.

Other teachers object at once. When Mr. B., an English teacher, says, "That will create chaos in my classes," other teachers voice their concerns. Lila is sympathetic to Mr. B.'s complaint, and she instantly realizes that he has considerable support from his colleagues. She responds, "I realize that it will necessitate some inconvenience, Mr. B., but doesn't that seem a small price to pay for helping someone stay in school who might otherwise drop out?"

Before Mr. B. can answer, another teacher, Ms. W., who is much respected as a voice of moderation in her school, jumps into the fray and begins softly, becoming more strident as she goes along: "It seems to me that every time we interrupt a class for any reason—announcements over the loudspeaker, taking students out of class to have their yearbook pictures taken, or something like the interruption Lila has suggested—we are communicating just one thing to our students: *Going to class is not important! This undermines everything we, as teachers, are trying to do. It is no wonder that students cut classes with impunity!*" By the time she is finished, Ms. W. is shouting passionately. As her voice fades, other teachers chime in with "Yes" and "Right on!" Then the room bursts into applause.

Questions

1. How do you react to classroom interruptions? Does your reaction tell you something about your personality?

2. If you are convinced you are right about something, as Lila is, but everyone in a meeting seems to oppose you, do you usually continue to defend your stand, do you give in to the will of others, or do you seek a middle ground? If you think you should try to change this facet of your personality, how might you begin?

3. Can you propose a compromise solution to the impasse that seems to be developing between Lila and her colleagues?

4. How would you feel if the principal asserted administrative prerogative, rose up in the meeting, and said, "I support fully what Ms. J. is doing with our high-risk students. You will do as she asks. It is

important to the school''? Would such an action benefit Lila in the long run? Why or why not?

Possible Solutions

1. On being attacked from every quarter, Lila, who has put her whole being into helping potential dropouts, bursts into tears and shouts, "You don't really care about these students! All you care about is the subjects you teach. It would do some of you good to remember that WE TEACH STUDENTS, NOT SUBJECTS." She turns and leaves a room that has been hushed by her outburst.

2. Lila stands up in an attempt to help bring order back to the meeting. When her colleagues have quieted down, she speaks softly, just barely audibly, and says, "I know how you feel about this. I was worried about causing a disruption in your classes, and I toyed with the idea of just asking that an hour be set aside so that I could talk to all of these students at once in the auditorium—that's the easy way; much easier than giving dozens of individual students essentially the same information over and over again. I rejected that idea, though, because it's too impersonal. I need to build a relationship with each of these kids. This is one way I can do it. I need your suggestions so that I can accomplish what I need to without disrupting our routine. I have to agree with Ms. W. that we send an undesirable message every time we interrupt a class for any reason."

3. Lila knows when she is licked. Enough people seem to be against her that she thinks the only thing to do is admit defeat. She stands and says to her colleagues, "Well, I can see that you are not willing to go along with this, so I won't push it. What I will ask instead is that you try to identify students who seem to be having particular problems and send their names to me. I will try to reach them during their study halls or homerooms." Lila's colleagues seem satisfied, and the meeting turns to other matters.

4. The scenario is the same as that in Possible Solution 3, except that when Lila finishes, Ms. W. says, "Wait a minute, Ms. J. I don't know that you should give up so easily. Our 'at-risk' students *are* important, and I think we need to get our heads together to figure out how you can meet them with the least possible disruption to school routine." Mr. B. chimes in, "Yeah, I'd go along with that. After all, Lila, we all know what you're doing for kids like that, and we appreciate it even if we do hassle you sometimes." All at once the room breaks into applause, and Lila knows that somehow, with the help of her colleagues, she will reach the students she needs to.

Consider This

No school has a single agenda. Each teacher, administrator, and student has an individual agenda, and the magic of a harmonious school is the melding of all those agendas into a single overall entity that allows everyone to accomplish as much of these individual agendas as possible.

Lila cannot impose her agenda upon her colleagues. She can speak for her agenda, but that is about as far as she can go individually. In Possible Solution 2, she makes her case, tells what alternative solutions she has considered, admits temporary defeat, and enlists the help of her colleagues to come up with a solution to her problem. Once people ask for help, they begin to share their burdens with others, and the people who accept part of their burdens join the team that will work toward a resolution of the dilemma involved.

Possible Solution 4 poses another approach, but one similar to that suggested in Possible Solution 2. Something similar happened to me once. I initially felt unloved, unappreciated, and defeated. Suddenly this feeling abated when I realized that those who opposed my proposal were not questioning the validity of what I had suggested but were at odds only with the logistics of how I might accomplish my aims. My emotions went from zero to 100 percent in one second when the colleagues who had opposed my initial suggestion suddenly burst into applause in appreciation of what I had done and vowed to help me work through the problem.

Obviously, the best schools are those in which teachers pull in the same direction rather than in opposite directions. Most teachers at some time find themselves in a conflict with one or another of their colleagues over something that seems to them quite fundamental. In such instances, it is certainly wise to ask yourself certain questions:

- Is the problem that is annoying me disruptive to my classes?
- Does the problem seem to be a one-time occurrence, or is there reason to think it will recur?
- Are any extenuating circumstances apparent?
- Do I have all the facts of the situation?
- Is it better to talk with the teacher(s) involved or to write a note detailing the problem?
- If an initial discussion fails to bring a resolution, can I turn to anyone except the principal for help?

1. List three annoyances in your situation that probably are one-time occurrences.
2. List three or four things you do that might annoy some other teacher(s). Why do you do these things?

CASE STUDY 5.2
Gym Teacher Makes Students Late for Class

Ramon L. teaches Spanish at Loma Prieta Senior High School. He has an annoying problem in his fifth-period class because five of his female students arrive late two days every week, always coming to class perspiring and breathless five to ten minutes after the lesson has begun. Standard policy in Ramon's school is to demand late notes from students who do not come to class on time. The principal often reiterates this policy in faculty meetings. In line with this requirement, Ramon told the girls the first time they came in late that they would have to return to wherever they came from to get the required late note.

Donna, one of Ramon's most dependable students and clearly a highly responsible person, replied, "But Mr. L., we have gym right before this class, and Ms. F. never lets us go to the showers until five minutes before the period ends—sometimes later!"

Ramon retorted, "In that case, you will have to go back to Ms. F. and ask her to give you late notes."

Ramon continued teaching his class. Ten or twelve minutes later the five girls returned, now having missed almost half the class. One of them said, "Ms. F. said she couldn't take time to write five late notes in the middle of her gym period."

Ramon, following established school policy, said, "In that case, I have no choice except to give you all detentions for next Tuesday. That means one hour after school in Room 213."

As soon as he could do so, Ramon went to see Ms. F. to check the girls' story. Ms. F. was cavalier about the whole affair, telling Ramon, "Well, I guess we were a few minutes late getting to the showers, but the girls dawdle sometimes. And I just can't be expected to stop a gym class with thirty-two students in it," she continued haughtily, "to give five people late notes."

The next day, Ramon called the girls aside and told them that he was going to cancel their detentions because he had talked with Ms. F., who had substantiated their stories. The girls were grateful. Later

144

that week, however, when they had Ms. F.'s class again, the same girls came into Ramon's Spanish class, huffing and puffing, eight minutes late. Ramon told them they would have to get notes from Ms. F. or go to the principal's office—and he told them to repeat to Ms. F. what he had said if she was reluctant to give them the notes they needed.

The girls came back to class fifteen minutes later, by this time having missed more than half their Spanish class, with one hastily scribbled note saying, "Late—five girls. E. F."

Ramon accepted the note, but he was outraged. He did not know how to deal with the situation. Ms. F. had taught at the school long enough to have become a legend. Ramon, although an experienced teacher, had been at Loma Prieta for only one year. He did not want to pick a fight with a colleague, but Ms. F. was placing him in an impossible position, forcing him to play the heavy with his students over something that clearly was not their fault.

The next week, when the girls came in six minutes late, Ramon, who by now was keeping a log of his students' lateness and of all of his contacts with Ms. F., said to them, "You have now missed the equivalent of almost two full periods of Spanish. On Thursday, instead of going to your gym class, I want the five of you to report to this room to begin making up the work you have missed."

The girls protested, "But Mr. L., Ms. F. will kill us if we cut gym! She gives detentions if you look at her wrong."

Ramon replied, "Don't let that worry you. I will square it with Ms. F. And don't think this extra session of Spanish is a punishment. I just need to help you catch up before our examination and before nine-week grades are due. You have done nothing that you should be punished for."

Questions

1. Was Ramon overreacting? Couldn't he just have lived with the situation and allowed the girls to come to class a few minutes late a couple of days a week?

2. Did Ramon act professionally when he told his students to cut the gym class and to come to his class for makeup work instead?

3. How should Ramon deal with any of the girls who go to their scheduled gym class rather than to his makeup session?

4. Suppose Ramon had sent these girls to the main office the first time they were late rather than sending them back to their gym teacher for notes? What might such an action have resulted in?

5. Has Ramon exhausted every possibility in dealing with this situ-

ation? If not, what other possible courses of action would you suggest to him?

6. When a teacher writes late notes for students, what information must they always contain?

Possible Solutions

1. At the end of his meeting with Ms. F., the gym teacher, Ramon says to her, "I don't want to cause trouble, Ms. F., but I must have my students in class for the whole class period. I am sure you can appreciate this. I am keeping a log, and if this situation persists, I will have no alternative other than to complain to the administration and to share my log with them." Ms. F. responds, "Make my day! I was teaching in this school when you were still a toddler. No one has interfered with me up to now, and you better not try!" Ramon says, "We shall see what we shall see," and leaves.

2. Ramon does not cancel the detentions he has given the girls. He decides that the only way to resolve the situation is to make them angry enough that they or their parents will complain to the administration, something Ramon doesn't want to do himself, knowing that Ms. F. has taught at the school for a long time and probably has more credibility with the administration than he, a relatively new faculty member, has. The girls all show up for their detentions, but they barely speak to Ramon, and the next day in class they are sullen and silent.

3. When the girls are late for his class the second time and eventually bring him Ms. F.'s makeshift excuse, Ramon decides that he must bring the matter before the administration. He does not have another meeting with Ms. F. because he considers her written excuse an admission that the girls were late because she kept them overtime. Lacking the written excuse, he likely would have told Ms. F. that he was forced to make a formal complaint about her just to make sure that the girls were not late for some other reason. Ramon schedules an appointment with his principal for the beginning of his lunch hour and takes with him his log indicating the repeated tardiness to which he is objecting as well as Ms. F.'s late note for the girls. He briefly outlines his case to the principal who says, "Oh, she's up to her old tricks, is she? I'll talk with her about it. You are in the right here. I hope I can work things out, but don't hold your breath."

Consider This

Students who are late for class usually miss the initial instructions the teacher gives that class. If four or five students come in simultaneously, as in this case, the teacher usually has to repeat instructions, thereby wasting the time of all the other students. If teachers insist on late notes and have to send students back to get them, a five-minute tardiness can turn into a fifteen-minute tardiness, and three of these are equivalent to missing a class period.

Other legal matters pervade situations like this one. Schools are expected to know where each student is at any given time. Most schools discourage students from walking around the halls, possibly disrupting classes in the rooms they pass, possibly going into a restroom to smoke or to fight. Teachers cannot permit the sort of tardiness that Ramon encountered in this case. If they permit it, their administrators have cause for action against them.

As difficult as this situation is, Ramon must fight his own battles. He cannot give the tardy students detentions in the hope that they will complain loudly enough to bring administrative attention to a situation the administration definitely has to be informed about. It is never fair to put students in the middle of a dispute of this sort, even though they are a part of that dispute. Ramon needs to document his case, present it openly and professionally to the offending teacher before he takes official action, and then take official action if the situation persists.

Ramon also cannot encourage students to be absent from another teacher's class to make up work for him even if they missed that work because of the other teacher. No administrator would be able to defend such an action. Ramon's relief can come only from one of two sources: (1) the offending teacher; or (2) the school's administration.

Proxemics:
Noise, Space, and Territoriality

E. T. Hall's *The Hidden Dimension* (Garden City, N.Y.: Doubleday, 1966) should have a place on the list of the five books every teacher or would-be teacher must read. The anthropologist who wrote this book deals with problems that confront most of us several times every day as we deal with space, noise, and distance. The situations he deals with essentially involve *proxemics*.

So much a part of all of us is our sense of territoriality that we perhaps have not thought much about it. If you are the sort of person who likes or hates to touch others or have them touch you, you are exhibiting a territorial or proxemic preference. If you are the sort of person who can shut out all the noise around you in a dank bus station and lose yourself

147

in your thoughts or your reading, you are reacting proxemically to your immediate environment.

Anyone who has lived in crowded conditions, like those in most dormitories or urban apartment houses, realizes that people can intrude upon others without ever physically setting foot in their space. Close neighbors can dance over your head in the middle of the night, can pound their typewriters early in the morning, can distress you with their cooking smells at any hour of the day or night, or can run chain saws outside your windows when you are on a long-distance telephone call. In all of these situations, your territory is being intruded upon. Nations have gone to war over proxemic issues, and governments deal with them every day in such matters as acid rain or the pollution of oceans. Warring neighbors abound in many neighborhoods, and most of them are at war over something proxemic.

Schools are crowded places, and noise sometimes intrudes penetratingly upon something we and our students need to do. Pity the poor teacher whose fourth- or fifth-period class meets directly over the school cafeteria with all of its clatter and wafting aromas, or who, because of overcrowding, has been assigned to teach a literature class directly beside the band room.

Sometimes we have no real way of controlling the noise or the smells around us, and we have to adjust to them. At other times, however, we can deal understandingly and tactfully with a situation that a colleague is willing and able to ameliorate as soon as he or she knows the problem exists. Before making a fuss, though, it is probably best to ask yourself if the problem you are forced to deal with is likely to be a one-time or a continuing problem.

Exercise 5.2

1. Sometimes teachers feel terribly strained and aren't sure why. The basic reasons may have something to do with how they deal with noise of various sorts. On a scale of 1 (this kind of noise doesn't bother me) to 6 (this kind of noise drives me up the wall), rank your reactions to the following noises:

   - A loud radio late at night in the apartment below you
   - Loud music on a tape deck in a closed automobile
   - A jackhammer on a street outside your window
   - A power lawn mower directly beneath your window
   - A dripping faucet in the bathroom off your bedroom
   - Loud shouting at a ball game
   - A baby screaming in anger
   - Loud organ music in a church or auditorium

- Students whispering in the back of the classroom
- Students talking when you are trying to talk
- Students all calling out at the same time in class
- One person about two feet away talking loudly
- The rumble of a jet plane taking off
- Loud noises in the classroom beside yours

2. In one paragraph using the data recorded above, try to assess whether your tolerance for noise is high or low.

CASE STUDY 5.3
One Teacher's Noise Disturbs Another's Class

Some kinds of noise bother Betty J., who has taught in the third and fourth grades at Cynthia Hughes Elementary School for the last five years. Betty loves a party and can be the life of any gathering, contributing as much to the noise as anyone else. It doesn't bother Betty to have all her students gather around her and talk all at the same time when they are excited about something they are working on.

But Betty suddenly becomes tense when noise comes from outside her immediate sphere. As a student she had one miserable semester in a college dormitory, unable to concentrate on her work because she always felt she was surrounded by other people's noise. She survived that semester only by going to her parents' home every weekend and doing most of her serious schoolwork there. The next semester she rented a room from a quiet widow and lived there for the rest of her college years.

Betty's classroom this year is beside Linda M.'s fifth-grade classroom, separated from it by a wall that, from Betty's standpoint, is too thin. Linda is probably the most dynamic teacher in the school. Everyone, including Betty, respects her for her energy and loves her for her warm personality. Betty and Linda have been friends from the day they met three years ago.

No friendship, however, is perfect, and Betty is discovering that Linda, whose room was not beside hers in past years, is a difficult neighbor. Betty is mature and reasonable. She realizes how low her noise threshold is, and she tries to assess the situation with that realization in mind and to view the problem as fairly and dispassionately as she can.

Wednesday afternoon was particularly taxing for Betty. Her students had written poetry, and she wanted to devote much of the afternoon to having them rehearse their poems and then read them into a tape recorder. On the same afternoon, Linda's students were playing a sentence structure game that involved a great deal of physical activity. The physical activity was accompanied by all kinds of yelling and cheering.

Betty's and Linda's classroom activities that day were both well conceived. Each made good pedagogical sense. Betty found the two activities incompatible, however, because every time one of her students was in the middle of reading a poem into the tape recorder, Linda's students would burst into the kind of enthusiastic cheering one would expect to hear at Churchill Downs on Derby Day. Linda, of course, was in no way bothered by the restrained activity that was going on in Betty's class.

On one level of response, Betty was furious. She could have knocked Linda down for letting her students produce so many decibels in their classroom activity. On a rational level, however, Betty knew that Linda was probably doing something that her students loved and from which they were learning something. Betty knew Linda well enough to assume that she never had her students participate in a gamelike activity that did not have some well-thought-out learning outcome.

As luck would have it, Betty's car was in the shop that day being repainted. She was going to take a taxicab home, but it occurred to her that she might ask Linda for a ride. Linda was glad to give Betty a lift. After they got into the car, Betty asked Linda, "What kind of day did you have?"

Linda was aglow. "Marvelous," she bubbled. "I taught my students prepositional phrases without ever using the term until the very end. They just played the game, working through it with prepositional phrases, and it wasn't until the very end that they realized they had been drilling in grammar for an hour and a half. I'm going to use the same technique tomorrow to teach punctuation. It should work like a charm."

Betty gulped, thinking to herself, "Oh, no, not another day of games!"

Linda continued, "What did your kids do today?"

"They wrote poems and then we rehearsed them and finally everyone tape-recorded an original poem. It was great. I'm going to play the tape again as soon as I get home," she said, holding up the cassette for Linda to see.

"Gee, I'd love to hear it," Linda volunteered. "Why don't you play it on the tape deck as we ride?"

"Sounds good," Betty answered as she pushed the cassette into the slot.

They listened for some minutes before Linda asked, "What's all that yelling in the background?"

Betty, seeing her opening, responded eagerly, "I think it's your lesson on prepositional phrases."

Linda looked dismayed as she said, "Oh, Betty honey, that's terrible. Why didn't you pound on my wall, or send a student over to tell me you were recording?"

Questions

1. How do you react to intrusions on your space? How do you react to various types of noise? Do instrusions of noise and space (proxemic intrusions) bother you in some contexts more than in others?

2. Do you think noise levels will get high in rooms that are under good teacher control? Does the case study give you cause to suspect that Linda's class was out of control? Discuss.

3. What solutions can you suggest to the problem the case study presents?

4. What measures can teachers take to minimize classroom noise or at least to minimize how far it carries?

5. Do you think Betty should have confronted Linda about the noise in her room when it was actually occurring? If not, should she have mentioned it immediately after that class had adjourned?

Possible Solutions

1. Betty took the noise coming from Linda's room as long as she could, but finally she decided it had to stop. She went to Linda's door and was about to knock when she saw through the window what was going on. It looked like such a productive activity that she could not bring herself to complain about it. She went back to her room and said to her students, "Come on, guys. We have to learn to live with a little noise sometimes. Let's just concentrate on our poems and get them recorded. The tape won't pick up much of the noise."

2. Betty became more and more tense as the noise from Linda's room continued. Her recording session was not going well because every time an enthusiastic howl came from next door, Betty's students would say things like, "Boy, it sounds like somebody scored a touchdown over there!" These comments got onto the tape. Finally, Betty admitted defeat and said to her class, "I'll tell you what. Let's copy our poems out on colored paper so I can post them around the

151

room tomorrow. Then, after they're posted around the room, we can read them into the cassette, and we can walk around and read everything that's up on the wall.'' Betty's students settle into this task, and she ponders the question of whether she should mention the noise to Linda.

3. Betty has her students continue their recording session, but she leaves her room for a minute to walk over to Linda's. She opens the door a crack and beckons. Linda comes over to her and steps into the hall. Betty says, ''Linda, honey, could you keep it down a little? My students are trying to read poetry into a cassette player, and the noise comes through the walls.'' Linda says, ''Gosh, Betty, I'm sorry. My students are so gung-ho for this grammar game I invented that it's gotten pretty loud. I'll do what I can.'' Linda goes back into her room and says, ''Look, guys, we have to keep the noise down a little—that doesn't mean you have to keep quiet. Just don't shout any more than you have to. If you're tempted to shout, just say to yourself, 'This is a grammar lesson.' That'll make you groan instead, right?'' The game goes on with a lower decibel count. Every time someone lets out a little yell, some other student says, ''Hey, man, did ya forget this is a grammar lesson?''

Consider This

Problems like this one are inevitable in most schools, but teachers usually come to some kind of accord among themselves so that learning can take place. None of the solutions suggested is really a long-term solution. Possible Solution 3, however, heightens Linda's awareness of the problem, and because she is a responsible teacher, she will try to minimize the noise her students make. She also thinks that if she is planning a noisy activity, she might let Betty know that she is, saying that she will do her best to keep the roof from blowing off. She hopes that by following this course, she might encourage Betty, who is more cautious than she, to try a few game activities herself.

In this situation, as long as Betty and Linda are in adjacent rooms between which the soundproofing is minimal, some problems will occur. Betty and Linda both seem capable of dealing with these problems on a mature level that will result in continued accord between them rather than discord.

Remember that noise as such is not a negative factor in some learning processes. Sometimes noise and enthusiasm go together just as learning and enthusiasm should. Teachers working in crowded schools, however, need to take into consideration the fact that other teachers are trying to teach at the same time they are and might be disturbed by their noise.

DEALING WITH ADMINISTRATORS

Administrators sometimes appear to act insensitively and unilaterally in situations that mean a great deal to teachers. We must always realize, however, that administrators have a broader view of the total school or district situation than most teachers have and that they may be acting quite reasonably on information that is not generally available to teachers. Sometimes they must also treat as confidential material that would help teachers to understand some of their decisions.

Before they let their exasperation control them, teachers should always tell themselves, "Principals want their schools to be as good as possible. I want my school to be as good as possible. We are working for the same outcomes, although perhaps in different ways."

Teachers must always remember that school administrators serve at the pleasure of their communities. If they have tenure, they have it as teachers, not as administrators. If they stray too far from what their community demands and is willing to tolerate educationally, they will soon be back in the classroom or on the job market. Many administrators are far more imaginative than the communities they serve. The best way they can serve such communities, and in the process perhaps lead them toward being more imaginative, is to provide a form of education that most of the citizens believe in. Collectively these citizens are the administrator's boss.

Over time, as school administrators win the confidence of their communities, they can begin to institute changes that will be for the ultimate benefit of the whole community. To try to bring about drastic changes overnight would be to resort to totalitarian tactics that would probably result in eventual dismissal.

This is not to suggest that no administrators are despots or tyrants. One can point to some who clearly are or have been. Such administrators can make life a misery for those who suffer under them. The only consolation to offer people who work in despotic or tyrannical environments is to point out that tyrants almost universally instigate their own undoing quite unwittingly. Teachers' patience, although sometimes tried almost to the breaking point, will usually be rewarded in the long term.

Consider whether the principal depicted in the case study below is acting prudently or tyrannically in dealing with a teacher's request.

CASE STUDY 5.4
Principal Vetoes Class Trip

It was a warm autumn day. Gilda L.'s fifth graders had been discussing how people make their living in ways that serve their communities. They had discussed the contributions that police officers, garbage collectors, and teachers make to the community. When someone mentioned firefighters, one student said, "Oh, they don't do much. There's hardly ever a fire, and mostly they just sit around the station house and play cards. They have a soft life."

Another student protested, "They do not. My uncle's a firefighter, and he works hard. Sometimes he even has to cook dinner for all the other firefighters. And if there's a fire before he gets it on the table, he just has to leave it, and he might get kilt in the fire."

This was the best controversy that Gilda had been able to get going among her students, and she wanted to capitalize on it. She asked her class, "How would you like to walk down to the fire station on Elm Street? It's a beautiful day, and it's only two blocks away. We can talk to some of the firefighters. I'm sure Ms. S. will let us go."

When the students responded with a chorus of approval, Gilda went across the hall to the principal's office to explain to Ms. S. what she wanted to do. Ms. S. listened patiently and then replied, "I am glad the youngsters have become so enthusiastic about firefighters, Gilda, but I cannot authorize your taking them down to the fire station. I have to say no. Why don't you drop by after school, and we will discuss my reasons?"

Gilda, crushed, returned to her class and had to tell her students that they could not go on the trip she had promised them. They were cross and resentful for the rest of the day.

Questions

1. Why do you think Ms. S. refused to allow Gilda to take her students outside the school for a school trip that could have demonstrably positive outcomes?

2. Had Ms. S. agreed to let Gilda take her students to the firehouse, how do you think the fire chief and the firefighters would have reacted to having twenty or so ten- and eleven-year-olds arrive unexpectedly for a tour of the facility?

3. Has Ms. S. damaged Gilda's standing as a teacher by placing her in the position of having to reneg on her promise to her students? What should Gilda tell her students when she informs them they will not be able to go on the trip?

4. What policy does your school have about school trips?

5. In your state, who is responsible if a student is injured or killed on a school trip? How do schools try to limit their liability in such situations?

Possible Solutions

1. When Gilda's students show a greater enthusiasm for this topic than they have for other things they have been doing, she tells them that she will try to arrange with the school librarian to get some books that tell more about what firefighters do. She asks whether any students would like to know more about other occupations, and soon she has a list of fourteen different jobs her students would like to know more about. She tells her students that if they would like her to, she will try to get a firefighter—perhaps even a fire chief—to come to their class and tell them about his job. She says that he might even be able to bring a fire truck with him so that they can go into the schoolyard and see a fire truck up close.

2. Gilda hates the thought of facing her students when she learns that she cannot take them to the firehouse. She goes back into a roomful of anticipatory students all yelling things like, "Can we go now?" "Do we have to wear our coats?" "Can we stay down there all day?" Gilda quiets them down and says, "I goofed, pals. I forgot a few things. Ms. S. is glad you're so excited about firefighters, but she thought we had better put our trip off." Groans from the students: "We never get to do nothin'." "Ms. S. is mean." "Why don't we go anyway? You're the teacher!" Gilda rescues the situation by asking, "Why do you think Ms. S. asked us to wait? Let's try to list as many reasons as we can. You tell me what you think, and I'll write it on the board." Hands go up all over the room.

3. When Gilda comes back from Ms. S.'s office, the situation is as described above. She finally gets her students quiet and says to them, "Ms. S. thought it would be more hospitable if we invited the fire chief and a firefighter or two to come down here with their fire truck and talk with you about their work. They might even let you sit in the fire truck. Ms. S. told me that she thinks the fire chief has never seen our school and she would like him to, so we are going to be the firefighters' hosts as soon as we can set up a time." One boy asks, "Can we ever go down to the firehouse?" Gilda says, "Why don't we be on our best behavior when the firefighters come to visit us? Maybe, if they know we would like to see the firehouse, they will ask us to come down there someday."

155

Consider This

Most principals, when their teachers make requests of them, would rather say yes than say no. Administrators prefer to appear benevolent, and saying yes is one way they have to assure themselves they will be perceived that way. They would be professionally remiss and legally culpable, however, if they acceded to requests that could place them, their teachers, or their students in danger of any sort or that could place any part of their physical plant in jeopardy. Principals are charged with assuring the safety and welfare of everyone in the school. If they are asked to do anything that might threaten the safety and welfare of anyone in the school, their automatic response has to be a resounding NO!

Because none of us likes to be denied something we have requested, the best way for teachers to make sure their requests are granted is to think carefully about what they are asking for. If the request involves taking students outside the school, they must consider the implications of doing so. They might ask themselves some of the following questions, for example, before they go to their principal to request permission to take students on a field trip:

- Might anyone conceivably be injured if my request is granted?
- Should I—or the school—have parental consent before we embark on the activity I have in mind?
- Does my principal know me well enough to be confident of my ability to handle the situation in question?
- Do I have absolute confidence in my ability to handle all aspects of the proposed activity?
- If the request is for something extraordinary and/or expensive, might some safer or less complicated activity accomplish comparable ends?
- Is what I am proposing likely to produce demonstrable and desirable educational outcomes?
- Do I have a backup plan if I am turned down?

Projects

1. Write a brief rationale for taking a group of your students on some trip away from school.

2. Write a memo to the parents or guardians of your students explaining to them the purpose of a trip that will take your students away from school.

CASE STUDY 5.5
Principal Assigns Extra Duty

Mike H. is a conscientious teacher who has been assigned to Technical High School for his first full-time teaching job. His field is social studies.

On Friday, Mike gave his second-period American history class an essay examination. He managed to read most of the papers and assign them grades over the weekend. He had five papers left to grade during first period on Monday, which was his free period. He wanted to distribute the graded papers to his second-period class and spend most of the period discussing them in detail with the class. Mike is convinced that examinations should be vital learning experiences for students, and he feels that it is incumbent on him to return papers as soon after an examination as possible and to discuss them as fully as possible with his students while the examination is still fresh in their minds.

On the Monday in question, Mike left his homeroom as soon as the bell rang and rushed to the social studies office, which he knew would be deserted during first period when all the other social studies teachers have classes. He had just sat down and taken out the remaining ungraded examinations when a secretary from the principal's office burst in and said, "Mr H., Mr. M. wants you to cover Ms. K.'s first-period French class until the substitute arrives. She should be here in about half an hour."

Mike has regularly sacrificed about two free periods a week to this sort of thing, but this day he was under pressure to finish grading his papers. To make the situation worse, Mike had not planned much for his second-period class other than going over the examination, so if he did not have all the papers ready to hand back, he would have to go into his own class and extemporize for fifty minutes. He said to the secretary, "I just can't do it today. I have to grade these examinations for next period."

The secretary replied, "I'm sorry, Mr. H., but those are Mr. M.'s orders. He has no one else to cover. You'll have to do it." She turned and walked away. Mike picked up his things and went dejectedly to room 213, where the situation was noisy and chaotic. Mike wondered whether he really wanted to be a teacher for the rest of his life.

Questions

1. Because it seems important that Mike get all of his examinations for his second-period class graded, can you suggest any way that

he might accomplish this and still accede to his principal's request?

2. Mike studied French in college but is not very confident in it. Do you think he should attempt to teach the class he has been asked to take? Why or why not?

3. If he decides not to teach the class, what might Mike ask the students in that class to do during the period he is with them?

4. Do you think Mike might have felt better about taking this assignment if the principal had come to him with the request rather than sending his secretary? Discuss.

5. Could Mike have outrightly refused to take this class, or could such a refusal be legitimate grounds for a charge of insubordination?

Possible Solutions

1. When Mike arrived in room 213, he found that the class was quite orderly and that Ms. K. had left detailed lesson plans in a folder, but that she also had a folder attached to her lesson plan folder that read, "Things To Do If You Don't Know French." Mike greeted the students and asked them if they had a French assignment they should be working on during this period. They did not. In Ms. K.'s second folder was a note that read, "Jennie W., Mel G., and Maria Y. all know where our boxes of objects are kept. Any one of these students can set the class up into groups—they are used to group work—in which one group member reaches into the box, feels an object, and, without looking at it, tries to describe it in French. The other students try to guess what the object is, giving their answers in French." Mike is extremely grateful for this note. He calls the names of the three designated students and asks whether they can take over the distribution of the boxes and the assignment of students into groups. They do, and the students stay busily engaged until three or four minutes before the bell rings, when one of the students Ms. K. has named calls time, and everyone gets busy straightening up the room. Mike has had time to read the remaining examinations for his second-period class and to record the grades.

2. Mike gets into room 213 five minutes after the period has officially begun. Chaos reigns, and Mike's heart sinks. He stands behind Ms. K.'s desk and says nothing at all. He just stares at the students, who begin to quiet down. Mike then says, "Ms. K. cannot be here today, but a substitute teacher will be arriving soon. I have work that I must have done by the end of this period, so I will ask that you work quietly on anything you have to do or that you read a magazine from the pile I see in the back of the room." One student asks, "Is it OK for me to go to the media center?" Mike sees no reason not to per-

mit this. When he does, everyone wants to be excused to the media center. Mike thinks it would be a mistake to let everyone go, although the prospect of doing that is tempting. Instead, he says, "I cannot let more than eight of you go, but I will write passes for the first eight to raise their hands." Hands shoot up, and Mike makes his choices. There is a little grumbling from the students who have to stay in the classroom as he writes a note to the director of the media center, but they calm down and work pretty well as soon as the other eight have left.

3. When Mike is asked to cover for the absent Ms. K., he tells the secretary for the second time that he just cannot do it. He asks, "Couldn't these students be sent to the media center or to the study hall for this period? If I don't get my examinations finished, I will be up a tree for second period." The secretary is sympathetic, but she says what she has to: "I know how you feel, but I have my orders, and I can't approve your sending the students to someplace outside the classroom. Why don't I do this? Mr. M. is talking with a parent right now. I can call him on the intercom and tell him your problem. You go to Ms. K.'s room. If Mr. M. goes along with your suggestion, I'll come down, and you can walk with the students to the media center or study hall and leave them there." Mike thanks her and says, "I'd be willing to sit with them in the study hall if Mr. M. wants me to. I could grade the rest of my exams there."

Consider This

Most public schools cannot function safely and effectively if groups of students are left unsupervised for extended periods. If students are left unsupervised and injuries or damages occur either to students or to property, the school and its chief administrator are generally liable. Under certain circumstances, then, nearly all principals must at some time or another assign extra duties to their teachers, and sometimes these duties have to be assigned with little forewarning.

Unfortunately, no matter how equally principals try to distribute this extra and—in most cases—unremunerated work, some teachers are drawn into it more regularly than others. Among those who are most vulnerable to it are teachers who do not have a teaching obligation during the first or second periods of the school day.

MAKING THE MOST OF SUPERVISORS

The title *supervisor* is perhaps an unfortunate one because it implies to most of us something judgmental—and a part of most supervisors'

159

jobs is to make judgments about people's performance. This, however, is not all they do. Some school districts, realizing the negative connotations of the term *supervisor*, have dropped the term altogether and have replaced it with a title such as *resource person* or *helping teacher*.

A popular jokes identifies three great lies:

1. I'll love you as much tomorrow as I do tonight.
2. The check is in the mail.
3. I'm your supervisor. I have come to help you.

The joke still brings a chuckle, but most teachers nowadays realize that supervisors (or whatever else they are called) are usually competent people who hold their jobs because they have been exceptionally good teachers and because they have special educational qualifications. Despite the cynicism of our joke, supervisors can help you and usually will go out of their way to do so.

How To Overcome One's Fear of Supervisors

Whether your supervisor is called a helping teacher or not, do not forget that those in a supervisory capacity are mature, seasoned people. Most of them have been exceptional teachers, and most of them have the sensitivity to remember what it was like to be a teacher and to feel an empathy with you as you struggle to find your way. Supervisors want to help, but they are not mind readers: they can help only if you let them know what your problems and insecurities are.

The best way for new teachers to feel secure in seeking such help is to ask whether it might be possible for the supervisor to meet with all new teachers under his/her jurisdiction at regular intervals, perhaps once a month until Christmas and once every two months thereafter. Just as reticent and retiring students gain self-confidence through group activities and become participants in such situations, so will a group of new teachers come to realize that they are not alone in their problems and come to gain security through this realization. No one is more isolated in our society than a teacher who teaches for all but an hour or so during a school day. Individual teachers may not know much about how anyone else teaches, not even the colleague next door; they do not always realize that, like themselves, half the teachers in the school may have to cope with significant discipline problems immediately before lunch period and with students falling asleep in class immediately after lunch period. Thinking that they alone are dealing with such problems may lead them to question their own worth and effectiveness as teachers. Knowing that others have the same problems helps them to view their own situations with objectivity and to bring a detachment that may help them to work out some solutions to their problems.

Among the things most supervisors can do to help you are the following:

- Suggest a variety of teaching methods to try with some of the classes you are teaching.
- Tell you about more effective textbooks or materials than the ones you are using.
- Help you to obtain materials better suited to your classes than the ones you are using.
- Suggest professional publications you might find useful.
- Tell you about media designed for class use.
- Suggest professional organizations you might join.
- Tell you about nearby conferences for teachers.
- Recommend to your principal that you be sent to conferences that would be of help to you.
- Arrange for you to swap classes with a teacher in another school for a day or a week.
- Arrange for you to have a day off to observe other teachers in your field.
- Tell you about summer programs available and about financial aid you might apply for to attend them.
- Listen to you when you let out your primal scream.
- Tell you what to do after you have let out your primal scream.

Exercise 5.3

1. What three services listed above would you most like to have right now from a supervisor?
2. If your school district does not have supervisors or similar personnel, who else in your school might help you with some of the items listed under things a supervisor can help you with?

If you ask specific help of a supervisor, remember that supervisors are busy people on tight, intricate schedules. Therefore, rather than telling your supervisor that it would be wonderful if you could find twenty-eight copies of Lewis Thomas's *The Lives of a Cell* (New York: Viking Press, 1974) to use with your biology class, put the request in writing. This is the businesslike way to handle this situation, and a written

161

request is much more likely to be acted on than an oral request. Your request should be brief and direct. It should contain the following items:

1. Teacher's name and school address
2. Designation of the class(es) with which the requested item(s) will be used
3. The number of items needed
4. The preferred date on which the item(s) should be available
5. The date on which the item(s) will be returned
6. Alternate dates that would work for you if the item(s) you want cannot be obtained on the preferred date
7. Alternate materials which might serve as substitutes if the first choice is not available.

Remember that supervisors are more likely to fill requests that they carry in their hands than requests that they carry in their heads. They are only human, and when their circuits become overloaded, they may forget things. Written requests obviate that problem.

Observation by a Supervisor

Most teachers will be observed periodically by their principals, by department chairpersons, and by district supervisors. It is understandable that they may be made somewhat apprehensive by such observations. However, the people who are doing the observing are well experienced and are observing you in the hope and expectation that they can help you deal with the problems common to nearly every teacher. Most supervisors will schedule their supervisory visits in advance, at least to the extent of telling you on what day you may expect them. In fairness to them, try to arrange not to spend the whole class period on the stipulated day giving an examination or showing a movie.

CASE STUDY 5.6
Supervisor Arrives in Middle of Class

Ms. N. is the district supervisor in social studies. She has just completed her third supervisory visit to Blair B.'s classes. She arrived twenty minutes before the end of his first-period class and was there for the end of a discussion on Manifest Destiny which was followed by a reading assignment and study questions to be begun in the remaining ten minutes of the period. Blair circulated among the stu-

162

dents during these last ten minutes, helping them with their work and answering their questions. One student was asleep in the back of the class the whole time Ms. N. was in the room. When the reading assignment was made, two students went to a worktable in the rear of the room and began to play chess.

After Ms. N. observed Blair's second-period class, they went to the teachers' lounge during third period when Blair had no class to teach. After getting coffee, Ms. N. said, "Let's concentrate first on what I observed in your first-period class, Blair. Can you fill me in on what happened during the first part of the class? I am sorry, incidentally, that I could not be there when the class began, but just as I was heading into the building, I received a message to call my office, and I had to deal with something rather complicated there. I thought I had better catch what I could of first period because that is rather a mixed class that might be a little frustrating to teach."

"Yes," Blair answered. "I am glad you got to see some of that class. They do put a gray hair on my head now and then." He then sketched in for Ms. N. two activities the class had done before her arrival: group work on Civil War projects and review of vocabulary words which might give them trouble in their reading. "Then," said Blair, "we began on the discussion of Manifest Destiny, which we were about halfway into when you arrived. I hope you did not mind that I failed to introduce you, but the kids were enough interested in the discussion that they didn't notice your appearance, so I decided just to let them continue."

"Yes, they *were* wrapped up in the discussion. I think you were wise to let them go on with it. I think they are getting used to having observers by this time."

"Yes. The principal and an associate superintendent have been in, as well as some students from the university. I guess by December they begin to think visitors are a natural part of things." Blair continued, "You may have wondered about the two students who did not begin on their assignment and went to the back of the room to play chess."

Ms. N. allowed that she was a little curious about this, and Blair explained, "They are two kids who should be in a much faster section. They landed with this group because of scheduling problems. They are so far ahead in everything that I have been allowing them to take advanced tests on the material, and I allow them certain privileges like playing chess."

"How do the other students feel about that?" Ms. N. queried.

"It was their idea. We did it town-meeting style one day, and they decided that students who wanted to work harder and get ahead

163

should be given certain privileges like playing chess, reading magazines, going to the library during the last fifteen minutes of class, or working on projects."

"Well, that sounds fair enough," said Ms. N., "as long as all the students in class know that they qualify for such privileges if they meet the requirements." She paused momentarily and then asked, rather hesitantly, "What about the student who was sleeping?"

"That is Donald," Blair told her. "He had a severe drinking problem, and the counselors have been working with the coach and me to see what we can do for him. He has made good headway—he says he hasn't had a beer in six weeks. He has a Christmas job in the stockroom of Perry's and puts in eight to ten hours a night. He comes from a poor family, and he needs the job if he is going to have clothes to wear. I have encouraged him to come to school, even if he has to sleep, because I don't want him to end up dropping out, which could happen. If he sleeps, I let him sleep. After Christmas, when he is under less pressure, I will work with him individually and make sure he is doing all right. Surprisingly, he is keeping up pretty well with his reading; he just runs out of steam by nine in the morning, having worked until eight, so he dozes off in class."

Questions

1. Does it bother you to have someone come into your class after it has begun? If so, try to think of three or four reasons that might give an observer no choice except to arrive late.

2. Did Blair show good judgment in not introducing Ms. N. to his first-period class or in any other way calling attention to her presence?

3. How do you feel about giving special privileges to students who are ahead in their work and who have completed it at a high level of achievement? Is it better for an activity like this to grow out of a suggestion from the class than to be suggested by the teacher?

4. How would you deal with a situation such as Donald's?

5. Do you think a teachers' lounge is the best place to have a conference with someone who has observed your class and wants to talk with you about the observation? Look around your school and try to identify four or five places that might be suitable for conferences of this sort.

Possibilities To Consider

1. Ms. N. enters the classroom and, nodding to the teacher, sits in the back just behind Donald, the student who is sleeping. She notices

him and wonders if Blair sees him. Finally, she puts her hand on Donald's shoulder and shakes him. Donald wakens, and Ms. N. says, "You'd better pay attention, young man. Take out your notebook, and pay attention to what's going on." Donald says, "I always sleep in here. I have a deal with Mr. B." Ms. N. is shocked and says to Blair, who is helping students with their project, "Mr. B., I need to talk with you. Can you step out into the hall?" Blair leaves his students and steps into the hall with Ms. N., who immediately says, "Were you not aware that one of your students was sleeping?" Blair responds, "Yes, I know Donald was sleeping. I let him sleep. I'll tell you about it after class, but I have to get back now and help those students figure out what reference books they need for their project." Ms. N. is far from pleased.

2. Upon entering Blair's room, Ms. N. notices the student who is sleeping. She makes a note to ask Blair about this in their conference. When she sees two students go to the back of the room and begin to play chess, however, this is too much for her. She walks over to where they are playing and just stands there looking at them. Finally, one of them asks, "Do you enjoy chess?" Ms. N. responds haughtily, "Not when I'm working!" She continues, "And you shouldn't either. I am sure you have something better to do during class than play games." The second student says, "But we've finished our work. Mr. B. always lets us play a game of chess when we're caught up on our work." Ms. N. sniffs but says nothing. Just then Blair comes over, and both boys talk at once: "It's OK for us to play chess when we're through with our assignment, isn't it, Mr. B.? Tell her, Mr. B. It's OK, isn't it?" Blair puts his hand on the shoulder of one of the boys and says, "Sure, it's OK. I'll explain it to our visitor."

3. Ms. N. comes into the room and is impressed by the fact that the atmosphere is free and informal but that nearly everyone seems to be engaged in some kind of work. She notices the sleeping student, but doesn't think much about him. He doesn't seem to be bothering anyone, and Blair doesn't seem distressed that he is sleeping. Blair catches Ms. N.'s eye and nods to her. She nods back, and he goes on working with a group that is intent on something. Other groups are working independently. All at once, a girl from one of the groups comes to Ms. N. and says, "My name is Nikki. Would you like to sit with our group?" Ms. N. replies, "Would you really like me to?" A chorus of students says, "Yes." Ms. N. joins the group, and before many minutes have passed, she is helping them to classify a group of famous Americans by the nature of their most outstanding contributions to society. She is having so much fun that she can hardly believe the hour is over when the bell rings.

Consider This

Regardless of what title one holds, people who observe in other teachers' classes must remember the following:

- This is not my class; I am a visitor and must behave like one.
- I cannot always judge with complete accuracy what is happening in a class I visit because I don't know what has preceded it.
- It is not my position to discipline another teacher's students no matter how strongly I am tempted to do so.
- I should not take offense at not being introduced, especially if introducing me would interrupt what is going on.
- I should offer no negative criticism about a class I have observed in the presence of anyone except the teacher whose class it is.
- If a teacher is having monumental problems, I must try to assess what the major problems and their causes are and to discuss these problems in our conference, rather than trying to discuss every problem I have noted.
- Before I mention any problem, I should try to have some solution to suggest to the teacher, although before I suggest anything, I should ask the teacher how he or she thinks the problem might be dealt with.

The best supervisors use more interrogatives than imperatives in the conference that follows their observations. If a teacher thinks the observer is not asking enough questions, it sometimes is well to volunteer answers to hypothetical questions. A typical scenario might be something like the following:

Teacher: You probably wondered why I cut short the discussion of suicide in that novel.

Supervisor: I did notice sort of an abrupt shift, but you made a nice recovery when you introduced the question about minor characters in the book.

Teacher: Thanks. I thought it was not the time to talk about suicide because the brother of one of the students in that class attempted suicide two nights ago, and the boy is terribly upset about it.

Supervisor: That was pretty perceptive of you. Thanks for explaining it to me.

Opinions are divided about whether an observer should participate in group work. If the teacher is engaged with one group and another group spontaneously asks a visitor in the classroom to join it or to help it with something, the visitor would sometimes seem ungracious to decline. In the conference, however, the visitor should say something like, "I hope you didn't mind my joining that group. They seemed to want me to work with them, and it really is fun for me to get back to working with students like that again. I really miss the classroom."

CASE STUDY 5.7
Teacher Seeks Supervisor's Help

Lois D. is in her first month of full-time teaching. Her assignment is to the third grade at William G. Simms Elementary School. She was a last-minute appointee and missed the orientation days for teachers late in August. She has had trouble getting organized and finally asked that the supervisor, Ms. G., come to observe her class and help her with her planning.

Ms. G. appeared in Lois's class at about ten in the morning, just when the students were going out for their milk break. Lois asked another teacher to supervise them so that she could greet Ms. G., telling her, "I am really glad you could come to see me today. I need help. As soon as the students return from their break, we will do some spelling drill, and then we will have a spelling bee. The students always seem to like this and to behave well during it. I saved the spelling bee until you got here so that you could see how well the students really can do."

At that point the students began to return to the room. One of them, Sheila, a usually quiet and retiring girl of eight, said, "Ms. D., I need to ask you something."

Lois went to a corner of the room with her where Sheila asked in a very loud whisper, audible to all, "Who is that old lady? Is she your mama?"

Lois replied, quite loudly, "Sheila, that is a terrible thing to say! I want you to apologize to Ms. G. right now. Do you understand? You apologize to her."

Sheila looked surprised and began to cry.

Questions

1. Why do you think Lois invited Ms. G. to pay a visit to her class? What did she want from Ms. G.?
2. Did Lois show good judgment in having another teacher take

167

her students for their milk break? How else might she have handled the situation?

3. Lois's last name is *Dornblazer*, which her students find hard to say. Do you think she should insist that they use that name in addressing her, or is "Ms. D." a reasonable alternative? Would "Lois" be a better choice?

4. Did Sheila mean to be rude to Ms. G.? How would you have dealt with that situation? How do you think Ms. G. viewed Sheila's overheard whisper?

5. Do you think Lois will be receptive to Ms. G.'s suggestions? Is she comfortable with Ms. G.'s presence? How can you tell?

Possibilities To Consider

1. When Ms. G. arrives, Lois is about to take her students to their milk break. These milk breaks have been a problem for Lois, largely because one boy who is repeating third grade and is bigger than the other children bullies his classmates and often a fight erupts. He fights with boys and girls alike, and if students have brought cookies or other snacks from home, he tries to take them for himself. Lois says to Ms. G., "Boy, am I glad you arrived right now when I really need you. My mornings go pretty well right up to milk break; then things begin to fall apart because of one boy. You'll see what he does." Ms. G. says, "I think I've spotted him already. Is he the big boy over there?" Lois tells her he is. Ms. G. says, "That kind of situation isn't easy to deal with. I've had a little experience with it. Maybe between us we can work something out."

2. After Ms. G. arrives, Lois takes her students to milk break. She asks Ms. G. whether she would prefer to come with them or remain in the room and look over the lesson plans Lois has generated. Ms. G. wants to accompany Lois because she wants to see her working with her students in a less formal setting than the classroom. As they walk along, Lois says, "I hope you don't mind, but I have saved the one activity I have trouble with until you got here. My kids do very well when I am up front teaching them things. They're great when we have a spelling bee or something gamelike. But I need to have them do group work, and whenever they get about five minutes into it, they begin to get silly and everything falls apart." Ms. G. inquires, "Have you tried having your group work at various times of the day to see whether that affects it?" Lois says, "Yes, I thought that might be the problem, so I've tried it the first thing in the morning, later in the morning, before lunch, after lunch, and right at the end of school. No

168

matter when I have it, things seem to get out of hand." Mrs. G. says, "I'm glad you saved your problem situation for me to see. Most teachers want me to see their successes, and it's not those they need help with, is it?"

3. The situation progresses as described in the case study up to the point that Sheila whispers to Lois her question about Ms. G. Lois would have preferred not to have this happen, but she takes it in stride, as she presumes Ms. G. can. She answers Sheila's question because it is a sincere, honest (if indiscreet) question. She merely says, "Heavens no, Sheila honey. My mother's a lot older than Ms. G." Sheila looks wide-eyed and says, "She is?" Ms. G. laughs and says to Sheila, "I'm Ms. D.'s friend, Ms. G. Ms. D. told me what a good group of students she has, and I wanted to meet all of you," and with that she extends her hand to shake hands with Sheila. In her conference with Lois afterward, Ms. G. says, "That kind of thing happens all the time; anyone over thirty looks ancient to students in the lower grades. A second grader last week told me that his mother is very old. I asked how old, and he said, 'Twenty-seven!' " Lois and Ms. G. have a good laugh at that.

Consider This

This case study poses two basic questions: (1) What should supervisors see when they visit? (2) How should a teacher deal with the innocent frankness of children when they say something embarrassing? Teachers need to remember that supervisors were once teachers—and usually exceptionally good ones. They have been through the same kinds of problems you probably have. They don't expect to walk through your door and see perfection. They know that you can be an outstanding teacher who has real problems that you need help with.

If you as a teacher want your supervisor to see only the best your students can do, then you really want the supervisor to praise rather than help you. In fact, if Ms. G. found fault with something Lois had done, Lois might have broken into tears of anxiety. Lois appears to be a perfectionist. That is the reason that Sheila's innocent question upsets her and makes her fly into a tirade that genuinely bewilders the unwitting student.

If teachers want to make the most effective use of their supervisors, they will seek help with their problems. They may also want to share some of their triumphs with them—we are all human, and we love praise. But teachers who remember that their problems are not necessarily signs of weakness and will not be regarded as such by people who have broad school experience will use supervisors to the best advantage and will be stronger teachers as a result. In an ideal situation, teachers and supervisors work in tandem to solve problems that interfere with effective teaching.

RELATIONSHIPS WITH SCHOOL STAFF

The effective and efficient running of any school depends largely on the nonteaching members of the school staff. These include school bus drivers, cafeteria workers, custodial staff, librarians and/or media specialists, school nurses, school secretaries, and a host of other people who serve the school in various ways.

School Bus Drivers

Your contact with school bus drivers may be limited, although most teachers who have bus duty one or two days a month at least become aware of some of the complexities of running the sort of transportation system many school districts operate.

Discipline may sometimes become a problem on school buses. Disciplinary problems on buses can do a great deal to reduce the safety with which the buses run. Drivers who must pay attention to the road cannot do so if six students are having a fight in the back of the bus. If you, as a teacher, work constantly to make your students feel the necessity to be responsible for their own actions, you will bring them closer to the point of being able to behave in all situations. If you become aware of problems involving discipline on school buses in which your students ride, it is wholly appropriate to take time out to discuss the implications of misbehavior in this sort of situation. The school bus drivers may not know what you have done, but any noticeable improvement in student behavior on their buses will relieve them and make their driving safer.

School buses sometimes arrive at school late, particularly during severe weather. If you see that it is raining heavily or that a light snow has begun to fall, try to anticipate that some buses will be late and begin your day with a review or with some other material that is not crucial. If you have scheduled an examination for that period, see if you can shift it to another time. If buses arrive late, the office will inform you. In most cases, you should admit students on late buses to class without a written excuse, provided the main office has made an announcement that a given bus has arrived late.

170

If you note that one or two buses are more frequently late than the others, you may have to approach the school administration to see whether something can be done about the situation. Such buses usually have long runs and serve remote areas. Perhaps their schedule has to be extended if they are to get students to school on time. Repeated lateness can have an adverse effect on students in first-period classes, and you, as a teacher, must make sure that the administration is fully aware of any such problems.

You can assist school bus drivers by dismissing your classes punctually at the end of the day. Remember that students who ride school buses probably have no other way to get home. If you delay them so that they miss their buses, then getting them home becomes your ethical—and in some states, legal—responsibility.

Cafeteria Workers

The best service teachers can render those who run the food services in the school is to see that students arrive at the school cafeteria on time. Do not keep classes beyond the lunch bell. Hundreds, sometimes thousands, of students must be served in a short time, and late dismissal from classes puts an added burden on both students and cafeteria staff.

Students whose teachers (including their earliest teachers, their parents) have engendered in them respect for others will treat everyone, including cafeteria workers, with consideration. If you observe any of your students doing otherwise, talk with them about their behavior.

Just as you expect students to clean up their room toward the end of class, so should you encourage them to clean up their tables at the end of a meal. Under no circumstances should students be permitted to eat in your classes before meals because they will likely spoil their appetites by doing so. Cafeteria workers like to see students enjoy the meals they have worked to prepare and serve. You, as the teacher, can do a great deal to assure the cafeteria staff that their work is appreciated.

Custodial Staff

As a teacher, you will probably have met your school janitor, who is normally on duty during school hours. Other members of the custodial staff may work during the times when school is not in session; therefore, you may not see them. You can cooperate with these people in ways that can make the school a pleasanter environment to teach in and to learn in.

Get to know the people who keep your school clean and who make the repairs necessary for its smooth operation. Seek them out, even if

171

you have to go to the boiler room an hour before school begins some day. Let your custodians know who you are and which room(s) you occupy. Let them know that you appreciate their services, understand some of their problems, and have come to meet them because you want to work with them to make their jobs easier and the outcomes of their work more visible. Encourage them to let you know what special problems they may have with your room or section of the building. You might help to bring some problems under control.

The most obvious thing you can do to help the custodial staff is to make sure that any room in which you teach is left in good condition when you are through using it. Make sure that paper is picked up from the floor. Check toward the back of the room to see that students have not immortalized themselves by carving up desks.

If you are strict about not allowing eating or the chewing of gum in your room, the problem of finding chewing gum under seats and half-eaten sandwiches crammed into desks will be eliminated. You can set an example for students by straightening up your own desk toward the end of each period or at the end of the school day and by erasing the chalkboard or having a student erase it for you.

Be sure to keep an eye out for broken chairs and desks. These items are hazardous. Often they can be repaired effectively if they are not used after the initial damage has been discovered. Exert your control to keep students from mistreating school property, and set a good example by showing respect for such property yourself.

If you have animal cages, aquaria, or any kinds of displays in your room, try to confine these to an area that can be cleaned around easily. Be especially sure to clean animal cages and aquaria frequently. It is not the job of the custodial staff to do this sort of work.

Lavatories are particularly abused parts of many schools where students smoke, throw paper around, leave water running, and decorate the walls with graffiti. Most schools try to control access to lavatories during class periods and to encourage students to use these areas only during designated times of the day. You can help the custodial staff and the school administration by checking the lavatory nearest your room during times of heavy use, as well as occasionally at other times. It takes only a minute to do this, but if students know that frequent checks are routine, they will be less likely to misuse lavatory areas. Remember that smoking is illegal in most states for students of school age; it also makes the work of the custodial staff much more difficult. You, as a teacher, can work toward the elimination of this almost universal problem simply by checking restrooms frequently.

Finally, let your students get to know the people who keep the school clean. If you are having a career day, invite the custodial staff to come in and tell your students about their jobs. This will help students to see from a different viewpoint the hard work these people do and to think twice about making their tasks more difficult than they already are.

School Librarians and/or Media Specialists

School librarians are well-trained professionals whose duties include maintaining the school library and its collection, helping students and teachers find necessary materials, ordering new materials and cataloging them when they arrive, giving students instruction about how to use the library, and maintaining an atmosphere conducive to study. Many school libraries are designated *media centers, learning resource centers,* or *study centers.* Most librarians are also trained media specialists.

Some schools have more than one librarian or media specialist. Nearly all schools encourage students to be library aides during free periods, and these aides are fundamental to the satisfactory operation of any library.

Large schools may have extensive learning resource centers that offer diverse materials and study areas. Some portions of such learning resource centers may be set aside for quiet study, and in them absolute quiet will be maintained. Other areas may be arranged for group work and for the sort of study that involves quiet discussion among students. Where this is the case, absolute quiet must be maintained in the area set aside for quiet study. This means that anyone in the designated area, including teachers and administrators, will be expected to remain silent.

Librarians and media specialists can perform the following services for you:

- Come to your classes to talk with students about the general use of the library.
- Come to your classes to talk with students about a specific matter, such as a term paper, that will require a whole class to use the library or learning resource center.
- Check out to you a classroom library of books to be used for a given period of time in a classroom study or learning center.
- Work with students sent to the library or learning resource center to do research on a project.
- Locate materials you need.
- Order materials you need.
- Arrange for you to borrow films, filmstrips, slides, records, and other software.
- Arrange for you to borrow such hardware as you may require to use the software.

173

- Set up library displays relevant to special learning units you might be dealing with.

Remember, however, that librarians serve the whole school and have many demands upon them. They must have ample lead time if they are to order the materials and/or equipment you request. Meet your librarian and/or media specialist early in the school year, and find out how much lead time is required to obtain, for example, a film your school district owns. Find out also the possibility of securing films and other software your school district does not own. Often state libraries will lend these materials free of cost except for return postage. Because the competition to obtain popular items is great, it is essential that you always plan ahead.

Let your librarian know when your students are likely to use the library extensively and for what purpose. Give the librarian a course syllabus if you have one. Find out your school's policy for checking out in quantity books that might be used as a classroom library.

Remember that librarians are not babysitters. Do not send students to the library just because you have run out of things for them to do in your room. If a day or more of library study is appropriate for your class, make prior arrangements with the librarian, take your students to the library at the beginning of the period, and stay with them throughout the period they are there, making every effort to control them and to keep them from disturbing other people. If, on the other hand, you are planning to give your class twenty minutes at the end of the period to do quiet work at their desks and you know that five or six responsible students would profit from spending that time in the library, explain the situation to your librarian and ask whether they might come in toward the end of the period. Make sure that such students have hall passes and that they do not dawdle en route to the library. Also make sure that they know what their responsibilities are within the library.

If you borrow films and/or equipment from the media center, be sure to return them promptly and in good condition. If a film has broken or if a piece of equipment is not working properly, report this problem in writing to the media specialist when you return the item. Also, you might wish to evaluate in writing an item that has gone over particularly well with your students or one that you considered a waste of time. Librarians like to be informed so that they can make suggestions to other teachers about effective materials for use with classes.

Your librarian or media specialist can be your staunchest ally in the school setting, but you must be considerate if you are to benefit from this alliance. You must be sufficiently well organized to let librarians know how best to serve you and your students.

School Nurses

Many schools have full-time nurses. If your school does not have a regular nurse, some person who has been trained in first aid is probably designated to be responsible in the event of sudden illness or injury. Find out who this person is. Know from your first day the location of the nurse's office and/or health room.

Nurses serve five basic functions in schools:

1. They attend to students and staff who are ill or injured.
2. They run routine examinations such as hearing and vision checks and checks for head lice and other such problems.
3. They maintain health records on students and supply teachers with necessary health information about their students.
4. They attempt to advise students and staff on health matters such as immunizations.
5. They work with health education teachers to inform students about such matters as AIDS and how to guard against getting it.

Remember that school nurses cannot prescribe and, in many states, cannot dispense even such simple drugs as aspirin. They cannot give teachers and staff routine shots except under the direction of a physician, usually during a mass immunization program. Do not embarrass school nurses by asking them to do things they are not empowered to do. They will either have to refuse you or have to violate an established rule of their job, so do not put them in the position of having to make that choice. If you unknowingly put them in such a position and they refuse to do what you ask, apologize for having asked, and do not hold the refusal against them.

School nurses usually identify for you any students in your classes who have chronic health problems that might cause difficulties. Epileptics can have seizures in class, although the likelihood of such occurrences has been dramatically reduced by the use of modern drugs. Diabetics can go into insulin shock from low blood sugar or into a coma from high blood sugar, and teachers have to know how to treat such emergencies should they occur. The school nurse can brief you on first aid if such crises occur and can also identify for you any students who may fall victim to other frightening manifestations of illness from previously diagnosed conditions.

Teachers should meet with the school nurse or with someone in the school who has had extensive training in first aid to discuss means of dealing on an emergency basis with situations relating to health and safety that might occur among students.

CASE STUDY 5.8
Student Diagnosed As Having AIDS

Mildred C. teaches fifth-grade English, social studies, and mathematics at the J. D. Daubs Middle School in a conservative northwestern community near Seattle. Her students are typical eleven- and twelve-year-olds going on twenty-five, but they all get along pretty well with Mildred and with each other.

One rainy November afternoon Mildred's principal asks to see her in his office after school. He begins the meeting by saying, "Millie, you probably noticed that Joanne W. has been away from class for the past ten days."

Mildred responds, "Yes. I tried to get her mother on the phone, but there was no answer. I hope it doesn't have anything to do with the surgery she had over the summer. She has seemed tired the last couple of weeks, and she has been bothered by some sort of skin rash."

"I am afraid, Millie, that you have spotted some early symptoms. Joanne's parents have just called from Seattle to tell me that a unit of blood Joanne was transfused with during her surgery was tainted."

"Tainted?" Mildred inquires, fearing the worst. "Tainted with what?"

"The AIDS virus," the principal responds sadly. "Joanne is still asymptomatic and might stay that way for some time. She is beginning AZT treatment that can offer a modicum of hope, but it means that she will be getting up every four hours all through the night to take her medication. She may tire easily and may even doze in class. That goes with the territory in cases like this. Right now all Joanne wants is to return to school and be treated like a normal human being."

Mildred is devastated. "Poor Joanne," she moans. Then she thinks of another question: "Will the other students know she's carrying the virus?"

"Yes," the principal responds. "I talked that out with her parents. We live in a small town, and no secret stays a secret for long. We decided that it's best to let it be known that Joanne has this problem."

"Do you think it will cause hysteria?" Mildred asks.

"It could," the principal says. "Here is our plan for now. Joanne will not return to school until your students and their parents have been told about the situation. We are going to call a meeting at seven o'clock tomorrow night. You and I and Ms. G. [the school nurse] need to plan this well. Ms. G. is waiting in her office now to talk with us."

When they get to the nurse's office, Ms. G. first shows Mildred and the principal pamphlets that explain AIDS. She has gotten special delivery on a thousand of them from the State Department of Public Health to meet this emergency. She says, "We will have two of these for everyone who comes to the meeting. We have to let people know first of all that AIDS cannot be contracted through the kind of casual contact students have with each other in classrooms. We also need to let them know that Joanne is at risk from infection because her immune system has been weakened. That means that if any of the students in your class are ill with a cold or with anything else infectious, they must be kept out of school. You will have to keep a sharp eye out for anyone who is sneezing or coughing. You will also have to be sure that there is no rough-housing with Joanne. A cut or scrape can result in infection if her blood gets on anyone else's cut."

"Do you think it would be best for me to read this pamphlet," Mildred asks, "and then introduce my students to it rather than have them learn about this situation at the meeting?"

"That's something we have to think through," says Ms. G. "If we decide to do it that way, I will come to your room and will be glad to stay there to answer questions throughout the discussion."

Questions

1. In this situation, would you prefer to discuss the matter with your students, or would you prefer to have someone else give them the initial information about AIDS and about their classmate? If you decide to talk with your students yourself, would you like to have the school nurse or anyone else present for your discussion?

2. What kinds of questions would you anticipate from your students in the course of or after a presentation of this sort?

3. Aside from questions, would you anticipate other reactions you might have to deal with in this instance?

4. On Joanne's first day back in your class, should you call attention to her presence by saying something like, "We are glad to have Joanne back with us and hope she is feeling better," or should you not call attention to her return?

5. One of the worst things that could happen to Joanne would be to have other students taunt her. What can you do before her return to limit the possibility of taunting?

Possibilities To Consider

1. On hearing about Joanne's illness, Mildred panics. She says to her principal, "I just don't think Joanne should be permitted to return to school. Can't she be taught at home by the visiting teacher?" The

principal says that such an arrangement is possible, but that Joanne is still feeling well and that she wants and needs to return to school. Mildred says, "Well, I just don't think she and her parents are the ones to make a decision that can put us all in danger. I have my own children to think about. And what happens if a fight breaks out in my class or something?"

2. On hearing the news, Mildred bursts into tears, sobbing, "Poor Joanne, the poor baby!" The principal finally succeeds in helping Mildred to regain her composure. Then he says, "Millie, I know that you have a big heart and that things like this affect you deeply. But remember that the best thing for Joanne is to help her go on as normally as possible. Her return to school should be as routine as the return of a student who has been out with a cold. If you let Joanne think you're upset, she's going to be upset." Mildred says, "I'll do my best, but every time I look at her, I know I'll think of all the problems that lie ahead." Her principal is worried because Mildred's emotional involvement, which her reaction seems to suggest, may very well be detrimental to Joanne's adjustment when she returns.

3. Mildred is pretty shrewd, and she is not wholly surprised at the news her principal has imparted to her about Joanne. In fact, long before Joanne had had her surgery, Mildred realized that, given the increasing number of AIDS cases that have been surfacing, she might one day have to confront this problem in her family, among her friends, or in her classroom. She had asked herself how she would want to be treated if she were ever diagnosed with this disease, and her answer was that she would want her life to go on as normally as it could despite her illness. As soon as she hears the news and knows that it is going to be made public, she tells her principal, "It's a heavy burden for Joanne and her parents to bear, but I think we have to make sure that Joanne has as normal a school experience as we can give her. Her classmates have to know, I agree, but once that is behind us, we have to look ahead and get Joanne involved in everything the other kids are involved in except for physical contact games where bleeding could be a danger." Mildred's principal breathes a sigh of relief and says, "Joanne is lucky in one way." "She is ?" Mildred asks. "Yes, " the principal responds, "she has you as her teacher, and you are going to help her immeasurably because you won't get overly sentimental." Mildred answers, "Well, my tears won't do Joanne's immune system any good, will they?"

Consider This

AIDS is the worst infectious disease widespread in the United States today. The bright sides of the situation are that (1) the disease is not easily communicated from one person to another, and (2) it has received so much publicity that strenuous efforts have been mounted to find a reliable way to treat the disease and a reliable vaccine to prevent it. It is just a matter of time before these efforts yield results.

People carrying the AIDS virus may remain asymptomatic for a time. They may become symptomatic and then go into remission. Young people suffering from this or any other life-threatening disease want to get on with their lives. Teachers need to help them do so. According to all the existing research and scientific information available, an AIDS victim in a typical classroom setting does not endanger the lives of other students, although the other students must know about any student who is known to carry the virus so that if any bleeding takes place—a nosebleed or bleeding from a cut or scrape—they will take precautions not to get the blood on them.

Whether or not a teacher has students in class who have been diagnosed as having the disease, all teachers, merely as the informed citizens they are expected to be, should learn as much about AIDS as they can. The best information is available free in publications from the U.S. Surgeon General's Office in Washington, D.C., or from your local department of public health. Teachers who are forewarned about the disease will be forearmed to deal with it if any of their students are diagnosed. They will also be in the best position to counsel students about ways to protect themselves from contracting this deadly virus.

School Secretaries

School secretaries are usually overworked. They prepare the official reports public schools are required to submit regularly. They meet the public, often when members of that public are at a peak of emotion—the angry parent who comes charging into the office, for example. They are the liaison between busy administrators and those who want to get through to them, including teachers. They answer telephone calls, often at the busiest time of the day. Sometimes they are in charge of dispensing supplies and of preparing teachers' materials on mimeograph or duplicating machines. They sometimes must deal with disruptive students whom desperate teachers send to the office to see a vice-principal. In short, they are on the firing line for eight hours a day receiving the kinds of barrages which would demolish the weak. Among school secretaries, the strong survive.

You can get along with and substantially assist school secretaries by

- Trying to understand the pressures they work under.
- Putting your requests for materials, supplies, appointments, and the like in writing.
- Getting your reports in on time.
- Thanking and praising them when they do something for you.
- Not sending students to the office without a note clearly indicating why they are there.
- Not making requests of them during their peak periods, which often come at the beginning and at the end of the school day.
- Informing them if you are expecting visitors, such as guest speakers or resource people, on a given day and providing them, in writing, with the names of such people.
- Smiling at them and greeting them warmly when you come into the school office, but respecting the fact that they have work to do and cannot have inconsequential conversation with each of the hundreds of people who pass through the school office every day.
- Treating them as the professionals that they are.

RELATIONSHIPS WITH VISITING CONSULTANTS

Most school districts engage specialists from outside the district to work with their teachers and administrators on matters of particular concern. Such consultants are sometimes in residence for extended periods of one week or more; however, they more often work with the district for one or two days, often conducting workshops on teacher workdays. Sometimes they offer in-service courses that might be conducted for two or three hours a day after school on five or six successive Tuesdays or Thursdays. Sometimes credit is offered to teachers when they attend such sessions.

Who Are the Consultants?

Most consultants are well-trained people with some particular expertise a school district is in need of. Some are professors from institutions of higher learning; some are from state departments of public instruction; some are from other school districts; yet others are independent consultants who have their own consulting firms. Most are well trained and experienced in their fields of expertise.

Attitudes Toward Consultants

Many teachers resent consultants and think that they cannot come to a school district for a short period and effectively solve the problems they were engaged to tackle. Such an attitude is understandable and is, in large degree, correct. Consultants are not brought into districts to solve problems, however; rather, they are brought in to help teachers and administrators in school districts work toward their own solutions. Consultants provide information on new techniques, research, and understandings. They assess situations, many of them similar to those with which they have dealt successfully before. They can point school districts in appropriate directions. They cannot deal single-handedly in a day or two with problems that have developed over a long time.

How To Profit Most from Consultants

Most consultants welcome input from teachers and administrators with whom they are dealing in workshop situations. Tell consultants of your specific educational concerns, and ask them to address those concerns. The best workshops are those in which everyone participates as fully as possible. Consultants work most effectively when the people they are working with are responsive and have a positive attitude. If a session with a consultant falls flat, it may be because local participants were unwilling to give all they might to make the session a success.

Remember it is not necessary for you to use every suggestion consultants make to benefit from their presence in a district. Listen critically to their suggestions, always considering what might work and what might not work in your immediate situation. You know your students, your school, and your community. Consultants know their fields. You, as a teacher, need to weigh what they say as fairly as possible and try to implement suggestions that stand a good chance of succeeding with your students.

Consultants can usually provide useful suggestions for resource materials and for additional reading in the fields of their expertise. Treasure these suggestions. Also, many consultants express a willingness to write to teachers who send them specific questions after a workshop has been held. If a consultant is generous enough to offer this kind of assistance, teachers would be wise, indeed, to avail themselves of such an opportunity.

6. WHY DIDN'T SOMEBODY WARN ME?

People who train teachers do their best to equip their students to cope with the range of experiences they are likely to encounter in their internships as well as in their teaching careers. Professors of general methods or special methods courses routinely meet with their interns at the end of the teaching internship. Usually they ask the returning interns to complete evaluations of the education courses they have taken before their actual teaching experiences.

Student responses to these follow-up questionnaires are often "figure-8" responses; that is, the responses cluster almost equally around two opposing extremes. On the one hand, interns who have had a wonderful internship in a school that seemed custom-made for someone with their approaches to teaching and with their educational philosophies often respond to the part of the questionnaire reserved for subjective comments by saying something like, "Why did you make us think things would be so bad before we went out to teach? The things you told us scared me to death, and I found that none of the problems we talked about ever surfaced."

In the other camp is an almost equal number of interns who took the same courses and who survived their internships with difficulty. Most of them write narrative comments that say something like, "My courses never prepared me for what schools and teaching are really like. My professors never told me about the kinds of discipline problems I encountered every day. And these problems were not just because I was a new teacher. Every teacher in the school had them."

It is impossible for teacher educators to anticipate how any given internship might turn out. Cooperating teachers who have had five previous interns, all of whom loved them and regularly keep in touch with them now that the internship is over, might be just the wrong people for their sixth intern. Some students can cope easily and maturely with discipline problems, whereas some others, who might in a different setting develop into exceptionally good teachers, are completely defeated by such problems, and they go from bad to worse during the internship.

No matter how strenuous an effort the director of teaching internships makes to put all the interns into their optimal settings, some internships do not work out well, and others work out extraordinarily well. A minimal performance in an internship is not necessarily an accurate predictor of how people will perform during their teaching careers. Most people gravitate eventually to settings in which they can perform at their highest capacities.

DEALING WITH EXTREME SITUATIONS

This chapter deals with some extreme and highly threatening situations. You may never encounter any of them in a whole lifetime of teaching. Still, each situation depicted in these case studies has actually happened, although some of the details given may, in order to make specific points, deviate slightly from the situations as they actually occurred. The author presents them to you because he is convinced that you will deal with any situation more effectively if you have given some advanced thought to similar occurrences than you would if the problem suddenly cropped up and you found yourself so startled or shocked by it that you could not collect your wits.

Some of the case studies are not pleasant to read. Teachers cannot ignore the realities that may face them in even the most remote, rural schools. The drug culture, the new sexual openness, social and geographic mobility, television, and all manner of other social and economic forces have conspired to create situations that have broad implications for all teachers. Each case study that follows represents an extreme, isolated case. Nevertheless, classroom teachers not unlike you have had to deal with each of them in one way or another.

CASE STUDY 6.1
Armed Parent Enters Classroom

Tamira P. considers herself fortunate. She teaches third grade at Lillian Helms Elementary School in an affluent residential community. The parents of most of her students are professionals, many of them involved in the computer industry. The community supports its schools well and has not rejected a bond issue for education in the past twenty-seven years. The parents of children who have difficulty with their studies usually hire tutors for them. Most of the children in the district are graduated from high school and continue to college.

One Tuesday afternoon, Tamira's students have finished doing mathematics problems on the chalkboard and are moving the furniture into a circle for their daily "read-in." All at once, the classroom door flies open, and the disheveled father of Linda M., one of Tamira's students, charges through it. Tamira knows Mr. M. One look at him is all it takes for her to realize he is not himself. She has heard rumors for months that he and his wife are on the brink of divorce, and only last week Linda said to her, "Ms. P., my daddy moved out of our house. He's going to live with his friend for a while. I sure do miss him."

183

Tamira says, "Hello, Mr. M. We are just going into our reading circle. Would you like to join us?"

Mr. M. snarls, "No. I can't stay. I've just come to get Linda. We're going on a trip for a few days."

Tamira answers, "I'm afraid I have orders not to release any of my students without clearance from the office. Have you seen Dr. F. [the principal] yet? He issues permits for early dismissals."

Mr. M. whips out a revolver and says, "This is my permit. I'm taking her. C'mon, Linda. We're getting out of here."

Several children scream, and two dive under a desk. Linda begins to cry. She sobs, "No, Daddy, I don't want to go away. Mommy needs me. I want Mommy."

Mr. M. moves toward Linda, still brandishing his gun. He grabs her and begins to pull her from the room. Tamira gets Linda's other arm and tries to pull her from her father's grip.

Questions

1. No school is totally secure from outside intrusion, although most schools require visitors to report first to the main office. What is your school's policy about this matter? If you, as a teacher, see a stranger walking through the halls or loitering on the school grounds, what should you do?

2. Is there any way teachers can prepare their students for an unexpected intrusion like the one in the case study? If so, what specifically can they do?

3. If a teacher in a class full of students is faced with the problem of dealing with an armed intruder, tell sequentially what he or she has to do from the time the intruder pulls the gun up to the five minutes after the intruder has left.

4. Tamira knew a little bit about Mr. M.'s situation, but teachers do not always know what is going on in their students' lives and homes. If a parent comes to your classroom and wants to take his or her child away, what should you do? Suppose the parent turns hostile or threatening, as Mr. M. did?

5. Did Tamira act wisely in trying to save Linda from this threatened abduction? Why or why not? Might she have tried to rescue her in a more effective way?

Possible Solutions

1. As soon as Mr. M. enters the room and Tamira realizes he is not acting in a wholly rational manner, she says, "How nice to see you, Mr. M. I had been wanting to talk with you about something.

184

Let's step out into the hall." Mr. M. looks rather surprised and asks, "What do you want to talk with me about?" Tamira says, "It's rather private. Let's step outside." She takes Mr. M.'s arm and leads him to the door. As they step into the hall, she closes the door, tripping the lock as she does, thereby locking herself out of the room.

2. The scenario is the same as in the case study except that when Mr. M. pulls his revolver, Tamira screams, "Get under your desks!" and she crouches behind hers. Mr. M. grabs Linda and drags her screaming from the classroom. As soon as he is out of sight, Tamira uses her intercom to call the main office, although Linda's screams have already attracted attention and the halls are filling with curious teachers and students.

3. When Mr. M. pulls his revolver, Tamira positions herself between him and his daughter. He advances toward her and she shouts, "You'll have to shoot me before you take Linda from this room." At that she grabs Linda and holds the girl in back of her. Mr. M. continues to advance and grabs Linda's arm, waving his revolver as he does so. He finally pulls her loose and bolts out the door, dragging Linda after him. Tamira rushes to her intercom and calls the main office. She makes a silent vow to be sure to lock her classroom door every day from now on so that no one can enter her room without being let in. She thinks it is best to minimize what has happened and goes on teaching the lesson she was beginning when Mr. M. arrived, although some of her students are crying.

4. As soon as Tamira realizes the situation, she bolts from her classroom, screaming to her students as she leaves, "Get under your desks!" She runs to the main office, screaming loudly all the way there to attract attention. Hearing her, other teachers rush into the hall. In the main office she shouts, "Call 911! There's a man in my room with a gun!" The chaos is intensified as students flock into the halls screaming. Mr. M. is rushing toward the exit dragging Linda by one arm. As soon as order is restored, Tamira returns to her roomful of badly shaken students, and she says, "What you have just seen is unfortunate and unusual. Let's talk about it now so we won't have nightmares about it." She then goes on to discuss what has happened and asks her students if they have any questions. All of them do.

Consider This

Domestic difficulties can lead parents to extreme behavior. Obviously, Tamira is not dealing with a rational person in this scenario, and there are no perfect solutions to situations that involve irrational people. The first thing teachers in extreme situations of this sort need to consider is the safety of their students. Tamira yielded to an understandable impulse when she tried to prevent Mr. M. from taking his daughter from her classroom, particularly when she knew the child was being taken away against her will.

In doing so, however, she placed all of her students in jeopardy. Mr. M.'s revolver could discharge, and bullets coming from it might land anywhere. One or more innocent children could be killed. It is difficult to think rationally when something as threatening as this situation occurs. It is preferable, therefore, for teachers to try to reason such situations out in advance and in the abstract so that if such an unfortunate event should ever occur, they can deal with it.

Tamira has no reason to keep Mr. M. from taking his daughter in this situation. She should let him take her and then should spring into action via her intercom. If she can lock her classroom door after Mr. M. has left, so much the better. If she notifies the office of what has happened, Mr. M. will not get very far. Linda is obviously in danger, but if Tamira tries to defend Linda, she will place all of her students and herself in danger. It is more likely as well that Linda will be shot accidentally if Tamira intervenes than if Mr. M. simply takes her from the classroom.

In a situation like this, it might be that the principal will dismiss school for the rest of the day, particularly if the halls have filled with students who witness what has happened. It is complicated, however, to dismiss school because with working parents, some students will have no place to go. It might be better for the principal to call an assembly and discuss the matter with all the students and teachers in the building. Before doing this, the principal should alert the superintendent of schools and should ask whether a psychologist can be sent to the school as soon as possible—preferably within the hour—to deal with distraught students and teachers. The fallout from an event like this can continue for some time, although children often put such matters from their minds more quickly than teachers do. Professional help and guidance must be made available to everyone in the school.

THE SINS OF THE PARENTS

Schoolchildren are sometimes the innocent victims of things their parents have done. It is extremely difficult for students to cope with the ridicule of their classmates if one of their parents has done something to attract notoriety. The student has probably been brought up to believe in honesty but also to believe that loyalty to a parent is a requisite virtue.

When parents are accused of doing something illegal and news of it becomes public knowledge, students are torn in opposing directions. At such times, their classmates can be incredibly cruel, as many a child has discovered. At times and in situations like this, teachers need to do all they can to be supportive of the innocent victim who has to bear more than any child should. No ideal solutions exist for dealing with situations like this, but teachers need to think about how to deal with such problems. They also need to realize that the student involved will need follow-up attention, particularly if a parent is found guilty of what he or she has been accused of. Teachers sometimes need to acknowledge that they cannot handle such situations completely on their own. School principals, guidance counselors, and superintendents of schools can tell teachers how to get suggestions from such people as psychiatric social workers.

DEALING WITH DEATH

In the course of any normal teaching career, teachers encounter students who have suffered the loss of a loved one—or even of a beloved household pet, which can also be terribly traumatic to a child. When the death is that of grandparents or favorite aunts or uncles, the usual platitudes might serve to comfort students and help them to go on with their lives. The death of a parent or sibling is somewhat harder to deal with because the relationship between the student and the person who has died is usually closer than is the relationship with a grandparent or some other relative who does not live in the student's home.

All of these deaths, however, evoke sympathy and understanding that might be absent in situations where a parent has been killed as a result of some illegal activity; yet deaths of this sort are on the increase in our society. Teachers need to remember that students who lose parents in ways like this require special attention, care, and understanding.

CASE STUDY 6.2
Student's Parents Killed in Shoot-Out

Cody B. has long had an interest in urban education because he realizes that many urban areas have experienced incredible social change over short periods of time. A sociology major in college, Cody studied communities in flux, doing neighborhood surveys once in a black ghetto and once in a Latino ghetto.

Now a social studies and physical education teacher in a large eastern city, Cody has survived the difficult adjustments beginning teachers have to make to such situations and is in his fourth year at a school that has had difficulty attracting and retaining teachers. The fact that he has lasted for so long has given him a special status among the students in the school.

One Wednesday morning as Cody is rushing down the hall to unlock his homeroom, Mr. D., the principal, calls to him, "Mr. B., come into my office." Cody knows that something must be terribly wrong because his principal is always civil to his teachers and would not shout out a command like this without so much as a "Please" unless he were under extreme duress.

The minute Cody sees Mr. D., his opinion is confirmed that something drastic has happened. Mr. D. is ashen. His hands are shaking. His first words are, "Lonnie T. is in your homeroom." Cody confirms that he is. Mr. D. then asks, "Did you hear all the sirens as you were coming in?"

"Yes," Cody answers. "I thought there must be a fire somewhere."

"Not a fire," Mr. D. volunteers. "A drug raid."

"Boy," Cody says, "that's going to mean a tough teaching day."

"Tougher than you think, I am afraid," Mr. D. says. "There was some shooting. A police officer was killed, and when that happened, the cops charged the building with their guns blazing. Lonnie's parents are both dead. He apparently is in school. It happened only twenty minutes ago, and he usually comes in early to shoot baskets in the gym."

Cody is dumbstruck. "What do you want me to do?"

Mr. D. says, "I'll get Ms. R. to cover your homeroom. You go up and get Lonnie. Bring him down here. We will have to tell him what happened."

Questions

1. The immediate problem Cody will have to deal with is apparent. What other problems will likely face Cody as a teacher in a school where many of the students will be affected in some immediate way by this tragic event?

2. Why do you think the principal wants Cody to go to the gym to get Lonnie? Why does he not go himself, or why does he not go with Cody?

3. Cody gets to the gym and finds Lonnie shooting baskets with some other boys. How should he approach Lonnie? What might he say to him?

How much information should Cody give Lonnie right at this moment?

4. Cody tells Lonnie that the principal wants to see the both of them. Lonnie asks him why. How might Cody respond to that question?

5. On the way to the principal's office, Lonnie keeps protesting that he didn't do anything. How might Cody deal with these comments?

Possible Solutions

1. Cody has a heavy heart as he makes his way to the gym. He wishes that he did not have to go on this particular mission alone. When he gets upstairs, there is Lonnie, intent on shooting baskets, yelling when he misses, bounding after the ball. Cody thinks to himself: "Lonnie's life will never be the same after the next few minutes." He catches Lonnie's eye, and Lonnie greets him with a "Hello, Mr. B. What you doin' up here?" Cody beckons him to come toward him and says, "Mr. D. needs to see you, Lonnie." Lonnie moves in his direction. "What for?" he asks. Cody tells him, "I guess we had better go down there and find out. He wants to see me, too."

2. Cody cannot face the thought of going upstairs to get Lonnie. He writes a note to him saying that the principal wants to see the both of them before homeroom and asking Lonnie to come to the main office as soon as he can. He sends the note to the gym with one of the office's student pages, who does not know what has happened. By the time Lonnie reaches the office, Cody, who has been working hard to control his emotions, lets loose. Tears begin to run down his face, and Lonnie asks, "Man, what'sa matter with you?" Cody puts his arm around Lonnie's shoulder and steers him toward the principal's office, hardly able to speak. Finally, he mutters, "Be strong, Lonnie. Be strong."

3. Cody finds Lonnie in the gym and beckons to him. Lonnie comes toward him, and Cody walks out part way on the floor to meet him. He gestures to a bench at the end of the gym, and says, "Let's go over there. I have something I have to tell you." When they sit down, Cody says, "I have some very bad news for you, Lonnie." Lonnie, looking terrified, demands, "What, what is it?" Cody puts his hand on Lonnie's shoulder and says, "Something really heavy has happened. Your parents have both been shot in a police shoot-out." A wail comes slowly from deep inside Lonnie. All the other students in the gym start in Lonnie's direction to find out what's wrong. Cody feels as though he is in the middle of a bad, slow-motion dream.

Consider This

Every ten years you teach, you will deal with well over two thousand students, sometimes with many more. The statistical probability of your having to break some sort of bad news to at least one of them is quite great. You will never feel prepared to be the deliverer of tidings like those Cody had to bring to Lonnie. You do, however, need to think of how you might deal with this sort of situation should you ever be called upon to inform one of your students of a tragedy of some sort.

You can be of the greatest help to a student suddenly numbed by news of this sort if you keep as calm and collected as you can. Your bursting into tears at a time like this will add to the problem rather than help to bring it under control. At this point you need to find a quiet place where you and the bereaved student can be away from other students until plans have been made for the student to leave school. In Lonnie's case, he cannot be sent home because that is the scene of the killing, and he should be spared the shock of seeing that scene unless he insists on doing so. A coordinated effort should be mounted to bring some relative to the school to take Lonnie away; if no such person is available, a social service agency should be asked to send someone out to help Lonnie cope with his grief. Meanwhile, Lonnie needs as much support and understanding from Cody and other school personnel as they can give him. He must not be left alone until someone has come to look after him, be it a relative or a social worker.

Cody must bear in mind that although Lonnie is the student who seems to be most directly and dramatically affected by what has happened, other students in the school are also going to be affected in some way by the drug bust and by the deaths that have ensued. Besides looking after Lonnie for a while, Cody has to be giving some thought to adjustments he might have to make in his classes because of this dire event.

THE LOSS OF CLASSMATES

The most frequent cause of death among people under eighteen is accidents. Rare is the school that does not have to face the death by accident or from illness of at least one or two students in a typical school year. Such situations are sad for everyone in the school. The matter is often discussed in a memorial assembly in the school auditorium. Although the students in the school do not forget their loss, they eventually put things into perspective and go on with their work.

Much more difficult is the sort of incredible disaster that wipes out a large number of students and that leaves others badly injured physically or psychologically. Few years pass in the United States in which some major accident of this sort does not make the national television news. When things of this sort occur, students and faculty alike are badly scarred, sometimes for long periods. Those who themselves survive the accident wonder why they have survived and feel guilty that their friends have been killed while they have been spared. Dealing with problems like this involves schoolwide effort and professional help for the entire surviving school community.

CASE STUDY 6.3
Almost Half of Senior Class Killed in Bus-Car Accident

Lowell Senior High School is a small school in the prairie country of the Midwest. The senior class has only fifty-four members; they have reached the itchy stage at the end of April when graduation is a little over a month away. Going to school seems anticlimactic.

The principal and teachers realize that this is not likely to be the most productive month these students have ever had. In a senior class assembly one day, Dr. G., the principal, tells the class that he has made arrangements for all of them to go to a theme park about three hours away from school. He has gotten a special price on the entry fee, and he will foot the bill for the school bus out of his own pocket. Several teachers will go along as chaperones, either riding on the bus or driving their own cars and taking some students with them.

On the appointed day the whole contingent except for two seniors who are ill is to leave at eleven in the morning after having had abbreviated meetings of all their classes. The cafeteria has put up box lunches, and the group will stop at a picnic area about thirty miles out of town for lunch. The seniors are excited to think of going to the theme park, and the other students in the school are envious. They complain, "Gee, they get to do everything. Why can't we ever do nothin' like that?"

The whole day is a howling success. All the students behave well, but not to the point that they aren't having fun. They are supposed to leave for home at eight, but by the time everyone is rounded up and sorted out, it is nine-thirty. The procession leaves for home, the bus full of singing students and the teachers' cars filled with students who doze off after their busy day.

191

Not far from the picnic area where they had lunched earlier disaster strikes. The bus is going south on the Interstate a little below the speed limit. All at once, a car appears through the haze going the wrong way on the three-lane road. The bus swerves, but not in time. The collision is head-on. The bus and car become tangles of steel. Fire breaks out. Some students get out through the broken windows. Others are trapped inside, many of them screaming as the flames advance.

When the tally comes in, it is determined that thirty-one students and three teachers died in the crash. The graduating class has almost been virtually wiped out.

Questions

1. What immediate problems might the surviving senior students have, particularly the two who were sick and could not go on the trip?

2. Under state compulsory attendance laws, schools have to continue even after a tragedy like the one written about here. How do you think the teachers in this school can best be helped to deal with the situation of facing their students immediately after an accident of this proportion?

3. If you were a teacher facing this situation, would you go back to school immediately, or would you simply say that you could not resume teaching for a while? Consider the pros and cons of each decision, remembering that good teachers try to act professionally at all times.

4. Commencement plans are already underway. The program has been sent to the printer, caps and gowns ordered, senior pictures taken, and the yearbook sent to press. The principal, who is as distraught as the teachers in the school, calls a meeting of the teachers to get their views on whether the school should go on with its commencement. How would you vote in this situation? What would your arguments be for going on as planned? For canceling the ceremony?

5. What agencies and civic organizations can be enlisted to offer help in a situation like this one?

Possibilities To Consider

1. Chandra H. was one of the teachers who was driving her own car on the day of the accident. She and four of her students were spared. All were taken to a local hospital and treated for shock. A civic organization in a nearby town immediately arranged for its members to drive survivors back to their homes, so Chandra and her stu-

dents were all transported back to their grief-stricken community within hours of the mishap. Chandra collapsed onto her bed and cried until her family thought she had no more sorrow left in her. She slept fitfully and was up at five. As she began to dress, her incredulous husband asked her, "Where are you going?" Chandra responded, "To school. It *is* a school day, you know." "But, honey," he argued, "you're in no condition to go to school." Chandra would not budge from her resolve: "Our students won't be in such great condition either. Someone's got to be there to help them through this." Her husband said, "Why don't you call to see if there is going to be school today?" Chandra said, "Whether there is school officially or not, my place is there. Some students will come, and someone has to be there for them. Besides," she adds, "I need to be busy today. Sitting at home wouldn't be good for me."

2. The accident took place on Wednesday night. The superintendent of schools announces a period of mourning that will last until the following Tuesday, by which time all of those lost in the accident will be buried. Meanwhile, the school will be open to anyone who needs psychiatric help. Four psychiatrists have volunteered their services for a few days, and several psychiatric social workers will also be present for counseling. Many of the town's clergy will hold counseling sessions at the school. As a teacher in the school who taught one senior class but who did not go with the senior group to the theme park, Burt G. is shaken by the accident. When he hears that school will not meet, his wife says, "Why don't we just go visit the folks for the weekend?" referring to her parents. Burt says, "No, I want to be here. I want to go to school and be there in case I am needed until classes start again." He goes to school, and although he does not feel the need to see one of the psychiatrists, he suggests to the principal that he might set up a group meeting for teachers who want to attend it and wonders whether one of the psychiatric social workers might sit in on the group session. The principal thinks this is a good idea and arranges a group session at 2:00 for the teachers who want to attend.

3. Mary Anne S. is a teacher in the school from which the dead students came. She has just been through a tragedy of her own. Her seven-year-old son was diagnosed as having bone marrow cancer. He was acutely ill for a year before his death five weeks ago. Mary Anne has managed to come back to school, and she and her family are trying to get on with their lives. When Mary Anne hears of this accident, however, she is disconsolate. All of the personal grief she has managed to control now overwhelms her. She cannot sleep at night; she sits for hours just staring into space; she is living in her own

world. She now thinks that she has no option except to ask for personal leave for the remainder of the school year. Her principal understands, but he tells her that he would like her to play the situation out day by day. He will hire a substitute teacher, but if Mary Anne decides she wants to come back to school before summer vacation, her job will be there for her. She is convinced that she will not return to school—perhaps that she never will—until the mother of one of her favorite students, one of the two students who missed the outing because of illness, calls to tell her that Betsy really needs her now. Betsy feels such incredible guilt at being alive when so many of her friends have been killed that her mother fears she may attempt suicide. When Mary Anne finds this out, she decides that the greatest monument she can build to her dead son and to the students who have been killed is to dedicate herself to helping those who have been left behind. Two weeks after the accident, she is back in her classroom.

Consider This

A problem like the one in the case study is too big for a school or school district to handle alone. Life must go on, but it certainly will go on with great difficulty after such a massive tragedy. Some of the school's most immediate needs can be met by volunteers from the psychiatric profession or by people provided by social agencies. Civic groups like the Rotarians, the Lions, the Knights of Columbus, and the Elks, as well as religious and veterans groups, can provide many services to schools that ask for them at a time like this.

The healthiest thing that can happen is for the school to reopen and to push on to finish the work of the school year. The atmosphere is likely to be subdued, and anyone who laughs at something might for a while feel guilty about laughing. Grief, however, must eventually yield to life and all of life's activities. The memory of the loss will linger, as will the sentiments the survivors have for those who died. They must be helped to see that the best way they can honor the dead is to go on with living and to live the best lives they can.

FILLING IN DURING AN EMERGENCY

Most teachers will be called upon occasionally to cover another teacher's class when that teacher becomes ill unexpectedly or has to leave school because of a family emergency. Covering classes in such situations is quite routine. Sometimes, however, teachers find themselves quite unexpectedly in situations that they could in no way anticipate and in which they have to function as well as they can. The easiest thing to do in such cases is to throw up one's hands, say, "I just can't handle it," and leave. Professionals, however, do not perform in that way. Teachers, as professionals, have to deal with the unexpected on a regular basis, and the unexpected can at times be extremely threatening to them. The job that Jerry R. suddenly found himself thrust into is, admittedly, extreme and unique. Jerry, however, was a real teacher who had to deal with the following situation on a few hours' notice.

CASE STUDY 6.4
Teacher Takes Over After Killing in School

Jerry R. loves adventure. His favorite category in *Trivial Pursuit* is geography, the subject that he always worked into his classes in social studies whether they were called geography classes or not. Jerry completed his MAT degree and stayed on as a teacher in the school where he had served a yearlong internship. For three years after he completed the internship, he lived frugally and saved enough money to take a year off and wander.

Before he left on his backpacking travels, he stopped by to see one of his former professors who applauded what Jerry planned to do and who gave him one bit of sage advice: "Be sure you carry your teaching certificate with you. Put it in a waterproof pouch and make sure you know where it is in your backpack. You never know when it might come in handy."

Jerry had not thought of teaching during his year away, but he followed his professor's advice, stashing the certificate where he could get at it. He pretty much forgot that he had it with him as he backpacked across the United States, up through the Canadian Northwest and on into Alaska. By mid-October, he was out in the Aleutian Islands not more than a hundred miles from the USSR. Someone offered to fly him from a population center of 750 people to a small town on an island fifteen miles away. Jerry was eager to see this small town that had about 250 inhabitants and a one-room schoolhouse. The people fished and farmed a little when the weather permitted it, but in winter, drinking became the major pastime.

Jerry arrived in town around noon and sat down on a bench outside the post office to have his lunch. It was a balmy day. He planned to stop by the school after lunch, but he ended up there shortly after he took the first bite of his beef jerky. A man, quite drunk, went roaring through the streets screaming, "Help me. My God, she got a knife. Help me!" He was pursued by a woman, also drunk, brandishing a large knife. Jerry ran along after them, as did about a dozen other people. The man ran into the school with the woman in hot pursuit. There, before the teacher and her seventeen students who were in nine different grades, the woman plunged the knife into the man. He died in minutes.

Betty P., the teacher, was in her first year of teaching and had come to Alaska because of the high salaries and the adventure. She was required to live in a room behind the classroom because someone had to keep the fire going all night, and that task traditionally fell to the teacher. After this event, Betty refused to go back into the building, even to retrieve her personal items. She was out on the next mail plane. No one in town had the education to be a teacher. Jerry showed the postmistress, who was also the mayor of the town and a justice of the peace, his teaching certificate. She hired him on the spot, and the salary was larger than Jerry had ever dreamed of making.

His immediate problem was that of figuring out how to pick up the pieces. He did not know the students he would be teaching, and he had to teach subjects he had never taught before. As it turned out, Jerry survived the year well and still considers it one of the most remarkable experiences in a life that has been extremely varied and interesting.

Questions

1. Teachers often face unexpected situations. Do you have a few general lessons you can fall back on for the first few days of teaching if you are suddenly thrust into a situation you had not anticipated?

2. Not many one-room schools exist, but sometimes teachers teach two grade levels together in the elementary schools of small communities. Can you point to any advantages in such a situation?

3. If a group of students has observed something as shocking as Jerry's new students have, how can a new teacher help them cope with their shock? How can Jerry use this dire event to lead to worthwhile learning outcomes?

4. List five or six of the first things Jerry has to be concerned with in this situation into which he has been so unceremoniously thrust.

Possible Solutions

1. When Jerry opens the school the morning after the murder, he begins by introducing himself and telling his students something about where he has come from. Some women in the town have

cleaned the school. Jerry learned that only two other people in the town have college educations. He learned from the postmistress/mayor that his children are mostly Aleuts and that few of them had been further away from their homes than to fly across the bay to the town from which Jerry had just arrived. He also observed that the people he met in the town were polite, friendly, private, extremely individualistic, and quite stoical. Because of what he has observed about the Aleuts, he decides it would be best to push right on with school. He, as a new teacher, can do that. The former teacher could not have proceeded in the same way. Jerry will deal with any questions his students ask him about the murder that has taken place in the school building. For the whole of the first morning, no one brings the matter up, and Jerry tries to get to know his students by asking all of them to tell something about themselves. Just before the students are to go home for lunch, one of them asks what many of them have apparently been thinking: "You don't think anyone else will break into the school that way, do you, Mr. R.?" Jerry answers, "Gosh, no, the chances of something like that happening are about one in a million. I think we're safe for a million more years at least." That answer seems to satisfy everyone.

2. The event depicted in the case study occurred on a Thursday. Jerry, shocked by the event and startled at the thought of teaching this handful of children strung through nearly all the elementary grades, agrees to take the job over, but he insists that he cannot hold school on Friday because he needs the weekend to get oriented and to prepare something for his students. He does not want to go in unprepared on his first day. The postmistress/mayor is not in a good bargaining position, so she accedes to Jerry's request, and a sign is soon nailed to the schoolhouse door that says, "No School Until Monday."

3. Jerry is on the brink of not accepting the position that has suddenly fallen into his lap. He doesn't know whether he can handle it, and he tells the postmistress/mayor so. She tells him, "If you don't take the job, we might have to close the school. These students need the school now. You expect too much of yourself. You will be the best qualified teacher we have ever had in this town. We have never had anyone with a master's degree, and especially with a master's degree from a school in the lower forty-eight." Jerry guesses that teaching here will be one more adventure for him, one more chapter—or perhaps several—in the book he keeps thinking he should write after the trip is over. He begins to think of all the exciting things that a one-room schoolhouse can lead to educationally, and he begins eagerly the very next morning, realizing that these students need

to get right back to their studies after this shocking event has interrupted their routines.

Consider This

Sometimes truth is harder to believe than fiction, but this event happened, and a teacher had to deal with it as well as he could. He knew immediately that the first thing he had to do was to put the shocking event as far behind him and his students as he could. He thought the best thing that could happened at this point was for a new teacher to take over. Student attention would be focused more on getting to know the new teacher than on reliving what happened immediately before he arrived.

Jerry soon learned that what had happened had been more shocking to him than it was to his students. They had observed more violence in their short lifetimes than he has seen in his. They were used to drunkenness and fights. Once he knew that this was the case, Jerry realized that the murder in the schoolhouse never had to be brought up with his students.

Jerry took control quickly, got his students into peer tutoring situations, and spent an exciting few months in the Aleutians teaching some of the most sincere, beguiling students he had ever encountered. Discipline problems almost never arose, and when they did, the older students usually took charge of eliminating them. He found that creative dramatics worked especially well with this group of students whose ages were so diverse.

THE GRIM REALITY OF JUVENILE SUICIDE

After death by accident, the second largest number of people under eighteen in the United States die from suicide. It is estimated that approximately five thousand juveniles commit suicide every year. As grim as suicide among young people is, the greater problem is that one suicide sometimes opens the floodgates for more such acts within a family or within a community.

Teachers need to be alert to physical conditions that suggest a student is perhaps engaging in dangerous experiments and should bring suspicions of this sort to the school nurse or counselor, making an objective report in writing. Teachers need also to be alert to behaviors that suggest presuicidal behavior, although it is sometimes impossible to distinguish such behavior from quite normal and usual teen-age moodiness. Particularly vulnerable to suicide are students whose parents are going through a divorce, students who experience frequent rejection and who have bad self-images, students who have little sense of direction, students who have been deeply involved in a love affair that is thwarted by the other person or by parents, and students who have recently been exposed to death, especially death by suicide.

When asked how one can distinguish between teen-age moodiness and suicidal behavior, the parent of a girl who killed herself responded, "You can't. You just have to be on the safe side and presume that anything that looks suicidal is suicidal. You may be wrong, but even if you are, you may still have your child with you rather than dead and buried."

Behaviors frequent in presuicidal juveniles are the following:

- Loss of interest in schoolwork
- Loss of interest in other people and rejection of former friends seemingly with no reason
- Continued loss of appetite over a substantial period
- Frequent conversation, perhaps in the form of jokes, about death and suicide
- A verbal questioning of one's self-worth
- Lack of concentration in class
- A need for excessive sleep
- A continued lack of vitality in the voice
- Social withdrawal despite physical presence
- Subconscious attempts at suicide through reckless behavior
- A general malaise or sadness that nothing alleviates.

Teachers need to pay special attention to youngsters who have recently lost someone they love through death or separation. If they have lost someone close to them through suicide, they can be at special risk. Such youngsters need to talk about what has happened, but this is a subject that most people avoid. Therefore, the youngster suffers and has no outlet for that suffering. Teen-age suicide is more common in affluent neighborhoods than in impoverished ones, although it is no respecter of social class.

If a student of yours has been deeply depressed, is unable to complete class assignments, is unwilling and unable to make commitments to do things a day or a week in advance, and suddenly seems to have turned the corner, this may be a danger sign. The teacher may be relieved. The student seems to have changed for the better and appears to be seeing things in a more optimistic light—and such, indeed, may be the case.

Often, however, people who have been grappling with depression will show just such behavior when they finally make the decision to kill themselves. Suddenly they will seem to shed the burden they have been carrying for weeks or months. They may even try to mislead their friends into thinking they have begun to control their problems by planning to do things with people several days hence or by talking about long-term projects that even a few days before they could not have contemplated. Be extremely wary of sudden changes in behavior. They may indicate that a once-tentative decision is now in place and about to become an immediate reality.

CASE STUDY 6.5
Teacher Hears of Student Suicide

Juan M. is a veteran teacher. He teaches senior high school science courses and is extremely popular with his students. He is the sort of teacher who gets to know each student as an individual. He lets them know that although he is stringent and demanding, he is utterly fair and that he has high expectations for all of his students. Juan has chosen to teach in a small town because he likes to live where he knows most of the people in the community. He feels that his teaching is enhanced by the fact that he knows his students and their parents and that he has all sorts of opportunities to interact with them.

This year, Juan has been worried. One of his best students, Jennie K., began the school year with a flourish and was active in extracurricular activities. Jennie always planned to follow in her mother's footsteps and become a psychiatrist. She received early admission to the college she most wanted to attend shortly before Christmas. Just when Juan would have expected her to be happy and enthusiastic, Jennie turned morose and apathetic. Juan knew that she and Howard L. had been practically inseparable for the last two years, but now Howard was dating other girls, and Jennie was simply withdrawing from most social activity, even during the Christmas holidays. She politely refused nearly every invitation to do anything with people, usually explaining that she had studying to do or that she didn't feel very well or that she was too tired.

After the Christmas break, Jennie's schoolwork began to fall off badly. Juan heard that Jennie, who was a very careful driver, had had two minor automobile accidents over the Christmas holidays and the second time had been charged with reckless driving. He also learned from her other teachers that she was doing barely passing work in their classes. He could not believe this was because she had already been admitted to college and had ceased to care about her grades. Grades had never been as important to Jennie as learning had, and Juan doubted that her personality had changed overnight.

One February morning, Juan was making appointments in his homeroom for his senior students to have their yearbook pictures taken. Jennie was not there that day, and it was unusual for her to be absent. About ten minutes before homeroom was to end, Ms. B., the vice-principal, opened Juan's door and asked him to step into the hall. This was a singular thing for Ms. B. to do because she felt she should never interrupt teachers when they were in the midst of doing something with their students.

When Juan got outside, Ms. B. said, "I think you had better close the door." He did, and Ms. B. put her hand on his arm and said, "I have some very bad news. Jennie K. is dead."

Juan was stunned. He muttered distractedly, "How? What happened? Was it an accident?"

"Suicide," Ms. B. responded.

"Are you sure?" Juan mumbled.

"She shot herself through the head with a shotgun she bought in a pawn shop two days ago."

Juan can hear his students through the closed door. They are beginning to get boistrous. He has to go back and face them.

Questions

1. If you, as a teacher, observe a sudden, unexplained change in a student's personality, how can you proceed to find explanations for that change without intruding unduly on the student's privacy?

2. If you suspect that one of your students is becoming severely depressed, should you keep this information to yourself, or should you inform someone in the school about it? Has your principal ever talked with your faculty about suicide problems?

3. Has someone in the counseling staff been designated as the person who should be alerted if you observe behaviors that make you fear one of your students is suicidal? Has your school had any suicides in recent memory?

4. If a suicide occurs in your school, what can the staff do to try to prevent further suicides? How can you, as a classroom teacher, work to prevent suicides?

Possible Solutions

1. Juan is confronted for the first time by a situation that other teachers have experienced. He is so stunned that he cannot think; he is incapable of reacting. Ms. B. observes his reaction and says to him, "Why don't you go somewhere and have a few minutes to your-

self? I'll go in and stay with your students until the bell rings." Juan says, "But the students in there will have to be told." Ms. B. says, "Do you think you should tell them?" Juan all at once regains his composure and tells her, "It's my responsibility to tell them. After all, we all knew Jennie." He turns and goes into the classroom. His students take one look at him and suddenly become eerily quiet, sensing that something is terribly wrong. Juan merely says, "I have just had some very sad news. Jennie K. has died." Students cry out, "No. Oh, no. Not Jennie." The bell rings, and not a student moves. Juan says, "It is very sad. You will find out the details soon. I should tell you that she took her own life." One student says, "Are you sure?" Juan responds, "Yes, I am sure." With that revelation, silent, stunned students move toward the door.

2. On hearing this terrible news, Juan knows that he cannot get through the day. He asks Ms. B. what he should do. He tells her, "I can't go back in there." Ms. B. says, "I'll stay with your homeroom. You go down to the office and see Mr. F. [the principal]. He knows what has happened. I think it might be best if you didn't try to get through today." Juan walks in a stupor to the main office. As soon as Mr. F. sees him, he says, "Juan, how are you doing?" Juan cannot speak. Tears well in his eyes. Mr. F. says, "Come into my office and sit down. I think we had better get someone to cover your classes today and give you a chance to deal with this tragedy." Juan reaches out and presses Mr. F.'s hand, still unable to speak.

3. When Juan hears the news, he goes back and tells his homeroom what has happened, as in Possible Solution 1. He does not know how he can get through the rest of the school day. His greatest need now is to see Jennie's family, to find out if they know what led to this act. He searches his own mind trying to remember recent conversations with the girl, digging to find clues to what she was contemplating in things she had said. He knew that her behavior had changed, but he kept asking himself, "What could I have done without being a busybody?" When his first-period students come in, they are subdued. He asks, "Have you all heard about Jennie?" They say they have. He says, "Why don't we just write today? Take out a sheet of paper, and write down everything you remember about Jennie." He takes out a sheet of paper and begins to write, wondering how he can get through the whole day with the grief that is pressing on his mind.

Consider This

Nothing can distress a teacher more than the loss of a student through suicide. When a student dies in an accident or from an illness, teachers are deeply distressed. When a student decides that life is not worth going on with, however, any teacher's distress will necessarily be mingled with guilt and with some inevitable questions: "What could I have done to prevent this? Where have I failed this student? What signs did I miss that would have given me a clue to what was coming?"

Teachers in a school where a suicide has occurred should meet soon after the event to discuss it and to assess with the school's administration the danger that this suicide will lead to others in the school. If such a possibility seems even remotely likely, the school must get a professional in to deal with teachers and to train them in ways to spot potential suicides.

Suicide often follows periods of deep depression that are marked by the characteristics of potential suicides listed earlier in this chapter. Depression can be dealt with through therapy and medication, but this means that the person who seems at risk must be made aware of what help is available and be willing to accept it. Teachers and administrators must also remember that depressed people are often incapable of much action. Help must be found for them—they will not find it for themselves. Once that help is found, someone must be sure that the patient goes to appointments and makes the effort required to turn the situation around. Depression is a cancer of the soul, and it requires the most skillful handling if it is not to result in suicide.

CASE STUDY 6.6
Shunned Student Kills Other Student and Self

Mindy W. felt privileged to teach in a high school in rural Kansas. Every time she read of the problems that teachers in urban schools had to cope with, she counted her blessings. Her students could be mischievous, but they were guileless, and she was well able to handle them.

Among her students in calculus is Paul J., son of a local pharmacist and his wife who teaches hearing-impaired students in a nearby town. A fine student, Paul usually maintains an "A" average in all his classes. Paul is quiet and retiring, but he seems in fairly good control of his life. He is obese and not attractive. He has a bad case of acne. He has few friends among the student body and is never invited to any of the social functions that take place nearly every weekend. This doesn't seem to bother him, however. He stays pretty much to himself and works.

One day Mindy decides to have her students work in groups of three or four on some inductive problems she has devised and is experimenting with. Students fall into place with other students, and only Paul is not attached to a group. Mindy says to one trio of students, "How about having Paul work with you people?" One of the girls in the group blurts out, "We don't want that fat slob working in our group." Paul bolts from the room, leaving his books behind.

The next day, Paul is back in class, and the unpleasantness of the last meeting seems to be forgotten. Mindy certainly is not going to make an issue of Paul's having left the room without permission after yesterday's outburst. She gets the lesson started, and everything goes pretty much as usual.

Fifteen minutes before the period is to end, Mindy tells her students they can start on their homework, and she will circulate to help them if they have trouble with any of it. All at once she hears Paul yell, "Fat slob, am I? Well, this fat slob can take care of you." She turns and sees that Paul has a pistol in his hand. He fires it, and the girl who struck out at him the day before falls down. Within two seconds, Paul puts the barrel of the gun in his mouth and pulls the trigger. He dies instantly. The girl also appears to be mortally wounded.

Questions

1. What can a teacher do to help students who are excluded by their classmates to improve their self-images and gradually to feel more as though they belong?

2. Might Mindy have used the fact of Paul's intelligence to help get other students to accept him more than they apparently did? How might she have done this?

3. Did Mindy make a difficult situation worse when she allowed students to select the people they would work with in their groups? Although she could hardly have anticipated that another student would call Paul a "fat slob," might she have anticipated that Paul would be left out?

4. Once Paul bolted from the class, what might Mindy have done to follow up on the situation? Would it have been appropriate for her to get in touch that evening with Paul's parents? Suppose she had decided on that course and Paul had answered his parents' telephone, recognizing her voice.

5. Realizing that Paul was not popular with his peers, might Mindy have talked with him about his problems in being accepted? Might she have suggested that someone else in the school talk with him?

Possible Solutions

1. It takes Mindy only a couple of weeks to realize that Paul feels like an outcast in school. He devotes himself to his studies because

he has nothing else in his life. He has a good mind, so his studying pays off in high grades. But Mindy senses the frustration he must feel when a school activity is going on, and he has not been invited to go with anyone. She also recalls that one night when he went alone to a basketball game, he sat alone. Other students pretended not to see him. Knowing this, Mindy went out of her way to get to know Paul. He often came to her room early in the morning before school to talk. One day he broke down and wept because the school was having a big dance on Saturday, and he could not get anyone to go with him. Mindy told him, "Paul, life isn't always easy. You will find that some of the most popular adults haven't been too popular in school. But I think you might at least touch base with more people if you were willing to share some of your knowledge with them. If I can arrange for you to work with a few students who don't know calculus from cacophony, will you help them?" Paul is pleased with this prospect and soon is tutoring four students.

2. On the day Paul rushes out of class, Mindy calls the main office to report that Paul has run out of her class. She asks that Paul be kept from leaving school and be detained in the office. She also asks whether one of the media center volunteers working in the building today might stay with her class for a few minutes because she needs time alone with Paul. Normally volunteers are not asked to do this sort of thing, but this is a unique circumstance. Mindy's class has work to do and is under control. The volunteer arrives almost instantly, and Mindy rushes to the office. Paul has been asked to wait in a small conference room. She goes in, and he is defiant: "I suppose you're going to give me a detention on top of everything else." Mindy puts her hand on Paul's shoulder and says, "Far from it, Paul. I am here to apologize that something like that happened to you in my class. You do, after all, have the highest average in that class." Paul answers, "Yeah, for all the good it does me. You don't know what it's like to . . ." He can't go on. Mindy says, "I think I know, Paul. At least I know a little bit about how you feel. There are some things that you just have to overlook sometimes. You're going to make it in life, and don't you ever forget it. I have to go back to my class, but why don't you go to the media center for the rest of the period and try to forget all this unpleasantness?"

3. When Paul storms out of the room, Mindy says to the girl who struck out at him, "There is no place for that kind of behavior in any class of mine, Jean. You owe Paul an apology, but more important than that, you owe it to yourself to get to know Paul. He is a wonderful student and a fine person." Jean looks at her desk and mumbles, "Yes, m'am." When the period is over, Mindy calls the school where

Paul's mother teaches and has her called from her hearing clinic. She tells her that she thinks it is urgent for them to talk about Paul. Knowing that her school gets out half an hour before the school where Paul's mother teaches, she suggests that she drive over there as soon as she can get away so that they can talk. She already knows what she has to suggest. She thinks that Paul needs some psychotherapy but also that he needs to go to a weight clinic and try to deal with his obesity, which accounts for a great many of the problems he is having.

Consider This

One cannot suggest possible solutions to this problem after Paul pulls his pistol out and begins shooting. If the situation is to be controlled, it must be prevented. It takes an acutely sensitive teacher to be able to enter a scenario like this one early enough to prevent its outcome—which is a recounting of an actual case that happened in small-town, midwestern America.

Unpopular students die a little bit each day. They may not show any overtly aggressive behaviors because of their dissatisfaction with themselves, but their constant solitary state and their withdrawal are often indications that something is festering inside them that might erupt if it is triggered, as it was in this case.

Teachers cannot control what their students say, but they can perhaps work with them constantly to help them to understand that all human beings deserve respect. We do not have to like or even accept everyone we meet, but as we move into adulthood, we at least make an attempt to be civil, even to people we might prefer not to have a social involvement with. Young people are not always civil in such situations, but teachers can help to civilize them if they are skillful enough in stressing to them the sanctity of every individual.

TEACHERS AS CITIZENS

It is expected that teachers will be concerned, responsible citizens. Most of them are informed voters, are active in community affairs, and have informed opinions about matters of public concern. Most teachers, however, keep their political views to themselves, sometimes even playing devil's advocate in class in order to get students thinking. Teachers certainly are well advised to keep their political and religious opinions personal. There is nothing inherently wrong, for example, with teachers' being socialists, but if those teachers step over the bounds and try to win their students over to their own political philosophy, they have acted unprofessionally, unfairly, and indefensibly.

Few teachers receive public attention for their views on political matters. It is their right, certainly, to hold their own views and to engage in political activities outside the school. Sometimes, if these political activities bring public attention to them, they are placed in an awkward position with their students, with their students' parents, and with their administrators and colleagues.

Even though they may have been scrupulously apolitical in class, they may face problems from their students if their political views on important issues become public knowledge. This does not mean that teachers should never involve themselves in political matters. As citizens it is their right to function politically. If they anticipate that difficulties might arise from publicity, however, they should begin to devise ways of dealing with the situations that are potentially disconcerting.

CASE STUDY 6.7
Teacher Takes Unpopular Public Stand

Zheng-Wu C. is a tough but popular teacher. Her certification is in secondary school social studies, but she was among the first teachers in her school nearly thirty years ago to teach driver education. She has spent most of her time doing that ever since. Nevertheless, she always insists on teaching at least one class of social studies every year, and she specifically requests to teach tenth-grade students with learning problems.

Zheng-Wu wants to work with students like this because she is deeply concerned about the dropout problem, and she feels that if she can work with youngsters about fifteen years old, she can prevail upon many of them to stay in school beyond the age mandated by compulsory attendance laws. Her students respect her enormously, and she has a good continuing relationship with them because most of them take driver education with her the year they take social studies with her or the year after.

In February one year, a state legislator from Zheng-Wu's district, a former student of hers, proposes in the state legislature that students who drop out of school not be permitted to get driver's licenses at age sixteen, as they are now able to do. His bill further stipulates that students who have less than a 2.5 average in their academic courses not be permitted to get driver's licenses. His argument is that driving is a privilege, not a right, and that this privilege should be withheld from those who do not serve society in specific ways.

Zheng-Wu's students are horrified at the proposal. They think it is their right to drive at sixteen, and many of them will get part-time jobs that require them to drive. They have all been grumbling about the proposed legislation.

The trouble really starts when Zheng-Wu, as an experienced teacher knowledgeable about driver education, is invited to testify about this bill before the state legislature. When she comes out in support of her former student's proposed legislation, the local press gives a full account of her testimony. Her students feel betrayed, and when she goes into her social studies class the next day, her students are stonily silent. They answer questions politely because they respect Zheng-Wu, but they answer in a cold, clipped way. When she leaves school that afternoon, Zheng-Wu finds that the tires of her car have been slashed. That night, she is wakened around midnight by squealing tires. She puts the lights on and looks around outside. She discovers that her house has been egged.

Questions

1. Do you have any personal feelings about public issues that you would prefer not to have widely known?

2. If, as a matter of conscience, you feel you must take a stand on a highly controversial issue like censorship, abortion, or homosexuality, should you alert your school's administration in advance that you are about to take such a stand?

3. If you have already taken such a stand, but it has not yet appeared in the media, should you forewarn your administrators? Why or why not?

4. If you go public on a highly charged, emotional issue, what are some of the consequences you might expect?

5. If you feel you must take a stand in favor of something your students are almost unanimously against, can you do anything to minimize student reaction to your stand?

Possible Solutions

1. Zheng-Wu sincerely thinks there is a degree of validity to her former student's legislative proposal, and she thinks that if it passes, it might keep some students from being high school dropouts. She knows, however, that the kinds of students she deals with regularly will feel terribly betrayed if she speaks publicly in favor of the bill. She decides that the best way to deal with the situation is to encourage her students to have a formal debate about this proposal. She likes this format because it will require some students to argue in support

of the legislation, some to oppose it. The day after the debate, which she records for her former student and which results in the side that opposes the legislation winning, Zheng-Wu tells her students that she has been invited to speak before the state legislature in favor of the bill. Her students are dismayed. She asks them, "Do you think that you and I need to think the same way about everything in order for us to get along well?" They say that they don't think that but that they think she has to be on their side in this debate. She tells them that she leans toward the other side and gives her reasons. She also tells them that she thinks they should all write essays defending their stand and promises to take this bundle of student essays to the state capital with her when she goes to give her presentation.

2. When Zheng-Wu's ex-student asks her to support his bill publicly before the state legislature, she tells him that although she does support the legislation, she knows that hers is such a minority view within the school—and particularly among the students she has the most direct contact with—that she cannot go public on the matter. She agrees to write to her legislators in favor of the bill, and she promises to try to make her students understand it, although she does not really believe that she will ever sway them to her side.

3. When Zheng-Wu's tires are slashed and her house is egged, she realizes that she is in the middle of a bad situation, and she wonders whether there is any way out of it. When she gets to class the next day, she tells her students that every political issue has two sides to it. She reminds them that although most Americans today deplore slavery, in the early days of this nation enough people supported it that half the nation seceded from the Union and that the two parts of the nation fought a four-year war over this matter. She tells her students that she does not want to fight a war with them, and she realizes there are two sides to this issue. The class work today is for everyone (including Zheng-Wu) to write an essay defending or attacking the proposed legislation. Zheng-Wu lets her students know that she values their opinions on the matter, and she offers to send their essays to the state legislature so that legislators can read them.

Consider This

In large, impersonal communities, teachers usually have much greater autonomy than they do in smaller towns. Large cities also are more likely to have significant groups of every political stripe from ultraconservative to ultraliberal. In such communities, the population has probably been exposed to a broader range of ideological viewpoints than one encounters in smaller towns.

Teachers succeed best if they understand the temper of the communities in which they teach and do their best to live within the limitations that exist in those communities. Teachers who become the center of public controversy often find it difficult to teach effectively because the community focuses on them as controversial public figures rather than as educators.

All of us espouse some heretical notions that we manage to nurture even though we live in communities that do not share these notions. The philosophy of live-and-let-live is a realistic one for teachers to adopt. This does not mean they cannot have their own ideas. It merely suggests that they do not have to spend their lives on a soapbox articulating their beliefs publicly.

TEACHERS, STUDENTS, AND SEXUALITY

Human beings, along with being thinking beings, are sexual beings. Sexuality is more on people's minds nowadays than it has been in the past largely because of the new sexual openness that pervades the country, but also because the media—particularly television—are increasingly sexually oriented. Also, because marriages are typically delayed now more than at any other time in history, many young people have to deal longer with sexual urges that a century ago would have been fulfilled for many of them by marriage between the ages of sixteen and eighteen.

Teachers must remember that nothing can destroy them more quickly than engaging in sexual activity with their students. Administrators cannot support teachers who engage in such activity; communities will not tolerate teachers who engage in it. Some students may be sexually aggressive with their teachers, but the teachers, as mature people in positions of leadership, must be prepared to deal with and fend off such advances. Some simple precautions will prevent many problems from occurring. For example, teachers should avoid meeting singly with students before or after school hours. If a student needs to linger after school to talk about something, leave the door of the room open or take the student to a place like the media center for the interview.

Most school districts are enjoined from denying employment to qualified applicants on the basis of race, religion, sex, age, or sexual orientation. This prohibition does not mean that someone hired to teach in a district may engage in sexual activity with students. It means rather that their sexuality is their own business but that it should not be manifested in the school setting.

CASE STUDY 6.8
Student Makes Homosexual Overture to Teacher

Frank D. teaches speech and English at the Amanda Streeper Senior High School in a town of about twenty thousand people in the Southwest. Frank lives with his male companion of nine years in a city of five hundred thousand people some twenty miles from where he teaches. He has never flaunted his homosexuality, nor has he denied it. His principal knows that he is gay but has never viewed this as a problem because Frank always acts professionally and is a fine teacher.

Frank has put together a remarkable debating team. The team has made it to the state finals and has taken first prize. This qualifies them for the nationals, and the town is as excited about this competition as it is about any athletic competition. Frank is to accompany five debaters from his school to the National Finals in Lincoln, Nebraska.

When he and his students arrive in Lincoln, he discovers that three motel rooms have been reserved for them. Four of the boys stake their claim to two of the rooms. The fifth boy, Nathan, is a sensitive boy, very thin and gangly. He is left to share Frank's room. Frank knows that Nathan has a terrible self-image. Although he is good-looking, he thinks of himself as skinny and unattractive. Although he is bright, he worries that he is not as bright as other people.

After having dinner and sightseeing until nearly midnight, Frank and Nathan part company with the other debaters and go to their room. Frank is tired, and he and Nathan go to bed and turn the lights out quite quickly. Frank falls into a sound sleep.

Sometime in the night, Nathan, who has not been able to sleep, gets up to have a drink of water. Frank hears him and is half awake. When Nathan comes back into the room, he leaps into Frank's bed, puts his arms around Frank, and says, "I love you. You are the only one who understands the way I am." Frank is dismayed. He has never had a conversation with Nathan about "the way he is." He puts the light on and says, "Nate, you know this can't go any further."

Nate sobs, "You think I'm ugly, too. I'm skinny! Everybody thinks I'm ugly."

Frank responds, "You aren't a bit ugly, Nate, but I am a teacher, you are a student. Let's get up. We need to have a long talk."

Questions

1. In this case study, might Frank have foreseen the possibilities and prevented this situation?
2. Would it be best for Frank to have prevented this situation, or

might it have been better for Nathan to get the matter into the open so that he can talk about it freely for the first time?

3. In their discussion, do you think that Frank should accept Nathan's sexual orientation and talk with him from that standpoint, or do you think he should try to convince Nathan that this is a period he is passing through and that as soon as the right girl comes along, he will probably overcome it? Consider the implications of each course.

4. Nathan is probably aware of Frank's sexual orientation. Do you think Frank should talk with him from the standpoint of his own orientation or from a more conventionally heterosexual base?

Possible Solutions

1. Frank gets out of the other side of his bed and puts his robe on. He knows at this point that he and Nate must have a long talk, but he thinks it would be preferable to have that talk somewhere other than in the motel room. He says, "I could do with a hamburger, and I noticed an all-night place down the block. Why don't we throw our clothes on and go get something to eat." Nate agrees, not too enthusiastically. He is obviously embarrassed. Once they get their hamburgers, Frank looks across the table at Nate and says, "Let's get one thing settled here and now, Nate. You don't have anything to apologize about in the looks department—and thin people usually live longer than fat ones, so don't call yourself skinny the way you do." Nate smiles a dejected smile. Then he says, "You must hate me for what I did." Frank says, "If I hated you, I wouldn't be buying you a hamburger—even on the school's travel money!" Then he says, "Have you ever had anyone you could talk to about your attraction to men?" Nate blushes crimson and says softly, "No." Frank says, "Well, it's a problem to keep secrets bottled up inside. You can talk to me and ask me anything you want to. I'm your friend, but I think you know I cannot and will not be more than that—and that doesn't mean I think you're ugly!" Nate asks, "Do you think I will always be this way?" Frank answers honestly: "Maybe. But most people have had feelings like this at one time or another, and most of them have grown in other directions."

2. Frank gets out of bed, and he and Nate sit down and start to talk. Nate says, "You won't tell anyone what I did, will you?" Frank says, "Of course not. You just got into the wrong bed. Anyone can do that in the dark." Nate answers, "But what about the things I said to you?" Frank says, "I was half asleep—and I have a rotten memory even when I'm awake." He pauses; then he says, "Look, Nate, don't make more out of this than you need to. Just know that you can always talk to me frankly about anything that's bothering you. Just re-

member that I am your teacher, and that means that our relationship has to remain a professional one, doesn't it?" Nate agrees that it does and thanks Frank for understanding: "You are the first person I have ever been able to talk to about my real feelings. Thanks!"

3. As soon as Nate gets into Frank's bed, Frank jumps up and switches the lights on. He says, "Listen, Nate, you get the hell out of my bed and don't ever try to pull anything like that again. I should throw you out of here right now, but it's too late to wake the other guys and arrange for you to stay with them." Nate is near tears. His lip trembles. Frank says, "Don't pull the tears routine with me. That's a girl's tactic. You need to straighten up." Nate finally says, "I never let anyone before know about me." Frank says, "Well, you had better not ever let anyone know again. This kind of stuff can get you into bad trouble." The two go back to bed, Frank in his bed, Nate in the other. Neither gets a wink of sleep all night.

Consider This

In situations involving a trip for students and teachers of the same sex, teachers sometimes end up sharing rooms with their students—and there usually is no harm in their doing so. In this situation, a student who is insecure and perhaps not wholly fixed in his sexual identity really needs someone to talk with—homosexuality is not an easy topic for adolescents to discuss with a counselor or teacher—and certainly not with fellow students.

Heterosexual students have as many adjustment problems as homosexual students at this level, but most of them feel less alien in their world, which is heterosexually oriented. All adolescents have sexual questions they want and need to have answered, and some of these questions are answered in health classes, by talks with parents, and, more likely, in talks with friends of their own age. They may not get accurate information every time they seek it, but they can at least seek it without risking ostracism.

At least one school district—Los Angeles—has a counselor who deals specifically with gay students in the district. This counselor is not trying to promote a gay life style; she is merely trying to help troubled kids sort out what to many of them is the biggest problem in their lives. Nevertheless, in most school districts in the country, homosexuality is a taboo topic—and in many districts, talk about matters sexual is proscribed. A narrow attitude toward sex education seems particularly dangerous in an age when AIDS, which is contracted through both straight and gay sexual contact, is increasing at an alarming rate.

7. WHADDID I GET?

Adults work for pay. It is true that some adults volunteer their services, but for most people, a job seems somehow not quite legitimate if it does not involve financial remuneration. In schools, the equivalent of pay is grades. Some schools have experimented with deemphasizing grades by not giving them to students, although all schools must keep records that reflect student performance because without such records, students often cannot qualify for passing from one educational level to another. Even in situations where instructors write narrative comments about students rather than giving them grades, the tradition of grading casts its long shadow over most teachers. Narrative comments often include such statements as, "If we were grading on a conventional basis, Frances D. would have received a high 'B' in my course."

WHAT ARE WE EVALUATING?

This question seems easy to answer: "We are evaluating our students' mastery of the work we did in this chapter/unit/nine-weeks/quarter/semester/etc." But this answer really is a nonanswer. The real question involves how well we design our evaluative instruments to interrelate our students' mastery of facts with their mastery of those broader concepts that will permit them to use their information for analyzing, projecting, solving problems, and doing other things that they will be expected to do when they get jobs. Some jobs require conformity and obedience; others require divergent thinking and a serious questioning of the validity of how things are usually done.

Good teachers evaluate their students on the whole range of abilities these students might be expected to develop in the subject area they are involved in learning more about. The highest levels of performance in any field require divergent thinking and analysis. These skills, however, are meaningless unless they are predicated on a strong base of factual information.

If one is discussing Shakepeare's *Romeo and Juliet*, for example, it is naive to condemn the parents of the star-crossed lovers as being insensitive to their children's needs unless one knows that in their society marriages were arranged and that this convention was then taken for granted, especially among people of property. One cannot use the argument that the children of socially prominent people in the United States today are free to marry whom they please. The argument has no meaning. Romeo and Juliet are not living today, they never lived in our society, and their parents—within their own contexts—responded quite predictably and acceptably to the romance that developed between these young lovers. Although it is legitimate to feel that modern parents should not act the way the Capulets and the Montagues acted, it is unhistorical to condemn them for having behaved the way they did, justifying that feeling merely on the basis that socially prominent parents in contemporary society act differently.

OBJECTIVE TESTS

Objective tests have many advantages, chief among them that they can be graded easily and quickly. Most can be machine-scored, so busy teachers can save time. On the other hand, it takes a long time to construct valid objective examinations, and teachers must remember that most objective exams test specific—often isolated—facts rather than deep understandings based upon making connections among facts. One danger of objective examinations is that an obvious correct answer is required if students are to receive credit. The student with a penetrating grasp of the subject may have a greater problem picking out the one correct answer than does a student whose knowledge is more superficial. Ask the typical person who discovered America, and the answer will be Christopher Columbus. Ask a well-informed American history professor, however, and you will likely hear the names of several reasonable candidates for that honor. You might also be told that we don't have a specific name, but it was undoubtedly an Oriental who walked over the land bridge across the Bering Straits that once connected our continent with Asia. A multiple-choice question that asks who discovered America might offer the following possible answers:

A. Sir John Manderville
B. Christopher Columbus
C. Ferdinand Magellan
D. Hernando Cortez
E. None of the above

The responses provide an obvious answer, Christopher Columbus, and one might cite several sources that support such a contention. The E response, however, is the only valid response in terms of what modern historians have discovered in their research, and an overwhelming number of reputable sources may be found to support that response.

215

CASE STUDY 7.1
Student Who Knows Too Much Gets Wrong Answer

Fiona Z. has been out of school raising her family, and now, more than a decade after her last teaching experience, she is back in the classroom. Fiona is interested in intellectual history, the history of ideas, and other related subjects. She is offering an elective course entitled "Leading Figures in Modern Thought." When she goes over her first examination with her students, one student, Joel A., objects because his answer to the item, "The first person to put forth the ideas of natural selection and evolution was...," has been marked wrong. The choices Joel was offered were

A. Karl Marx
B. Sigmund Freud
C. Charles Darwin
D. Alexis de Tocqueville
E. None of the above

Joel's answer was E.

Joel raised his hand, and when Fiona called on him, he said that he didn't believe that Charles Darwin was the first person to espouse these theories. He could not remember the name of someone he had read about in *Smithsonian* recently whose work, according to the article, although not published as early as Darwin's, had predated his. He remembered one statement from the article: "One thing is certain. During Darwin's time, the ideas of natural selection and evolution were much in the scientific air. It is impossible to credit Charles Darwin alone with having made the discoveries with which he is usually credited."

Had Joel not read the article, he would probably have received full credit for this answer which would, likely, have been "Charles Darwin." Joel, however, had more information than some of the other students in the class, and this surplus information was his undoing.

Fiona, realizing the situation, told Joel that his explanation was valid. She had read similar things. She gave him full credit for his E response. After class, five more students with E responses clustered around her desk wanting credit, and she had no recourse except to give it to them.

The next time she gave an objective examination, however, Fiona told her students that if they had reason to think that more than one answer was possible for any question, they should mark the answer they thought was most valid, but that they should indicate with an ar-

row that they had written on the back of the answer sheet an explanation of why they answered as they did. If the explanation made
sense, the student could receive full credit for the answer.

Questions

1. Do you think Fiona's encouraging students to explain answers
they think are controversial is a good idea, or will it lead students to
think there are no right answers? Discuss.

2. In this instance, was Fiona correct in giving credit to the other
students who marked E as their selection for the question Joel
brought to her attention? Might her new policy help her to overcome
this problem?

3. Do you think Fiona might have future difficulty explaining to her
subject matter supervisor that one student received full credit for an
answer that other students had not received credit for? Might Fiona
be confronted by angry parents about her policy?

4. How do you react if you tell your students something in class,
possibly a fact that is also presented in their textbooks, and a student
tells you that he or she thinks you are wrong?

5. Sometimes you will have a student or two—usually a very bright
student or two—who will challenge a great deal that you say. How
would you deal with students like this?

Possible Solutions

1. Fiona knows the various controversies that have brewed about
whether Darwin or Wallace or somebody else was first to come up
with the theory of evolution and natural selection. She thinks that to
introduce this question into her class will divert her students' attention
and that it is safer to go with what is in their textbooks. She listens to
Joel and notices that a couple of other students are nodding in
agreement as he makes his point. This makes her nervous because
she doesn't want her class to get out of control. She finally says to
Joel, "Joel, I think you've been in school long enough to know that in
multiple-choice examinations, there is one right answer—the one that
coincides with what is in your book. I am not unaware of some other
theories, but our job is to learn the material the school asks us to
learn from the textbooks the school requires us to use." Joel begins,
"But, Ms. Z. . . .," but that is as far as he gets. Fearful of having her
authority challenged and fearful that other students might join Joel
and gang up on her if she does not stand her ground, she says,

"One answer, Joel. The answer in the book, from now on. Is that understood?" Joel is seething. He does not answer.

2. Fiona is thrilled to have a student who reads a magazine like *Smithsonian*. She has been planning to bring up some of the theories that paralleled Darwin's, but she was going to do this in a couple of weeks after she had covered more of the material in the unit. She actually wanted to challenge several of the statements made in the textbook because some of them were questionable. After Joel spoke, she said, "Well, Joel, you're beating me to it. I was going to bring this matter up eventually. As long as you have brought it up, we can say a few words about it now, and I wonder whether you would be willing to read the *Smithsonian* article again and give us an oral report on it?" Joel says, "Sure, I'd like to. Do I still lose credit for my answer?" Fiona feigns annoyance and says, "Well, you dirty grade-grubber, I guess you deserve your two points. I'll bring your grade up two notches." Joel smiles.

3. Fiona has been wondering what kind of term project she might give her students. They are bright, eager kids. She wants them to do papers that make them think, that involve persuasion and analysis, and that will not be a drag to read. When Joel questions the item mentioned in the case study, Fiona gets an idea. She doesn't say anything about it because she wants to think it through for a day or two. But she thinks it would be appropriate in this course to have every student do a documented paper on exploding truths the world has accepted. After all, the greatest human progress occurs when some brilliant maverick takes a commonly accepted truth and disproves it—the earliest sailors who headed for the horizon were thought to be fools because all right-thinking, common-sensical people knew the earth was flat and that beyond the horizon was the great drop into the abyss. Every time a sailor sailed beyond the horizon and lived to tell about it, the commonly held truth must have been disproved. Fiona's mother had told her that when she was a girl, everyone knew that humans could never get to the moon because even if they could maintain the unlikely speed of a hundred miles an hour, it would take more than a lifetime to get there. Fiona rejoices that Joel put her on the track of a good idea.

Consider This

No student should be penalized for knowing more than the rest of the students in class—although this still happens to some students, and it can be extremely discouraging. Discussing the validity of items on an examination can be almost as good a learning experience as studying for the examination.

Once students know the form of the examinations a teacher gives, they might be invited to submit a few questions for each future examination. Teachers who do this should make it clear to their students that not all the questions submitted will be used, but that some of them probably will be. Teachers should reserve the right to revise questions students have submitted. One of the best ways to study for an examination that covers a large body of work is to make up an examination for that material. Students who take the time to do that will likely learn quite a bit of material and will also learn to differentiate between salient and incidental information.

ARE THE RULES THE SAME FOR EVERYONE?

Teachers owe it to their students to make new examinations specifically for them rather than to use a test they gave to their students a year or two earlier. Nevertheless, when a body of material is to be covered and mastery of it evaluated in an examination of some sort, even a new test will correspond to earlier tests of the same or similar material. Copies of old tests have a way of floating around, of being passed clandestinely from one student to another, thereby giving some students an advantage other students do not have.

One way to make the situation more equal is for teachers to staple copies of old tests into a manila folder and make these copies available to students under controlled conditions. Such folders could be kept in a filing cabinet in the classroom for students to peruse when they have finished their other work or during a free period. In some schools, such folders could be put on one-hour reserve in the media center and made available to students there. In this way, all students have access to information that previously belonged only to the those in the inner circle.

CASE STUDY 7.2
Some Students See Last Year's Tests

Geng-Sheng C. teaches mathematics in a middle school. He tries to construct his examinations so that they will test concepts his students must know in order to go on to more sophisticated concepts in his courses. He varies his examinations from year to year, but the basic material he covers remains the same, so the emphases in his examinations can vary only slightly.

After the second examination of the school year, four students ask

Geng-Sheng if they can see him after school. Each of these students has done poorly on an examination in which the results were in a "figure-8" configuration—a substantial number of students had high "B"s and "A"s and an almost equal number had low "D"s and "F"s.

Geng-Sheng learned from the students who came to see him that four students who had had siblings in his class at some time within the past five years had gotten copies of past examinations. They had study sessions with their friends in the class, and it is these students who ended up with the high grades. Geng-Sheng's students asked him, "Isn't that cheating, Mr. C.?"

He responded, "Well, no, I wouldn't exactly call it cheating. Our examination was different from the ones those students studied from. But it certainly gave them an advantage to know as precisely as they did what to expect." He mused on the problem; then he said, "I'll tell you what I am go to do. I have copies of all of my old examinations on file. I am going to put them on reserve in the media center for anyone who wants to use them." The students are pleased at this decision, but one of them, seemingly speaking for all of them, asks, "But what about this exam? That will help us with the next exam, but I have an 'F' on this one."

Geng-Sheng says, "I'm really sorry about that, Denny, but there's not much I can do about it. I'll certainly give all of you the benefit of the doubt when I compute final grades in May."

Questions

1. If you were in Geng-Sheng's situation, would you make some adjustment for the students who received low grades because they had not had the advantage of seeing past examinations?

2. Do you think Geng-Sheng's decision to make his past examinations available to all students would work for you? Why or why not?

3. Do you think students who use the examinations in the media center should be permitted to make photocopies of them? Why or why not? How would you control the situation if you did not want the examinations to be photocopied?

4. Some students like to study together for their examinations. Do you think that you, as a teacher, can help them set up study groups, acting as coordinator to get students together for study sessions outside school hours?

Possible Solutions

1. Realizing that some of his students have had a great advantage over the others, Geng-Sheng, who plans to give five examinations

during the term, tells his students that he will count the highest four of the five examinations when he computes final grades. He warns, however, that he will not permit makeup examinations; that is, students who miss an examination and, therefore, have only four grades will be judged on those four grades. Most of his students think this solution is fair, but a few think he should let those with low grades take the examination again. Geng-Sheng points out to them that doing this really would not be fair because they have already seen the actual examination and he does not have time to make up another one.

2. Given the problem that has surfaced with the examination, Geng-Sheng thinks the best thing to do is simply not to allow it to count for anyone. He announces to the class, "We are going to regard this examination as a practice run. The grade will not count. We will move our third examination up two weeks and have it next Thursday." Some students cheer, but at least as many say things like, "That's not fair! I got an 'A.' Why do I have to give that up?" Geng-Sheng feels pressed to the wall, and he says, "Well, let me sleep on it, and we will make a final decision in a couple of days." Then, as an afterthought, he says, "Why doesn't each of you write me your suggestions about how to handle this matter and hand them in tomorrow? See how persuasive you can be. I won't make a decision until I've read your arguments."

3. When the situation is brought to Geng-Sheng's attention, he realizes that he has a problem on his hands. He doesn't see how he can handle it equitably, so after he announces that from now on copies of past examinations will be put on reserve in the media center and finds that the students who received low grades are still complaining, he says, "Look, life isn't always fair. This exam is behind us. If you don't like your grade on it, work hard to do better on the next three and you will probably pull your grades up." One student says, "But it's hard to pull an 'F' up to an 'A' by the end of the term. I'm trying to get into engineering school." Geng-Sheng reminds the student that he has promised to give his students the benefit of the doubt when he assigns final grades. He says, "That's the best I can do. It's an imperfect world!"

Consider This

In most cases, grades—quite understandably—are more important to students than they are to teachers. It is your students who have the most to lose if their grades are disappointing. It is, therefore, important that teachers keep a few matters in the forefront of their minds when they assign grades:

- Every student should be treated equally when grades are assigned.
- Grades ideally reflect performance rather than such ancillary matters as attendance, behavior, affability, and conformity.
- All students must have available to them equal study materials for examinations, even though some students may not use the items that are available to them.
- Examinations should be major learning experiences for those who take them.
- Going over graded examinations should be a significant part of the learning experience.

If students have a legitimate objection to a grade, teachers need to let them know that the door is open to discussion, as time consuming as that is. Well-constructed exams will leave little room for doubt about what is expected and will provide opportunities for students to perform on both objective and subjective questions. Teachers must decide before they administer an examination what their grading standards will be and should inform their students accordingly. For example, if an unanswered item does not affect the overall grade but an incorrect answer represents a value of −1, students must have this information because it might be better for them to answer only the questions they are completely sure of rather than to make educated guesses.

WHAT IS WORTH KNOWING?

Facts are meaningless unless they are used as building blocks to understanding. Teachers can get fairly good ideas of the information their students have mastered by testing them objectively on factual information, but this is only a first step to learning. The second, more important step comes when students begin to put facts together, to see patterns in them, and to analyze the development of thought patterns.

In *Teaching as a Subversive Activity* (New York: Delacorte, 1969), Neil Postman and Charles Weingartner suggest that things that are really worth knowing do not lend themselves to objective testing. Their statement may be too categorical, but it touches on a truth that many teachers—particularly those in nonscientific teaching areas—have discovered on their own. It is one thing to know that Robert Frost wrote "Mending

222

Wall''; it is another thing to know when he wrote "Mending Wall.'' But these two pieces of information give no indication of whether a student knows what Frost is trying to communicate in this poem, certainly one of his most popular.

Frost's poem can be seen to have implications for international relationships: strong borders keep one's international neighbors at peace. It can also be shown to contain a diabolical contradiction to this sentiment because the poem revolves around a subtle pun: "Something there is that doesn't love a wall, that wants it down.'' That something is the frost that gets into the damp ground and contributes to its contraction. Then in the warmth of day the ground expands, only to contract again the next time there is a heavy freeze. This alternation of contraction and expansion brings the wall down eventually, and it has been caused in part by frost as well as by Frost—Robert, that is.

An objective examination might test the broad international implications of Frost's poem and might test as well one's knowledge of the inherent contradiction in the poem, but it could test such matters only after the fact. In writing an analytical essay about the poem, students might make discoveries like this on their own, and in doing so, they would be using cognitive material to reach highly sophisticated ends, to bring themselves to rewarding epiphanies, as James Joyce might call them. Their reasoning would be of a higher order than that required to answer questions about Frost or about his times or about specific lines in the poem.

In most subjects, it is a good idea for teachers to include on their examinations some multiple-choice questions, some identifications, some other sorts of questions such as map questions, short-answer questions, and at least one brief essay question. Examinations of this sort allow teachers to test a fuller range of student knowledge and understanding than a test that is all multiple choice or all essay or all short answer can.

CASE STUDY 7.3
Teacher Downgrades for Mechanics, Gets Flak

Luccia W. subscribes generally to the idea of having her students write as much as possible. She has attended a writing-across-the-curriculum workshop in her district and has come back from it fired up about the idea of having her students write every day. She is convinced that students understand best the things they write about. She has always included some short-answer and brief essay questions in examinations she has given her fourth-grade students because she thinks that it is never too early for students to learn how to organize their thoughts and get them down on paper.

223

Luccia's students have just completed an extremely interesting unit on the scientific accomplishments of native American Indians in the Southwest prior to European settlement in the United States. Luccia used the same unit with her students two years before, and it went well. When she tested her students on the unit, however, she was disappointed with the results. Student enthusiasm for the unit seemed to be greater than student accomplishment in it. Her examination had consisted of five essay questions. Her students were invited to write on any two of the five topics, and they had forty-five minutes to complete their work. At her workshop, Luccia had heard a great deal about the necessity of prewriting if one expected to get good writing results from students, and she began to realize that this had been one basic defect in her previous handling of the evaluative part of the unit.

Other problems also plagued her the last time. Students wanted to know whether they could use dictionaries as they wrote their essays. Luccia favored in principle letting them do so, but she also realized that they could use the dictionary to get partial answers to some of the questions that called for definitions of terms on which she specifically wished to test them. She solved that problem by telling her students that she would keep a pad in her hand and that students who didn't know how to spell a word could ask her. She would then write the word down on a slip of paper and leave the slip on their desks. That arrangement worked out pretty well.

An additional problem arose, however, when the papers were returned. Luccia had downgraded for such errors as sentence fragments, lack of agreement of subject and verb or of pronouns and their antecedents, and slang usage. Her students felt cheated and told her so: "I got the answer right. You never told us we had to pay attention to our writing. I don't see why you gave me a 'C' just because I didn't write too good."

This time Luccia decides to incorporate prewriting into her evaluative scheme. By doing so, she can also give her students a good lesson in the actual and practical use of an outline. On the Monday before the examination, which is scheduled for Thursday, Luccia tells her students that she wants them to think about what they are going to write on their examinations. Therefore, she tells them, "I am going to hand out today five essay topics. You will write on the two that interest you most. You will be graded on the basis of the information your answer provides, on the organization you use in presenting facts and relating them to each other, and on the general elements of writing that good papers usually reflect—spelling, agreement, word choice, punctuation, and so forth. The reason we learned these things was so that we could use them, wasn't it? They apply to all our work, not just to our work in English."

She then tells her students that she will help them with their spelling in exactly the same way she had helped her students two years before and that when they write their essays, their desks must be clear of everything except a one-page outline for each essay. This outline is to be handed in with their papers.

Luccia is gratified by the results on these essays. The ideas are much better thought out than those expressed in the essays she received two years ago. Also, her students did a fine job of outlining, and enough of them came to her in the days before the examination for help in outlining effectively that she spent forty-five minutes on Wednesday teaching a special lesson on how to outline.

Questions

1. Do you think it is fair to give students essay questions they are going to write on in a test situation in advance of that test? Discuss.

2. What is prewriting? What forms of prewriting did Luccia use to help her students prepare themselves for the examination?

3. Do you think it is better to teach such skills as outlining when the occasion arises rather than simply to teach a new skill every week or two and expect that students will be able to use these skills when the occasion to use them occurs?

4. Luccia's idea of helping students with their spelling during an examination makes sense. Might she go one step further and use this technique as a way of individualizing spelling? Think of what students might do with the slips of paper Luccia gives them rather than merely throwing them away.

Possibilities To Consider

1. Having been disappointed with the writing skills her students demonstrated in their examination in this unit of study two years ago, Luccia decides that this year she will let her students know that they will receive a split grade—something like a "B+/D." The top grade will be for content, the bottom grade for writing skills. Each grade will count equally. When she announces this grading system to her students, a number of them are upset. They say things like: "I know the stuff, but my writing isn't too good. It's not fair to knock my grade down for that!" Luccia sticks to her guns because she thinks it is important for students to pay close attention to effective writing, correctly spelled and well punctuated.

2. Luccia wants her students to know a body of material on which

she will test them. She values good writing, but she knows that her students will be working under pressure, so she tells them she will mark problems in usage, punctuation, and spelling, but that she will not deduct any credit for these problems. She will expect, however, that every student will pay close attention to them and will use her comments as an indication of things they must study on their own. When the papers come in, Luccia spends more than twice the time grading them that she would have had she graded only for content. She hands the papers back and finds that a number of her students have seen their grades and then have crumpled the papers up and thrown them away.

3. The situation is the same as in Possibility 2, except that before she hands the papers back, Luccia tells her students that they will have two days to work on the problems she has marked in usage, punctuation, and spelling. They should make the necessary corrections and hand their papers back. She will record no grade until she has the returned paper with corrections. To make sure that students will not lose their papers, she allows them fifteen minutes of class time to work on their corrections and then collects them. The next day, she hands them out and allows fifteen more minutes to students who need that much time. Other students are free to play quiet games or to go to the reading corner to read or look at magazines.

Consider This

Writing and thinking are closely interrelated. If we grade student essays strictly on the basis of content, we are sending an inaccurate message to our students. We are saying that we live in a world in which facts are all that matter—the way these facts are presented is inconsequential. This is not the case in the real world. Students who have received this message may be in line for a rude awakening when they go to college or enter the job market. College professors and people's bosses demand literacy of the people who hand written reports to them.

Some teachers use split grades, as Luccia did in Possibility 1. In a way, the split grade sends an inaccurate message because it divides something that is essentially indivisibie. Marshall McLuhan uttered a profound statement when he said, "The medium *is* the message." Everyone really knows that this statement is true. If you begin reading a newspaper and suddenly notice misspellings and unjustified punctuations, even though that newspaper's contents may be significant and accurately presented, you will soon begin to question its reliability. Anyone who reads something you or one of your students has written will question its credibility if it is prepared with errors in the three areas on which the public judges most writing: usage, punctuation, and spelling.

UNDERSTANDING VS. MEMORIZATION

We live in a world of factual information, and those who are not privy to such information lead extremely limited lives. Some cornerstones of knowledge lend themselves better to memorization than to inductive procedures. Life is easier for people who know the multiplication tables, for example, than for those who do not. People are also well served who memorize their Social Security and telephone numbers because these are things you either know or do not know; there is no way to figure out either of these numbers in any specific way, even if you know that a certain part of town has telephone numbers that begin with "356" or that people born in New York and New Jersey have Social Security numbers that begin with "1."

On the other hand, it is doubtful that many students will ever really need to know that George Washington was born in 1732 and died in 1799 or that James Watt received a patent for the first steam engine in 1769. Some teachers like to test on facts like these because there is one right answer to such questions. Before they ask students to regurgitate this sort of information, however, teachers must ask themselves whether there is a real purpose in requiring students to clutter their minds with specific dates, even though some specific dates, like 1066 or 1776, are perhaps worth knowing.

It is important that students understand the sequence of some major historical events. One might, for example, ask students in the upper elementary grades or in middle school to make certain rough divisions. Using Jesus Christ as a central figure because our system of dates is connected with his birth, one might present students with the names of various historical figures written on cards. Their first task would be to place each of the cards either to their left (born before Jesus) or to their right (born after Jesus). Such a pack of cards might include the names of anyone those students are studying at a given time—Pythagoras, Plato, Socrates, Aristotle, Alexander the Great, King Tut, Julius Caesar, Ovid, King Arthur, Charlemagne, Chaucer, Shakespeare, Emerson, Thoreau, etc. The cards should be well shuffled before the students get them.

Once the first task has been accomplished, students can then make further discriminations, using source books that will help them. Did Plato come before or after Alexander the Great? Did Charlemagne come before or after King Arthur? Working with time sequences rather than spe-

227

cific dates will help students avoid the sorts of anachronisms that some-times creep into student writing and discussion—things like criticizing Oedipus or Creon for not having a Christian value system, when, indeed, each lived in the era before Christ.

It is equally important for students to know that the Norman conquest came before Chaucer was writing, for example, because a great deal in Chaucer, including his use of English in his writing rather than the French that most socially prominent English citizens spoke in his day, cannot be understood without having this historical information.

CASE STUDY 7.4
Teacher Wonders Whether Students Must Know Exact Dates

As Luccia W. thought through some other things she was doing with her students, she began to realize that she had sometimes expected them to memorize information they really would never need to know. This year, rather than asking for specific dates, she adopted a new policy. On examinations, she would give her students lists of four or five events and ask them to arrange these events in chronological order from the earliest to the latest.

For dates that Luccia considered really important in what she was then teaching—things like the first landing of the Pilgrims at Plymouth Rock or the dates of the American Revolution—she would give full credit for any date that was within five years of the actual date and half credit for any date that was within fifteen years of it.

Essentially Luccia wanted to prevent her students from falling into traps that lack of chronological information could create. For example, Eugene O'Neill in 1936 became the first American playwright to win the Nobel Prize in Literature. He was in the State of Washington when he received news of his selection. He was not feeling well, so he decided not to go to Stockholm, Sweden, for the awards ceremony.

A contemporary student might think that O'Neill should have hopped on a jet and gone to this illustrious ceremony and might condemn O'Neill for not having done so, without realizing that in 1936 one crossed the United States by train and got to Europe by steamship, so that what would be a six- or seven-hour trip from Seattle today would have been a two- to three-week trip in O'Neill's day.

Having adopted this new policy in her examinations, Luccia found that her students developed a positive attitude toward learning historical events and also began to see them as interrelated events rather than as isolated islands in the chronological stream that represents history.

Questions

1. In the situation described, do you think Luccia is justified? After all, the date of the Pilgrims' landing at Plymouth *is* 1620. In your opinion, should a student receive full credit for 1617 or 1625? Defend your answer.

2. Does the fact that Luccia is teaching students in the fourth grade make a difference? Do you think high school or college instructors should proceed differently? Why or why not?

3. Luccia has used the birth of Jesus as her broad point of demarcation. Can you think of other significant events that mark the start of a new era, like the birth of Jesus did?

4. Can you think of situations in which Luccia's method is justified and other situations in which exact dates should be demanded, even of fourth-grade students?

Possibilities To Consider

1. Some of the parents of Luccia's students express concern to her about her method of dealing with dates. Luccia thinks that her students know more chronology than most sixth or seventh graders she knows, and she is convinced that her method is working. She tries to let parents know this. However, some of the parents have heard about E. D. Hirsch's *Cultural Literacy* (Boston: Houghton Mifflin, 1987) and are worried because Hirsch seems to be calling for specific, not approximate information. Reluctant to abandon a method that she is convinced is working and that her students like, she tells them that she is going to begin a new policy. The grading will be the same as it has been; however, all the students who get the exact date will receive a gold star on their papers. She buys a couple of boxes of gold stars, and soon finds that her students are competing avidly with each other to see who has the most stars.

2. One day Luccia's principal asks to see her before school. The principal has heard of the way Luccia is dealing with dates and asks her about it. Luccia explains what she is doing, but the principal says, "Ms. W., we try to deal in facts, not approximations. If you go to the bank and cash a check for $20, you don't expect to get $19 or $22." Luccia protests that this is hardly a fair comparison, but the principal is unmoved. She then says, "I have told my students that this is the way they will be graded. If I change that policy now, they're going to lose confidence in me." The principal's answer is, "If you don't change it, I will." Luccia leaves the office feeling quite defeated, but she realizes two things:

1. If you are going to try something new, clear it administratively before you do it; and

2. Do not promise your students anything for the whole school term or school year. Rather tell them you think it would be a good idea to try something for the next two weeks or for the next month. A promise is no longer binding after the time has run out!

3. One day one of Luccia's most dutiful students comes into the classroom ten minutes before school is to begin. Luccia is at her desk reading. Tina, the student, asks, "Ms. W., can I talk to you about something?" Luccia says, "Sure, Tina, what is it?" Tina tells her, "Well, you know how hard I work." Luccia affirms that she does. Tina continues, "I study and study to remember dates and facts. Whenever we have to use dates, mine are the right ones. But other people in class who don't have the right ones get the same grade I do. Do you think that's fair?" Luccia says, "Of course, it's always best to know the exact date, Tina, but some people have awful trouble with dates, and I think we have to help them, don't you?" Tina says, "I guess so, but. . ." Luccia interrupts and says, "You see, Tina, the problem I had with some of my students before was that they just didn't have any idea about when things happened. Some of them thought President Eisenhower had been a general in the Civil War and things like that. The way we are doing it now, no one in the class is confused about who goes with what event. I am glad you are working so hard to remember your dates. You keep on with it because you have a better head for dates than some people have."

Consider This

Many American students are shockingly deficient when it comes to understanding the sequences of history. This deficiency can prevent them from understanding why and how certain things in history occurred and from making accurate analytical judgments about history. People lacking a sense of historical chronology can misinterpret facts badly. For example, one might read somewhere that in 1920, 27 percent of public officials in Poland were Jewish. In 1945, no public officials were Jewish. If one did not realize that Hitler's campaigns against Jews had led to the Holocaust, the bare facts might suggest that in the twenty-five-year period between 1920 and 1945, Polish Jews lost interest in politics, obviously a fallacious conclusion.

Similarly, one might discover that between 1911 and 1930, six Germans won Nobel Prizes in Physics, but between 1931 and 1950, no Germans won Nobel Prizes in Physics. The conclusion could be that the study of physics declined in Germany in the years after 1931. Such was not the case. In Hitler's Germany, a number of people who were named to win the prize were forbidden by the government to accept it, thereby precluding their names from the list of recipients.

One extremely interesting way to deal with important dates with more mature students is to pose a question like, "In 1776, when the American colonists were fighting their revolution, what was going on in England? In Germany? In France? In Italy? In Egypt? In Japan? In Cuba? In Panama? In China?" It is also interesting to pose such questions as, "Did you know that in 1900, the year Queen Victoria died, Sigmund Freud was practicing psychoanalysis in Vienna, Tchaikovsky was composing music in Russia, and Eugene O'Neill was still in grade school?"

Facts out of sequence, facts unrelated to complementary events, are mere ornaments. Facts must bear a relationship to something to have meaning. Luccia's method moves toward realizing such an ideal.

WORK COMPLETED OUTSIDE THE CLASSROOM

It is worthwhile to have students work on projects outside school hours. Doing varied independent projects permits students to use abilities that may not be tested in the average classroom and to set their own pace. Artistic students who have trouble reading and writing, for instance, might create a collage that indicates their understanding of or insight about some element of what is going on in class that the teacher would not otherwise have realized they had arrived at.

Students should not be graded excessively for work of this sort, however, because some of them will get so much help from parents, siblings, or friends that the work is not actually theirs. If students write outside reports on something—and this can be a valuable learning experience for students who do it honestly—teachers have to make sure that they understand what they have written about. One way to assess their understandings is to have them talk to the whole class about their reports without actually reading them to the class and then entertaining questions about their presentations.

Before their work on projects like this begins, students should know it is expected that the work they submit will be their own. They should understand what plagiarism is not only by being told about it but also by being asked to write their own definition of plagiarism after the matter has been discussed in class and after they have discussed it—possibly in small groups. Teachers must emphasize that outside work will be judged on its content. An outside report that contains misinformation, is beset by recurring inaccuracies, and is badly written will not be graded leniently because it has been stapled into a handmade, well-decorated folder that took the student five hours to create.

CASE STUDY 7.5
Teacher Deals with Substandard Student Report

The science class Bart B. teaches in Logan Middle School is quite cooperative. It is a class whose students range from below average to average in ability. Bart is trying to give them an overview of the various sciences they will be exposed to in senior high school. He is not expected to go into great depth with them, but to provide them with what is essentially a scientific overview.

The class has kept up with its work pretty well, and as March approaches, Bart decides that he will ask each student to select one scientist whom they have studied in class and to do an outside paper on that scientist. Having completed the paper, which will be handed in for grading, all students are expected to give a five- to ten-minute oral presentation on the person about whom they wrote and to field questions the class asks.

Jack M., a student who has done "C" work up until now, is the first to give his presentation. He is to speak on the work of Marie Curie. He gives a quite flat presentation, capturing little of the excitement of what Marie discovered, and he did not mention her husband and collaborator, Pierre Curie, at all. When Jack called for questions, the room was still. Finally, one student asked, "When did she die?" Jack did not know and had to search through his paper to find the date, 1939. Finally, Bart thought he should ask a question, and he inquired, "Were many other women working in the French laboratory where Marie worked at that time?"

Jack looked bewildered for a moment and then said, "I guess so."

When Bart read Jack's paper that night, he knew that the language of the paper was not Jack's. He looked in the "C" volume of his *World Book Encyclopedia* and found that Jack's paper corresponded almost exactly to the *World Book* article on Marie Curie. The only difference was that Jack had left out some material and, in doing so, had omitted some of the facts most pertinent to anyone who really wanted to understand Marie Curie's singular contribution to society. Bart has to decide how to deal with Jack in this situation. This is the first out-of-class paper Jack has ever been called upon to write, and Bart is sure that the boy really thought he was doing research when he copied his information down and typed it up neatly. His paper had an elaborate cover, a collage made of cut-out microscopes, beakers, and other scientific equipment.

Questions

1. What specific things might Bart have done to help his students understand the kinds of papers they were expected to write? Might he have invited someone in his school to spend a class period with them discussing how to write a paper? If so, whom should he have invited?

2. If students are assigned papers like the one Jack did, should they be required to provide documentation? If so, should a specific number of sources be required?

3. What is the difference between a research paper and a resource paper? Which of the two do you think Bart's students have been asked to do?

4. Can you think of any kinds of papers that middle school students might do that do not require them to use sources but that still expose them to putting a paper together? Discuss.

Possible Solutions

1. Realizing that Jack has copied his paper from an encyclopedia and that he has not even copied it very well, Bart decides that he has to spend a day with his students setting up new rules for doing papers. He drafts those rules the night before and has them mimeographed, as he now realizes he should have done in the first place. His rules are as follows:

1. You will be writing a paper about one important person in science. You must write this paper from an outline that you submit to me one week before the paper is due.

2. Two days before your paper is due, I need to see your rough draft and your notes.

3. You should check a minimum of three sources on your subject; one of these should be a periodical source like a journal or magazine.

4. Indicate what resources you used as you gathered information—things like the card catalog, the Union List, the *Readers' Guide to Periodical Literature*, etc.

5. Remember that your sources should help you to write your paper and to make your presentation. I do not want you to copy from them directly. Read your sources; then construct your presentation based on them.

6. All papers will be submitted in plain folders—no decorations.

2. Bart realizes that Jack's paper and presentation have been unsatisfactory, but few of his students realize this. He knows that he has to do two things: (1) he has to convey to the rest of the class exactly what is expected of them; and (2) he has to deal with Jack, whose plagiarism cannot be overlooked but who genuinely did not know that he was plagiarizing. One other matter soon comes to light that Bart will have to deal with. After school, he goes to the media center to check some textbooks, and he discovers they have been mutilated and that all kinds of pictures are missing. Some of the missing pictures appear to have provided Jack with the illustrations for his elaborate cover. He reluctantly decides that this matter is serious enough to warrant administrative intervention, and he reluctantly goes in to talk with the vice-principal.

3. When Jack is halfway through his paper, Bart realizes that the other students are bored and are not following well. He says to Jack, "I think that's enough, Jack. You still have some work to do on this paper. We'll talk about it, and you can tell us more about Marie Curie sometime later." As Jack gathers his things up, a couple of his classmates stick their tongues out at him, and one girl says, "I'll bet you get an 'F' on your paper!" Jack is visibly unhappy.

Consider This

Students' first ventures into writing a resource paper outside of class are shots in the dark for most of them. They have no idea what is expected of them unless teachers provide them with guidelines. In Bart's situation, he might have tried to work with the English teacher who teaches this very class two periods after they have science. If he and their English teacher combine their efforts, the students should learn a great deal more, and Bart will be able to share the burden of evaluating the papers.

One of the most important lessons of early research was lost on Jack because of Bart's approach. Jack did not learn to discriminate between valuable information about his subject and incidental information. Jack never pointed out how unusual it was for a woman to work in the sciences when Marie Curie was doing her work. He did not point out that she was the first person in history to win two Nobel prizes, one in Physics in 1903 and one in Chemistry in 1911. He did not mention the chemical elements, radium and plutonium, she discovered, and he did not relate her work to anything that served the good of humankind, although her work with X-ray technology has directly affected most humans living today.

Jack's research was lifeless and uninteresting—probably to him as well as to his classmates. Had Bart spent more time at the prewriting stage, the results could have been dramatically different. His colleague who teaches English could likely have helped him in this important area.

RESOURCE PAPERS VS. RESEARCH PAPERS

Public school media centers are not research libraries. Therefore, if secondary school teachers assign research papers to their students, they may be inviting trouble, encouraging plagiarism, and expecting the impossible. This is not to suggest that teachers should not work to prepare their students for the research papers they will likely be called upon to write in college. Rather, teachers need to ask themselves what they can best teach their college-bound students to prepare for what lies ahead.

Among the things secondary school teachers can realistically hope to achieve, the following are important:

- How does one locate sources?
- What indexes are available to lead researchers to sources?
- How does one document interviews?
- How does one take notes effectively?
- How does one outline a proposed research project?
- How does one decide on a topic?
- How does one find out whether that subject has been written about previously?
- How does one limit that topic and make it manageable?
- How does one write a footnote or an endnote?
- What kinds of footnotes and endnotes are there?
- What style sheets are appropriate to what kinds of research?
- How does one compile a bibliography?
- When should a bibliography be divided into categories?
- What should a bibliography include? Not include?

Students will benefit from spending two or three days in the media center looking for specific information. Teachers can devise worksheets so that all students have some obscure fact to look up during their time in the media center. One might ask, for example, "What is the first name of American novelist Reynolds Price?" or "What are the first and middle names of N. Northcutt who did research in adult illiteracy?" or "What was the third largest export of New Zealand in 1984?" The specific information demanded is not important. All the students, however, should keep track of exactly how they went about answering their assigned questions. Teachers should make sure the answer to each question is available in their school's media center. Students should keep track of every source they consulted, of every dead end they found themselves in. By pursuing this assignment, students will begin to get the feel of a library and its resources. They will enjoy the challenge.

Students should begin to work on assignments that demand them to use their analytical abilities and their reasoning skills. They can be guided in this direction by being asked to do resource papers rather than research papers. For example, a student might be asked to find three reviews—one positive, one negative, and one mixed—of a recent movie or of a book they are reading in one of their classes. They should read these reviews and then write a paper in which they analyze the arguments of the three reviewers. Is one more fair than another? Is one obviously better informed than the other two? Are any of the reviewers guilty of making factual errors that affect their interpretations? Did any of the reviewers change your opinions about the movie or book being reviewed? In what ways did this/these reviewer(s) bring about a change in you?

CASE STUDY 7.6
Teacher Adjusts Research Paper Assignment

Westside High School demands that English teachers of college-bound students have their students do research papers in both the junior and the senior years. Maria W., who teaches two senior sections and one junior section of such students, wants to stay within school rules. Her husband, Ben, who heads the freshman English program in a nearby university, is dubious about the requirement, however. He deals every semester with bewildered students who are accused of plagiarism for doing exactly what they did in preparing so-called research papers in high school, and they often had these papers—usually graded "A"—to show him.

At her husband's urging, Maria has decided to teach her students research techniques and conventions, but not to have them do research papers as such. Rather she decides to try having them write a paper about their favorite sport or about the hobby they are most enthusiastic about, and then to give them a resource assignment based on the interests revealed in these papers.

A student who ties trout flies and has begun to have some success in selling them is asked to compose a dictionary of at least thirty terms used in fly tying and/or in trout fishing. This student must identify each term according to the part(s) of speech it might be and must do an etymological study of one of the thirty words, using the *Oxford English Dictionary*, which the media center has both in a multivolume set and on microfilm. The report is to be fully documented in the form prescribed by the Modern Language Association (MLA).

A student whose hobby is reading about research in diabetes and who is herself diabetic is asked to find medical reports written within the last seven years on two drastically different approaches in the medical management of diabetes—something like injected insulin versus insulin dispersed through a treated patch attached to the patient's skin—and to write analytically about the validity of each treatment as it is reflected in her reading. She is to document her paper according to the style sheet of the American Psychological Association (APA).

Another student is trying to decide between getting hard or soft contact lenses and, because of this interest, is asked to present data about the virtues and limitations of both types of lens, taking into account as well long-term, gas-permeable lenses versus lenses that are removed every night.

Maria's only worry is that she does not know much about some of the topics her students will be writing about. In the past she has had all her students write on literary topics, and she felt equipped by training to evaluate these papers fairly.

Questions

1. How much do you think you need to know about a topic in order to assess student resource papers at the secondary school level? If you insist on having your students write about things you know well, what limitation does this place on them?

2. Should all students be taught the same conventions of documentation, or does it make sense to teach people the conventions they will be expected to know in their main areas of interest?

3. What are the main points of having students go to the library or media center, each with an assignment to find some relatively obscure fact?

4. If you took your students to the library for a meeting with the librarian immediately before they begin work on their resource papers, what sorts of things would you hope the librarian might tell them?

5. What specific prewriting lessons might you use to assure your getting the best possible papers?

Possible Solutions

1. Maria talks over with her husband the course she has decided to follow, and he thinks it makes good sense. When she expresses her insecurity about not knowing much about some of her students'

topics, Ben reminds her, "You know more than you think about a lot of things. Look at all the reading you do—*National Geographic, New Yorker, Smithsonian, Time, Money,* the Sunday *New York Times*— what all else do we take?" Ben continues, "You know, if you make all your students write about things you know about, you'll stunt their mental growth. Now is the time for them to strike out and explore their interests. They should be doing live investigation instead of dead research. That's why I like your idea." Maria feels better, and when the papers come in, she feels much better because they are interesting to read. They still have their rough spots, but they have vitality, and that counts for a great deal.

2. Maria investigates her school library, and she finds that it is pretty inadequate to handle a hundred students who have papers to do. She is at her wits' end until she remembers some controlled resource books she has seen in her department's book storage room. She goes down and finds a treasure trove of controlled resource books that are specifically designed to enable students to set up a resource paper without having to use library resources. The resources required are all incorporated in the controlled text. She pulls out two sets, one on Twain's *The Adventures of Tom Sawyer,* the other on the raid at Harpers Ferry, and decides to let her students get their research feet wet by using these books.

3. Maria decides that she will lead into the resource paper gradually by having her students do an assignment that will require them to make judgments based on the analysis of some data. The national press is filled with news of how a train wreck occurred. Some sources are convinced that mechanical failure was to blame. Other more inflammatory sources are convinced that the train crew was impaired at the time of the accident either by drugs or by alcohol. Still others believe that someone had disconnected a crucial signal a mile south of where the northbound train ran off the track. Maria's students all will analyze the reporting of this accident in three different types of sources and will attempt to reach generalizations, in a three- or four-page paper, about the reliability of each source, asking themselves such questions as these: (1) Does the most reliable report contain any inaccurate or speculative information? (2) Does the least reliable report contain any accurate information? (3) Which report is the most subjective? The most objective? (4) At what kinds of audiences is each report aimed?

Consider This

Students who are eased into doing extensive projects like resource papers can be totally bewildered by the assignment if they have never tackled anything like it before. Skillful teachers will analyze various skills students have to develop to do this sort of paper and then will incorporate some of these skills into the classwork that precedes the long paper. The day spent in the library tracking down some bit of information will help students to see how to locate the resources they will need in order to locate one small fact in one big library.

At this stage in their development, some students have not yet learned how to assess the validity of things they read. Many middle school and high school students think that anything in print must be true. It takes some direction to make them see that falsehoods frequently exist in print. Once they learn this lesson, they will be unlikely to cite authorities without first establishing the validity of what those authorities are saying. Many students are surprised to learn that quoting directly from something in print and writing a footnote that cites the writer of the quotation do not *per se* make that person an authority.

IS BIGGER BETTER?

Students usually like to know what is expected of them, so it is helpful for teachers to spell out in writing exactly what is required in written assignments done outside the classroom. Because of the pressure teachers are under, they usually assign relatively short papers. Assignments should be made in terms of the number of words rather than the number of pages because margins, handwriting, typefaces, and other elements of papers vary. Some students think they can ignore the directions they have received regarding the length of papers to be submitted. Some also think that the longer the paper is, the better it will be. Everyone who writes, however, has to conform to certain stipulations, and students are being badly trained if they are not forced to complete their assignments within the stipulations their teachers impose.

If *Time* asks one of its reviewers to do a 250-word review of Barry Lopez's *Crossing Open Ground* (New York: Scribner's, 1988), they will not accept a thousand-word review simply because the reviewer got carried away. The reviewer may begin by writing a thousand-word review; but if this happens, the next job to be done is to cut that review down to within a few words of the stipulated length. Learning proportion in writing and commenting is of singular importance. We have all been to conferences where four speakers were scheduled for a two-hour session, allowing essentially for four twenty-minute speeches followed by a question-answer session of ten minutes after each speech. If the first speaker rambles on for an hour, the audience is being cheated, and the other presenters are being treated badly. No matter how global a topic one is speaking or writing about, that topic must be confined to the stipulated length, and making the discriminations that are necessary to keep it to that length is part of any presenter's self-discipline and control.

CASE STUDY 7.7
Teacher Downgrades Paper for Being Too Long

Casey M. teaches a sociology course to high school juniors in his school's college preparatory program. Each of his students is expected to do a documented paper on a topic that can be researched in the school's media center or in the local public library. Casey spends a full week team teaching his course with Linda V., an English supervisor in his district, who tries at least twice a year to get back into a high school classroom, so that she will not lose touch with the realities of teaching. Linda essentially teaches Casey's students methods of note taking and documentation. Casey teaches them how to locate resources in sociology and how to track down those sources.

Before Casey's students embark on their own resource projects, each of which Casey has approved in advance, they are provided with a mimeographed guide for doing the sort of work Casey expects. He specifies that all papers must be typed, that margins must be one inch all around except for the top margin of the first page, which will be two inches, and that the stipulated length is one thousand words, which he also defines as being about three typed, double-spaced pages. He is clear to say that 975 words will be all right with him and that 1050 words will not upset him, but that students should keep the one-thousand-word length in mind as they prepare their final drafts.

When the papers come in, most conform to Casey's specifications. Susan Y., however, has produced a thirty-seven page behemoth on sources of income among Chicago's homeless. The documentation in Susan's paper is commendable, and the effort she put forth is an honest effort. The paper, however, does not meet the instructor's stipulations, and Casey, after considerable inner struggle, decides not to put any grade on the paper, but rather to return it to Susan as unacceptable. He writes a note to her, which he attaches to the paper, in which he says, "Your effort here is obvious, Susan, and I applaud your industry. You have, however, not met the requirements of this assignment. Your paper is ten thousand words longer than what the assignment sheet called for (see Section B of the direction packet you received). I am returning the paper unread. You will have a seven-day extension to complete this assignment." When Susan gets her paper back, she puts her head down on her desk and sobs. As soon as the period ends, she bolts from the room.

Susan is a fine student, much interested in sociology. Her father is a member of the Board of Education. It is presumed that Susan will attend Bryn Mawr, her mother's alma mater. Casey knows all of this. Therefore, he is not surprised that Susan's parents schedule an appointment to see him after school the next day. Susan's mother is quite reasonable, but her father is furious. He rants at Casey, "Susan did nothing for two weeks but work on that paper. No wonder our schools are in such sorry shape if teachers like you discourage students who put forth a great effort!"

Casey says, "I think we really need to discuss this in Dr. W.'s [the school principal's] office. I told him you were coming to see me, and he is expecting us."

Questions

1. Why, aside from having more to read than they can handle, do you think people who assign papers stipulate a length? How would you deal with a student who either comes to you and asks permission to exceed that length substantially or exceeds it without talking it over with you?

2. If you were required to write a paper of 750 words, for example, on the audience of *Beowulf* or on the Monroe Doctrine or on the turbine engine, all the subjects of book-length studies, what skills would you be learning as you worked to remain within the limitations of your assignment?

3. In the world of book reviewing, some periodicals publish multi-page reviews of a book, and others publish 150-word reviews of the same book. What do you think accounts for this kind of disparity?

4. Do you think it is preferable to downgrade a paper that is either much too short or much too long to satisfy your requirement or to return it as not having met the conditions of the assignment? If you did the latter, would you penalize the paper that comes in to replace this one?

Possible Solutions

1. Casey realizes that although he led into this writing assignment clearly and well, he might have spared Susan the disappointment she is now suffering had he asked students to hand in drafts a week before the final paper was due or had he in some other way kept a clos-

er check on what his students were doing. It had not occurred to him that a problem of this sort would arise or he would have guarded against it, as he will the next time he makes an assignment of this kind.

2. Casey knows how much effort Susan has put into this paper, and he is convinced that the paper is her own work. He calls her at home the night before he is to return the graded papers and asks if she can see him fifteen minutes before homeroom begins the next day. Susan asks, "Is it about my paper?" and Casey responds, "Yes, it is." Susan immediately says, "I know it was long, but I did it all by myself. I swear I didn't have any help with it!" Casey says, "I know it's your work, Susan. It's something else. We need to talk about it." Susan has a restless night, wondering what she could have done wrong. The next morning she is at school half an hour before homeroom, getting there just as Casey comes in. They go to the departmental office and sit down. Casey says, "I glanced through your paper, Susan, and it is impressive and well documented. The only problem is that it does not do what the assignment asks for. I am not going to penalize you for not staying within the word limit, but I am gong to have to ask you to reduce this paper to a thousand words and resubmit it." Susan says, "But there's too much in it to say in a thousand words." Casey answers, "I know there is. That means that you are going to have to work hard to decide what the most important and salient facts in your paper are and then to write a paper that emphasizes those facts. Let's put it this way, Susan. If the president visited our high school someday when he was making a seven-state tour, you could probably write a hundred pages about what happened here that day. No one would print that much. If a newspaper wanted your story, they would want it in about 200 words. You would have to decide what two or three things that happened in the visit were most important for you to write about."

3. Casey thinks that students must learn from their mistakes. He stated explicitly and in writing what was required. When he received Susan's mammoth fulfillment of his lean requirement, he simply wrote across the top of it, "Too long. Unresponsive to assignment. F." He handed it back with the rest of the papers. Susan, who had expected her work to earn her the highest grade in the class, ended up with the lowest, and she began to sob hysterically, muttering about how Casey was destroying her life and ruining her chances of going to Bryn Mawr. Finally, when she is more composed, she asks if she can do the paper over. Casey tells her that she can't. He says, "If you were writing this for a magazine, the magazine would have gone to press already. You have to learn to follow instructions."

Consider This

Mishaps of the kind depicted in this case study will occur, especially in highly competitive situations. Teachers can guard against them by requiring that papers come in a little bit at a time—notes, outlines, drafts, etc. Had Casey done this, Susan probably would not have gotten into this situation. The best way to deal with a situation of this sort once it has happened is to give the student involved a reasonable amount of time to do the assignment according to specification, most likely without exacting a penalty if this is the first time such a problem has surfaced.

Susan will learn a great deal from honing this paper down into something manageable. Once I asked a prolific writer of scholarly books, "Why is it that you have written so many books but almost no articles?" Her response was, "I never had time to write articles. They are much harder work because they have to be controlled so much more." It is just that sort of control that Susan will learn when she finally gets a thousand or so words from her huge paper.

FINAL EXAMINATIONS

As students yourselves, you probably have come to the end of classes in many a semester and wished there were no final examination. Final examinations can be threatening. They often require one to review a whole semester's work in a course rather than to review just the few chapters that were covered on each examination as the course progressed.

The extensive review most finals require, however, is one of the best justifications for giving comprehensive final examinations. The courses many students take remain patchworks of information until they review the entire course and come to see how one part of it interrelates to other parts of it. Organizing one's information about a subject in preparation for a final examination can be one of the most rewarding experiences in students' lives, even though it may be a while before they realize what has happened to them intellectually as they prepared for an examination that hung over them like the sword of Damocles.

CASE STUDY 7.8
Teacher Preplans Final Exam for First Time

Joyce W. always gives her fifth-grade students final examinations in all their subjects because her school expects her to and also because this is her students' last year in elementary school. Next year they will be in the middle school where they will be expected to take final examinations.

Nevertheless, Joyce was not wholly satisfied with the way her examinations had gone in the past. As a less-experienced teacher, she realized that she did not give enough thought to final examinations. Instead, it was suddenly time for finals, and she dashed off exams that she hoped were fair. This year, however, is her eighth year of teaching, and she is determined to take a new approach.

Right after Easter vacation, a full two months before the end of the school year, Joyce tells her students that they will have the kind of mathematics examination they have always had, a combination of regular problems and word problems, but that she is going to combine their English and social studies examination. This examination will consist of thirty multiple-choice questions, of which they may answer any twenty-five. There will be ten short-answer questions, of which they may answer any seven. This part of the examination will count for 40 percent of their grades in the two courses. The other part of the evaluation will be an essay examination with a difference.

One week before the final examination, each student will be expected to hand in five essay questions, any two of which they would be willing to respond to. Each question should be broad and searching. To make sure that they are, Joyce is going to allow up to fifteen points for the quality of the questions. Any student who receives less than 5 percent on this part of the assignment will be arbitrarily assigned two teacher-composed essay questions to write on.

On the day of the final, Joyce will return to all of her students the essay question sheets they turned in to her the week before. She will have marked the two essay questions she wants each student to write about. The two essays will count for a possible total of forty-five points. Students will return their essay topic sheets with their completed essays.

Questions

1. What safeguard has Joyce built into her system of having her students write their own essay examinations? Can you think of any other safeguards that might assure the integrity of an examination of this sort?

2. Do you think Joyce's students will study as much material when they prepare for this examination as they might cover had she given more conventional examinations in English and social studies?

3. What do you think about giving final examinations in the upper elementary or early middle grades?

4. How would you deal with a student who had done reasonable work throughout the term but had fallen apart completely on the final examination?

Possibilities To Consider

1. Joyce decides that the final examination should be a joint effort. She divides her classes into groups of four or five students each, and each group works on making an examination for the course. Joyce will finally make up her own final examination, but she will see all of her students' work before she does, and she has told them that she might use actual items from the material they have given her. She is convinced that the best way for them to review the material they are responsible for is to devise examinations that will test it adequately. She also knows that in framing their questions, they will engage in a good lesson in the exact use of language.

2. Joyce reacts against giving students at this level final examinations. She decides that it just places too much emphasis on grades, not enough on learning. She decides that she will just give a last major examination for each subject, but that it will cover only the material her classes have covered since their last major examination. Now she has to decide whether to share her decision with her students or to let them study for a final examination and end up taking a much less comprehensive test. A friend tries to discourage her from the latter course, telling her that her students will feel cheated if they have studied all the material and are tested on only a tenth or so of it. Also, they might have concentrated their studying on the early part of the material, much of which they feel they have forgotten the details of, only to be tested on the material they studied less well.

3. Joyce can understand why the school wants to get its students used to having comprehensive final examinations. She agrees in principle with the idea. She decides, however, to let each of her students decide how much the final examination will count for him or her. She is willing to allow the final to count for anywhere from 15 to 45 percent of the grade in the course. Two days before the examination, she has all students indicate on a piece of paper how much they want the examination to count for them. To her surprise, all but two of her thirty-one students opt for 15 percent, even though some of her weaker students could get significantly higher grades by taking a greater risk.

Consider This

Anything that will help students to develop a comprehensive view of something they are studying is likely to be of help to them. Using the technique Joyce employed in the case study takes some of the mystique out of final examinations and makes them less scary. Joyce has not abdicated control, but she has given her students options, and she has involved them in the process of composing the examination. She has imposed an excellent control in allowing credit for the quality of the essay questions the students devise. This control will discourage students from asking narrow questions that reveal only minimally what a student has learned.

Giving students some options and allowing them some voice in determining what they will be responsible for has an incalculably positive effect on classroom environment and morale. Joyce's standards have remained high, but she has approached her students with a good sense of their feelings and insecurities.

WHAT IS AN EDUCATION?

It has been said, perhaps a little flippantly, that anyone's education is what remains with the person ten or fifteen years after he or she has left school. Certainly as our students go into the world to live their own lives, they will forget a great deal that we have struggled to teach them. The bewildering part is that they will all remember different things, all of them in effect having a very different education from their peers even though they may have taken many of the same classes together.

Students who become surgeons will know intimately the parts of the nervous system that their biology teacher forced them to learn as high school sophomores. The students who sat on each side of the surgeon in the biology class may well have forgotten the nervous system, but the one who became an engineer will still remember and be able to apply the binomial theorem and the one who became a commercial pilot will remember a great deal about where the stars are placed in the heavens. As teachers who routinely compose tests for students, we probably need to ask ourselves constantly, "What do my students have to know?" The only problem with this question is that there are as many legitimate answers to it as there are students in any class. The best we can do is to make sure that in the course of any school term we allow all our students some opportunity to demonstrate the best they can do in our subject fields. This means that we need to construct tests that allow students who excel at rote memory to demonstrate their ability to remember, but that we also provide opportunities for those who excel at problem solving or reasoning to demonstrate those high-level skills.

We need also to help students to become "test-savvy." The students we deal with will live in a world filled with tests of one sort or another. If we equip them to take tests, we perform a great service for them. We need to let them know that the subconscious mind is a huge container of specific information, not all of which can necessarily be retrieved on command. However, students who read over a test before beginning to answer questions and who then go back and answer the questions they are sure of will find that while they are performing one task—answering questions—their subconscious mind will be sorting through all it knows and bringing a great deal of information to the fore. Once students have handled what they are sure of in the test, they can usually then go back and answer with increased confidence questions they might not initially have been able to remember the answers to.

One of the best ways for students to prepare for objective examinations over a specific body of material is to compose objective examinations on the material. Students who study their readings and their notes with an eye toward composing an objective examination from the material may discover that their dummy examinations pose many of the same questions that appear on the official examination.

Teachers will find that students are extremely grateful for the opportunity to be involved in devising some of their own means of evaluation. Some students do well on objective examinations but cannot write essay examinations very well, and vice versa. Throughout any semester, all students should be exposed to both kinds of examinations, but why should students not have a choice in the all-important final examination of writing either an objective or a subjective examination?

Many subjects lend themselves easily to this sort of choice, and students—even those who end up not doing too well—are deeply grateful for having options made available to them, as we all are. Also, when students are permitted to complete two or more types of examinations, teachers will find the grading of these examinations less boring than the grading of fifty or a hundred papers that are all essentially the same.

The most important thing teachers can do as they decide upon the most effective testing techniques to use with their students is to develop a philosophy of testing based on the question, "What do my students need to know when they leave this course?" Once teachers have arrived at reasonable, tentative answers to this question, they are well on the way to testing students in a meaningful professional context.

8. I GUESS I *WOULD* DO IT ALL OVER AGAIN!

Every profession has its bleak days as well as its days of incredible satisfaction. Sometimes we go through long periods wishing that Saturday came immediately after Monday every week, but for most of us there are also periods when we hate to see Friday come and are eager to get back on Monday morning to doing something we were in the midst of when we left school on Friday. If you are to be the most effective kind of teacher, you will pay attention to your personal needs, and you will work hard to keep intellectually vital and excited about ideas. Sometimes you may even have to neglect your work for a weekend and do something totally divorced from school and from youngsters. If you do not do this occasionally, you may thwart your own development as an adult and gradually turn into an overgrown child. As a teacher, you cannot afford to allow this to happen.

Teachers have to keep in mind that some of the rewards in the profession are slow to come. Even if you deal consistently and fairly with every student you teach, some students will go away hating you, perhaps because you demanded that they be punctual or that they do their work more neatly than they have or that they sit apart from other students because they do not have the self-control to pay attention when they sit immediately beside someone they can talk to or play tricks on.

Even students like this may eventually come around to appreciating you. It may take them a decade or more to discover that you treated them the way you did because you were trying to prepare them to face the realities of the world in which they now find themselves.

Teachers are among a small group of professionals who usually consider themselves failures if they do not succeed 100 percent. All surgeons expect to lose some of their patients; indeed, the best surgeons lose the largest number of patients because the best surgeons end up handling the most difficult—at times, the most hopeless—cases. These surgeons deplore losing patients, but few of them develop a negative self-image because some patients die. They know that surgeons are judged on how appropriate their procedures are for the patients they treat.

The best attorneys, especially those who practice criminal law, lose cases, but are still excellent attorneys. They do the best job they can for their clients given the limitations of each case they defend. An accused mass murderer has the constitutional right to be deemed innocent until proved guilty and to have access to a legal defense. If that person is indisputably guilty, a good lawyer will not bring about an acquittal, nor should an acquittal be considered the only successful outcome for an attorney who is handling such a case.

Teachers are admirable, lovable people because of all professionals, they are probably the most idealistic. They do not become teachers because they want to get rich. They do not become teachers because they expect to receive enormous recognition. They do not become teachers because they want to have easy lives. Rather, they become teachers because they are giving, socially concerned people who believe they can make changes for the better in society. They realize that as teachers they may be able to turn a few lives around. If teachers have any universal flaw, it is that so many of them are perfectionists when it comes to their own performance, and this very perfectionism drives some teachers from the profession prematurely.

The author hopes that this book will help teachers and prospective teachers to realize that all teachers have limitations common to the human animal generally. The case studies should help equip teachers to deal with typical situations that confront them in every day of their professional careers. The situations you encounter will not be exactly as I have depicted them, but working with the problems presented in the case studies should help you to cope with matters that come up in your own classrooms.

SOMETHING TO THINK ABOUT ON A GLUM DAY

If this is one of those days on which you feel unappreciated, unloved, and unlovely—as all of us occasionally will—think of a teacher who has irritated many of her grammar school students throughout the years of a long teaching career, the fictional Miss Dove, a teacher based upon an actual veteran in the classroom and depicted with tremendous fidelity by Frances Gray Patton in *Good Morning, Miss Dove* (New York: Garrett Price, 1954).

Miss Dove insisted on obedience, but this insistence was not to satisfy her own ego; it was to help her students learn something about self-control, although she never articulated this motive to her classes in any direct way. Miss Dove was a legend in her community. She had taught three generations of some families. Many students, especially boy students who wanted their own ways and were in the process of developing the macho characteristics often encouraged in boys, breathed a sign of relief when they finished the fourth grade and did not have to put up with Miss Dove any more.

Somehow, though, these boys, when they grew into men, usually realized that Miss Dove had been an important ingredient in their development, in their coming of age. She was part of an initiatory process that boys probably need to go through.

As World War II raged, Miss Dove was near retirement age. She probably had her own moments of doubt about what her contributions to society had been. She probably asked herself at least a few times, "Have I lived my life well? Have I made an impact upon society?" Because people often ask such questions of themselves when a slight downturn in their spirits has made them reflective and introspective, Miss Dove probably concluded more than once that her life had not really meant very much to anyone.

It was then that she received a letter from one of her former students, now a sailor in the U.S. Navy, whose ship had been torpedoed and sunk in combat. This sailor, who has resented Miss Dove for a few years after the year he spent in her fourth grade, had found himself on a life raft bobbing around in the Pacific Ocean after his ship was destroyed, and it was weeks before he was rescued. How had he survived? By remembering that when he was in the fourth grade and would ask Miss Dove to be excused to get a drink of water, she would always tell him he could not leave the room: "You have work to do. You wait until the bell rings. Your thirst won't kill you."

Miss Dove was right. He always survived until the bell rang, and on the raft—sunburned, feverish, totally bereft—he could still hear Miss Dove telling him that his thirst would not kill him, that he could wait until the bell rang. The bell in this larger context was the rescue ship that eventually appeared on the horizon and picked up a sailor who had been without water long enough that he really should long ago have gone mad from his overwhelming thirst and jumped overboard.

FINDING YOUR TEACHING STYLE

What would you say if someone asked you what a good teacher looks like? You would probably be at a loss for words because good teachers can be short or tall, thin or fat, tense or relaxed, male or female, swarthy or pale. What makes teachers good or bad, successful or unsuccessful is their ability to interact meaningfully with students and to communicate learning behaviors to these students in ways they can understand and adopt. Teachers' looks have nothing to do with how successful they will be, although teachers who have ready smiles sometimes get along better with students than those who do not.

Part of any teacher's task is to help students correct errors they make in their work, and this is a negative kind of responsibility. A larger and more important task, however, is to help students understand the errors they have made so that they will be able to find general ways to avoid making such errors in future work. The most effective teachers realize that more important than their search for errors in student work is their ability to help students see the strengths apparent in their work. If students begin to build on their strengths, sometimes their errors diminish.

Effective teachers are fair and consistent when they deal with students. They are also clear in telling each student exactly what is expected of him or her in the specific assignments they give. Students have considerable confidence in teachers who give their directions in writing and who let students know in advance—also in writing—what will be going on in class for two- or three-week periods. Good teachers deviate from their lesson plans when it is appropriate for them to do so, but if students know their teachers have overall plans, they feel secure about studying with them.

Research has shown that most of us teach much as we have been taught. We respect and value certain teachers, and, understandably, we model much of our own teaching on theirs. Such modeling is not inherently wrong as long as we remember that we are individuals, that we cannot *be* someone else. The best teachers are those who have learned from the people who taught them but who also strive consciously and calculatedly to experiment with various approaches to teaching in order to arrive at teaching styles that are best for them.

If any single teaching style were the *right* one, then everyone could be programmed to teach that way, and everyone would teach in the same way. How boring our schools would be if that happened! Some of us teach by moving all over the room as we conduct class; others sit down behind a desk and talk. Some involve their students in a broad range of group activities; others stand before their students and lecture for class hour after class hour. None of these styles is basically wrong, although some of them might be wrong for you or for your students. If your style succeeds in helping students to learn, your style can be adjudged effective. But a successful style is a style one believes in and is comfortable with.

If you have assessed what your individual style is, don't hesitate to adopt that style in your teaching. Also, don't be reluctant to look for ways to broaden your style. If, for example, group work makes you nervous, even though you have read a great deal about the benefits it offers and even though you know that several of your friends have wonderful results when they use it, don't plunge headlong into group work simply because you think it is a good idea. Rather, move gradually into it, reserving perhaps the last ten minutes of class every Tuesday and Thursday for it over a month-long period. Once you have tried group work, you might feel better about using it as a regular teaching technique than you initially did. If this is the case, then you should begin to increase your use of it.

If, on the other hand, the ten minutes two days a week that you devote to group work leaves you with a migraine, don't go on with it. Enough teachers in your school will be using group work as an instructional device that your students will not be deprived if you adopt an approach with which you feel more comfortable personally. Students are quick to discover the things that make their teachers feel insecure and apprehensive, so teach them from the strongest, most secure personal base you can establish.

A FINAL WORD

My final word is really a final wish, a sincerely articulated hope. I want you to succeed as teachers. I want this to happen because I am convinced that education is important for society, particularly for a society as participatory as ours in the United States.

Teachers are second only to parents in helping to mold the raw human material from which our nation is made. Without strong human resources, a nation, no matter how great its other resources, is bankrupt. It is up to schools and families more than to any other social institutions to provide our society with the means by which it can continue to prosper and prevail as a bastion of freedom in a troubled, sometimes divided, and frequently dangerous and threatening world.

ANNOTATED BIBLIOGRAPHY

Alabiso, Frank P., and James C. Hansen. *The Hyperactive Child in the Classroom.* Springfield, Ill.: Charles C. Thomas Publishers, 1977. Especially useful for what it has to say in its chapter on concepts of distractability and for its comments on hyperactivity as a cognitive dysfunction.

Bloom, Allan. *The Closing of the American Mind.* New York: Simon and Schuster, 1987. One of the most frequently read and cited books about education in the 1980s, Bloom's attack on U.S. schools reflects a nearly total misunderstanding of the purposes of mass education in a society as diverse as that in the United States. He would cure the nation's educational ills by returning to the educational ideals of Plato's Athens, a slave state in which only 10 percent of the residents held citizenry. An approach so elitist as to be irrelevant.

Brown, Muriel, ed. *The Structure of Disadvantage.* London: Heinemann, 1983. The essays focus on the disadvantaged in Britain, but they have strong implications for readers in the United States. The discussion of family structure among the disadvantaged provides a few unique insights.

Chamberlin, Leslie J., and Joseph B. Carnot, eds. *Improving Classroom Discipline.* Springfield, Ill.: Charles C. Thomas Publishers, 1974. The fifty-two individual contributors to this volume cover about everything that needs to be said about the topic of discipline, focusing on every level from nearly every possible angle.

Cleaver, Betty P., Barbara Chatton, and Shirley Vittum Morrison. *Creating Connections: Books, Kits and Games for Children: A Sourcebook.* New York: Garland Press, 1986. An indispensable sourcebook for elementary school teachers who want to introduce inductive activities into their classrooms. Its suggestions for locating sources are comprehensive.

Coleman, Margaret Cecil. *Behavior Disorders: Theory and Practice.* Englewood Cliffs, N.J.: Prentice-Hall, 1986. Teachers will find all of this book down to earth and sensible. Its chapters on adolescence (Chapter 9) and severe behavior disorders (Chapter 10) are of particular interest.

Dick, Walter, and Nancy Hargerty. *Topics in Measurement: Reliability and Validity.* New York: McGraw-Hill, 1971. Despite its age, the material in this book has held up well and provides excellent guidance for teachers who want to know more about valid test construction.

Diekstra, Rene F. W., and Keith Hawton, eds. *Suicide in Adolescence.* Boston: Martinus Nijhoff Publishers, 1987. This treatment not only deals with the problem of teen-age suicide but also offers perceptive advice in the kind of after-care those who have attempted suicide should receive if they do not succeed. Also gives good information about how to deal with friends and members of the families of suicides.

Draves, William A. *How To Teach Adults*. Manhattan, Kans.: Learning Resources Network, 1984. Based on a televised presentation of the topic, this book offers information useful not only for those who teach adults but also for those who teach any students who are in the work force.

Galloway, David, and Carole Goodwin. *The Education of Disturbing Children: Pupils with Learning and Adjustment Difficulties*. London and New York: Longman's, 1987. Although the focus is on British schools, the information will prove valuable to American teachers who deal with children who are continually disruptive. Discusses well various dysfunctions—physical, psychological, and sociological—that can result in disturbing behavior. Chapter 7 on handling disturbing children in the ordinary school setting is directly pertinent.

Gartner, Alan, Mary Conway Kohler, and Frank Reissman. *Children Teach Children: Learning by Teaching*. New York: Harper and Row, 1971. Although this book is a bit dated, its basic premise that students learn a great deal about subject matter and about responsibility by teaching other students remains valid.

Gibbs, G. I. *Handbook of Games and Simulation Exercises*. Beverly Hills, Calif.: Sage Publications, 1974. The activities suggested in this book are realistic, and most of them can be implemented easily within the typical classroom.

Goslin, David. *Teachers and Testing*. New York: Russell Sage Foundation, 1967. Despite its age, this small book has not been superseded. Its suggestions are direct, clear, and sensible.

Green, John A. *Teacher-Made Tests*. New York: Harper and Row, 1975. A clear, concise presentation in language teachers tired of educational jargon will appreciate.

Gronlund, Norman E. *Measurement and Evaluation in Teaching,* 3d ed. New York: Macmillan, 1976. The most comprehensive book to date on the subject.

Hall, Edward T. *The Hidden Dimension*. Garden City, N.Y.: Doubleday, 1966. Hall examines how people from different cultures relate to space and time. A penetrating, well-written study.

_____. *The Silent Language*. Greenwich, Conn.: Fawcett, 1959. One of the most perceptive anthropological studies of how humans communicate. An important book for teachers in all fields.

Hammill, Donald D., ed. *Assessing the Abilities and Instructional Needs of Students*. Austin, Tex.: Pro-Ed, 1987. Poses questions that will cause teachers to articulate their own philosophies of assessing student progress.

Hirsch, E. D., Jr. *Cultural Literacy: What Every American Needs To Know*. Boston: Houghton Mifflin, 1987. Hirsch contends that students have trouble reading with meaning because they do not have the common information about their society that writers demand of their readers. His list of some 4,400 names, terms, and dates he thinks people need if they are to read such items as the daily newspaper with reasonable comprehension has presented a challenge to many readers.

Holt, John. *How Children Fail.* New York: Pitman, 1968. One of the more intelligent and humane books of the educational revolution that developed in the United States in the 1960s.

Jeffries, Derwin J. *Lesson Planning and Lesson Teaching.* Titusville, N.J.: Home and School Press, 1966. Although much of the information in this book is terribly dated, the basic mechanics it gives for making effective lesson plans remain valid.

Kohl, Herbert. *The Open Classroom.* New York: Random House, 1970. The classic resource on the concept of open education as it relates to open space as well as open attitude in settings where open space is not available.

Kozol, Jonathan. *Death at an Early Age.* Boston: Houghton Mifflin, 1967. One of the better books that grew out of the educational revolution of the 1960s. It focuses notably on the educationally disadvantaged.

Labov, William. *The Structure of Nonstandard English.* Champaign, Ill.: National Council of Teachers of English, 1970. Labov demonstrates how members of some cultural groups in schools resent having to replace their language patterns with patterns that are foreign to them to the extent that they divorce themselves from the school setting.

Lindsay, Geoff, ed. *Problems of Adolescence in Secondary School.* London: Croom Helm, 1983. Of particular value are the chapters on abnormal students (Chapter 6), sex and adolescence (Chapter 7), drugs and adolescence (Chapter 8), and vandalism in adolescence (Chapter 10). The approach is British, but much of it is valid for the United States.

Lindvall, C. M. *Measuring Pupil Achievement and Attitude.* New York: Harcourt, Brace and World, 1967. Although the portions of this book about measuring student achievement have been superseded, the information about measuring student attitude remains valuable and pertinent.

Morrow, Gertrude. *The Compassionate School: A Practical Guide to Educating Abused and Traumatized Children.* Englewood Cliffs, N.J.: Prentice-Hall, 1987. This is one of the most sensitively reported and carefully observed books on the topic of child abuse and the school's role in dealing with its victims.

Postman, Neil. *Amusing Ourselves to Death: Public Discourse in an Age of Show Business.* New York: Viking, 1985. Postman considers the passivity that the media have imposed upon a generation of people used to viewing rather than participating.

Postman, Neil, and Charles Weingartner. *Teaching as a Subversive Activity.* New York: Delacorte Press, 1969. In many ways the most influential educational book in the educational revolution that began in the 1960s. The authors challenge most of the assumptions on which education has conventionally been based.

Romano, Louis G., Nicholas P. Georgiady, and James E. Heald, eds. *The Middle School: Selected Readings on an Emerging School Program.* Chicago: Nelson-Hall, 1973. This early book on middle-level education contains some of the best thinking on the topic.

Sarup, Madon. *The Politics of Multiracial Education.* London: Routledge and Kegan Paul, 1986. The focus is on multiracial education in Britain, but the implications for American readers make the book worthwhile for those who teach in schools with large groups of first-generation students. The chapters on racism and on how children develop their early racial attitudes are of special value.

Sharan, Shlomo, et al., eds. *Cooperative Learning in the Classroom: Research in Desegregated Schools.* Hillsdale, N.J.: Lawrence Erlbaum, 1984. The considerations of cooperative vs. competitive behavior found in Chapter 3 are excellent.

Shulman, Lee S., and Evan R. Keisler, eds. *Learning by Discovery: A Critical Approach.* Chicago: Rand McNally, 1966. A good introduction to inductive teaching, particularly at the elementary level.

Symington, Neville. *The Analytical Experience.* New York: St. Martin's Press, 1986. Symington does a fine job of relating Freud to Darwin and the founders of the physicalist theory. Chapter 10, which deals with the crucial significance of transference, is relevant to teachers.

Taub-Bynum, E. Bruce. *The Family Unconscious: "An Invisible Bond."* Wheaton, Ill.: Theosophical Publishing House, 1984. Although this book is not notable for its scientific detachment, Chapter 18, "The Self and Perception," is of some value to teachers.

Warren, Neil, ed. *Studies in Cross-Cultural Psychology.* New York: Academic Press, 1980. Of unique value to teachers in intercultural settings will be Chapter 6, "Culture and Achievement Motivation: A Second Look."

Wilson, Richard W. *The Moral State: A Study of the Political Socialization of Chinese and American School Children.* New York: Free Press, 1974. The book makes interesting comparisons between two cultural groups in relation to attitudes and behavior as well as to shame, guilt, and socialization.